POWER AND POLITICS
IN THE PERSIAN GULF MONARCHIES

POWER AND POLITICS IN THE GULF

Christopher Davidson and Dirk Vanderwalle (editors)

After decades of sitting on the sidelines of the international system, the energy-exporting traditional monarchies of the Arab Gulf (Saudi Arabia, the United Arab Emirates, Kuwait, Bahrain, Qatar and Oman) are gradually transforming themselves into regional, and potentially global, economic powerhouses. This series aims to examine this trend while also bringing a consistent focus to the much wider range of other social, political, and economic issues currently facing Arab Gulf societies.

Quality research monographs, country case studies, and comprehensive edited volumes have been carefully selected by the series editors in an effort to assemble the most rigorous collection of work on the region

CHRISTOPHER M. DAVIDSON

(editor)

Power and Politics in the Persian Gulf Monarchies

HURST & COMPANY, LONDON

First published in the United Kingdom in 2011 by
C. Hurst & Co. (Publishers) Ltd.,
41 Great Russell Street, London, WC1B 3PL
© Christopher M. Davidson and the Contributors, 2011
All rights reserved.
Printed in India by Imprint Digital

The right of Christopher M. Davidson and the Contributors to be
identified as the author of this publication is asserted by them in
accordance with the Copyright, Designs and Patents Act, 1988.

A Cataloguing-in-Publication data record for this book
is available from the British Library.

ISBN: 978-1-84904-121-8 *paperback*
978-1-84904-122-5 *hardback*

This book is printed using paper from registered sustainable
and managed sources.

www.hurstpub.co.uk

CONTENTS

v

The Persian Gulf

ACRONYMS

ADAT	Abu Dhabi Aircraft Technologies
ADFEC	Abu Dhabi Future Energy Company
ADIA	Abu Dhabi Investments Authority
ADSB	Abu Dhabi Shipbuilding Company
AMD	Advanced Micro Devices
APOC	Anglo-Persian Oil Company
Aramco	Arabian American Oil Company
Bapco	Bahrain Petroleum Company
BCHR	Bahrain Centre for Human Rights
BFM	Bahrain Islamic Freedom Movement
BHRS	Bahrain Human Rights Society
CIO	Central Informatics Organisation of Bahrain
COM	Council of Ministers of the United Arab Emirates
CNU	Committee of National Unity of Bahrain
DLF	Dhofar Liberation Front
EADS	European Aeronautic Defence and Space Company
EDB	Economic Development Board of Bahrain
FDI	Foreign Direct Investment
FFFG	Fund for Future Generations of Kuwait
FNC	Federal National Council of the United Arab Emirates
GCC	Gulf Cooperation Council
GDP	Gross Domestic Product
GTL	Gas to Liquid Fuels
HEC	Higher Executive Committee of Bahrain
IFLB	Islamic Front for the Liberation of Bahrain
IMF	International Monetary Fund

ACRONYMS

KAUST	King Abdullah University of Science and Technology
KFAED	Kuwait Fund for Arab Economic Development
KIO	Kuwait Investment Office
KOC	Kuwait Oil Company
LNG	Liquefied Natural Gas
MP	Member of Parliament
NAC	National Action Charter of Bahrain
NATO	North Atlantic Treaty Organisation
NGO	Non-Governmental Organisation
NOGA	National Oil and Gas Authority of Bahrain
OPEC	Organisation of the Petroleum Exporting Countries
PDO	Petroleum Development Oman
PFLOAG	Popular Front for the Liberation of the Occupied Arabian Gulf
QFC	Qatar Financial Centre
SABIC	Saudi Arabian Basic Industries Company
SAMA	Saudi Arabian Monetary Agency
SCR	Supreme Council of Rulers of the United Arab Emirates
THAAD	Terminal High Altitude Area Defence system
UAE	United Arab Emirates
UN	United Nations
UNCTAD	United Nations Conference on Trade and Development
US	United States of America
WTO	World Trade Organisation

INTRODUCTION

Christopher M. Davidson

In command of the world's largest hydrocarbon reserves and occupying an increasingly central role in both Middle Eastern and global politics, the six monarchies comprising the Gulf Cooperation Council (GCC)[1]— Saudi Arabia, Bahrain, Kuwait, Oman, Qatar, and the United Arab Emirates (UAE)—are now among the most heavily researched yet most commonly misunderstood actors in the international system. Bringing together six experts on the fast moving politics and economics of the Persian Gulf, this edited collection provides a comprehensive yet highly accessible analysis of these states. Following an overview of their various achievements, opportunities, and collective challenges, each chapter then discusses the individual historical backgrounds of the states, their political structures, economic diversification efforts, foreign policy and security environments, and future threats.

The six studies begin by demonstrating how the respective ruling families of these territories managed their early encounters with external powers—namely the British and Ottoman Empires—in the nineteenth century. In most cases these relationships helped secure legitimacy and protection for the governing sheikhs and their sons, often in exchange for exclusive imperial control over trade routes and foreign relations. The British Empire in particular was responsible for bringing stability to the region, as its agents rarely tolerated aggression between the tribes and rulers that had signed up to the various imperial peace treaties. An important exception, however, was the interior of the Arabian Peninsula. By the twentieth century a powerful ruling entity—founded on a well-established alliance between adherents of purist Wahhabi Islam and the tribal muscle of the Al-Saud dynasty—was able to position itself as an independent state and, consequently, as both a threat and an opportunity to its smaller British-backed neighbours. By the 1960s the political landscape was changing once again, with substantial oil exports commencing and with Britain's imminent retreat from the region, as part of severe imperial retrenchment, prompting a period of hurried state formation, national identity building, and preparation for an uncertain future.

The chapters all then move on to demonstrate how the resulting modern states—three of which only became independent in 1971—managed to graft seemingly modern administrative departments and institutions onto existing traditional political structures. In this way, hybrid governments were established that fused centuries-old sheikhly and monarchical powers with new, rational-legal ministries and appointed bureaucrats.[2]

Since then, little has changed, as although there have been various experiments with political reform—ranging from Kuwait's and Bahrain's parliamentary elections to Saudi Arabia's municipal council ballots—the GCC's ruling families undoubtedly still dominate most aspects of political life, and in all cases retain monopolies over the key power bases of foreign policy, defence and national security.

While there has been variation in the individual popularity and competence of the Gulf's monarchs, all have been able to derive considerable legitimacy from unwritten (and often unspoken) social contracts or 'ruling bargains' that bind citizens to all-providing regimes.[3] Essentially, in exchange for packages of oil-financed benefits, which often include direct wealth transfers, free houses, welfare benefits and guaranteed public sector employment, the rulers have managed to purchase the political acquiescence of their indigenous populations. And as for the legions of expatriate workers who have been imported in lieu of productive national labour forces, generous tax free salaries have usually been enough to guarantee satisfaction. In all cases, but especially in the smallest and wealthiest of the monarchies—Qatar and the UAE—the rulers have also been able to offer their nationals extra benefits, including a sponsorship system that allows regular citizens to build rent-generating business empires on the backs of foreign workers and, less tangibly, the maintenance of a subtle social hierarchy that invariably elevates the 'locals' above Arab and Asian immigrants.

The chapters then outline how oil and gas exports have been the primary forces in shaping the economies of the six Gulf states over the past four decades, with the most successful industries being those that have exploited their comparative advantage of access to cheap and abundant energy. Meanwhile significant chunks of the hydrocarbon surpluses have been placed under the management of government-run sovereign wealth funds, some of which are among the world's largest. It is also shown, however, that in recent years a number of the Gulf monarchies have had to grapple with declining hydrocarbon reserves. This has placed enormous pressure on their manufacturing sectors—as energy now has to be imported—and has led to a number of post-oil diversification efforts. The UAE's second wealthiest emirate of Dubai—historically a successful trade hub—has most famously tried to reinvigorate its commercial and transport sectors, while also building up new tourism and real estate sectors, albeit with mixed success. But there is strong evidence of diversification elsewhere too, with Bahrain having long tried to build up a financial sector and Oman also opening up to foreign property investors and tourists. While there has been much less pressure to diversify in Saudi Arabia, Qatar, Kuwait and Abu Dhabi—the UAE's oil-rich and largest emirate—these monarchies are nonetheless also introducing new sectors with the threefold aims of improving vibrancy in national economies, creating appropriate employment opportunities for citizens, and building international linkages.

The Gulf states have had a number of shared security concerns in recent years, most notably a fear of either military aggression or fifth column activity generated by the Islamic Republic of Iran. Iraq too has been a cause of concern, especially for its most immediate neighbours, Kuwait and Saudi Arabia. However, the GCC has done little to promote a united front in the face of such threats, with the liberation of Kuwait in 1991 and the current containment of Iran relying almost entirely on the deployment of Western troops or the presence of United States bases. Moreover, the six monarchies have regularly pursued their own foreign policy and security strategies, and this remains an area of great divergence. Saudi Arabia and the UAE have invested in some of the world's most advanced military hardware—mostly sourced from the US, France, and Britain—and have built up the most powerful conventional armed forces in the developing world. Both states have also been taking hawkish stances on Iran[4] and now seem willing to play the role of regional hegemons. In contrast, despite housing US naval and air bases, Bahrain and Qatar have pursued active neutrality, carefully maintaining channels of communication with both Iran and the Western powers. Qatar in particular appears willing to play the role of an Arab Switzerland, now regularly positioning itself as a mediator in regional disputes. What the Gulf states do have in common, though, is that those with hydrocarbon surpluses still view foreign aid to beleaguered Arab or Muslim states as an important component of their foreign policy and security building. Very public efforts to get aid to embattled Palestinian communities in the West Bank, war-torn Somalia, tsunami-hit Indonesia and impoverished Kosovo have not only boosted the domestic legitimacy of Gulf rulers and their governments, but also served to win friends and buy off enemies in both their neighbourhoods and their own constituencies.

The future challenges facing the Gulf states are, again, both shared and diverse. As all of the chapters indicate, the rulers must prepare for a fast-changing political landscape. This has become particularly pressing following the 'Arab Spring' of 2011 and the pro-democracy revolutions that have swept the region, beginning in Tunisia, Egypt and Libya. With serious unrest spreading eastwards to the GCC's borders, notably in Syria and Yemen, and a full blown revolt having already begun in the poorest GCC member, Bahrain, the situation could rapidly develop into an existential crisis for the surviving monarchies. As yet, no proper roadmaps are in place for genuine democratic openings, and this renders the existing polities brittle and highly vulnerable to rapidly mounting pressures for reform from their fast growing and increasingly educated youthful populations. Most acute is the strengthening opposition to the monarchies' routine reliance on censorship and their perceived lack of accountability. Blocking Internet sites, pulping newspapers, and co-opting journalists, academics and other would-be civil society actors may reduce the immediate need for heavy-handed security apparatuses, but the methods and rationale behind this Gulf-wide strategy are being increasingly criticised, and often in the open. The lack of any meaningful indigenisation of the labour force also remains a concern, as repeated attempts to hold in check the stream of immigrant workers and push nationals into the workforce have routinely failed. At the root of the problem is the unwillingness of citizens to compete on a level playing field with foreign workers, given their social contract with ruling families and their preference for maintaining hierarchy-based, rent collecting economic structures.[5] In time, this may prove to the ultimate weakness for these states, as post-oil economic realities will require reforms that strike at the core of the ruling bargain and particularly its reliance on distributive practices.

Individually, Bahrain presently faces the toughest challenges, given that its government no longer has either wealth or economic advantages to transfer to its citizens. Recent elections have exposed resentment over an increasing wealth gap between the state's various communities, with its substantial Shia population having been particularly vocal. Having resorted to a public and deadly crackdown on its opponents in early 2011, and having invited Saudi Arabia and the UAE to deploy troops to Bahrain to help suppress the rebellion, the Sunni ruling family's legitimacy has been greatly and perhaps irrecoverably damaged. Although at the helm of a much more powerful economy, the ruling family of Saudi Arabia is also facing a looming crisis. Many Saudis consider themselves poor and disenfranchised, and the country's substantial Shia population undoubtedly sympathises with the Bahraini people's plight. Women too are becoming increasingly vocal, with many beginning to publicly condemn their status as second class citizens. Moreover, with an aged ruler surrounded by almost equally aged potential successors, there is concern that the kingdom's political stability may deteriorate as factionalism surfaces within the inner circle. The situation is likely to be exacerbated by an ongoing struggle between reformers and religious conservatives—the latter still commanding great loyalty across the state, even if their political power has been carefully contained in recent years. Oman too faces a succession question, with its childless ruler having taken much personal credit for the sultanate's various modernisation programmes. If his successor proves less progressive, there is a danger that the measures which have been taken to liberalise Oman's economy—and which have delivered largely positive results—may be reversed.

As the chapters on Kuwait, Qatar and the UAE demonstrate, these monarchies also face parochial challenges. Kuwait's unusual parliamentary political culture—an awkward mishmash of pork barrel politics and public chest-beating—is now deeply entrenched, and it will prove difficult to push through genuine democratic reforms without significant instability. Meanwhile Kuwait will probably remain unable to develop its economy properly or emerge from the sidelines of the regional system. With the smallest but wealthiest per capita population of all the

GCC states, Qatar is the most vulnerable to invasion or coup d'état. Its energetic, rather high risk foreign policy may at some point backfire, especially if regional or international powers deem that its usefulness has expired. In this scenario, the country will be left unprotected and will represent a valuable prize. The UAE is the most complicated of the six states given that it is a federation of seven emirates. Only one of these still commands significant hydrocarbon reserves, and it is likely that this will lead to increasing economic and political centralisation. Given the proud histories and carefully guarded autonomies of the other constituent emirates, this may result in significant tension within the state. Already there have been signs of growing unrest in the poorer, outlying emirates, as significant numbers within their populations are uneasy over the ambitions of the current generation of Abu Dhabi rulers.

THE UNITED ARAB EMIRATES

Christopher M. Davidson

State formation

Following a series of truces signed with Britain in the early nineteenth century and formalised in 1853 as the *Perpetual Maritime Truce*, the sheikhdoms of the lower Persian Gulf or the 'Trucial States' remained de facto protectorates of the British Empire well into the twentieth century. Keen to avoid expensive troop deployments or colonial administrations, Britain implemented an informal, low-cost imperial solution: in exchange for guaranteeing that their towns and ports would never host pirates that might attack British or British-Indian shipping, the various signatory sheikhs enjoyed the promise of full support from Britain, not only in the event of an external threat, but also against internal dissidents.[1] In this way, the same ruling families that Britain chose to do business with in the nineteenth century and managed to sign peace treaties were able to resist multiple challenges through the following century, and are the same families that remain in power today.

One of the earliest threats to the trucial sheikhs came from their merchant community, which was suffering a severe recession in the 1930s in the wake of global economic depression and declining interest in the region's principal industry, the export of pearls. Leading merchants were frustrated with their rulers' close relations with Britain, as the latter effectively restricted access to foreign markets and foreign technologies in an effort to maintain the Gulf as a 'British lake'. Resentment was exacerbated by the rulers' personal enrichment from rents being paid directly to them by British companies in return for approving oil exploration concession agreements and air landing rights. In 1938 matters came to a head in Dubai, which was the region's busiest port at that time. Dubai's merchants had taken control of half the city and were pressing the ruler to limit his personal income and distribute rents in the name of the state. Viewing this as a challenge to the entire trucial system and the informal empire, Britain intervened in favour of the ruler by flying aircraft low over Dubai and distributing pamphlets that encouraged residents to respect the status quo.[2]

By the 1950s the trucial sheikhs again faced internal challenges, when many young nationals—some having been taught by imported schoolteachers from Syria and Egypt—began to embrace the cause of Arab nationalism. Revolution in Egypt in 1952 and the Suez Canal crisis of 1956 further emboldened the activists. Some formed a National Front, while others began visiting Cairo and Damascus to discuss their plans. Violence broke out, with British vehicles and members of the ruling families being targeted, often with explosive mines. Most spectacularly, in 1961 the *MV Dara* was blown up off the coast of Dubai and over 200 were killed. By the late 1960s, however, much of the threat had subsided, as the loss of prestige by the Arab cause following defeat by Israel in 1967 coincided with a period of unprecedented economic boom. Oil exports had commenced in the three largest sheikhdoms of Abu Dhabi, Dubai and Sharjah, thus providing their ruling families with a powerful ability not only to distribute wealth directly to their citizens, but also to assign lucrative import monopolies to various merchant families. In turn, these were well placed to supply goods to the rapidly expanding urban populations and the thousands of arriving foreign workers. In many cases the same families that had supported the National Front's activities suddenly became enriched and busy with the demands of establishing substantial business empires. Britain also moved to reduce the influence of Arab nationalist schoolteachers in the region, by appointing new school directors from the Sudan and other pro-British Arab territories.[3]

There were also significant external threats to the Trucial States during this period, as the independent Kingdom of Saudi Arabia sought to renew historical claims to large swathes of Abu Dhabi's territory. Backed by United States oil companies that were unable to seek exploration concessions in Britain's zone of influence, in 1952 the Al-Saud family despatched a small force to occupy villages around the Buraimi oasis, close to Abu Dhabi's border with Oman. Claiming that Buraimi tribesmen had historically paid tribute to Al-Saud sheikhs, the Saudis offered gifts upon their arrival at the oasis, and their leader even married the daughter of a local dignitary. Eventually, Britain headed off the challenge on behalf of Abu Dhabi by mobilising its tiny Sharjah-based Trucial Oman Scouts.[4] Britain also limited opportunities for further US or Saudi interference by formally incorporating the Indian Ocean coastline sheikhdom of Fujairah into the trucial system, as it was understood that Fujairah's elders had already established relations with US companies.[5] In the northern sheikhdoms the threat of invasion was of equal concern, especially in the 1960s, as the Shah of Iran had reinvigorated earlier Persian claims to a number of islands belonging to Sharjah and Ra's al-Khaimah. A few hundred tribesmen inhabited the largest of these islands—Abu Musa—and it was feared that conflict would break out.[6] In 1968 the Trucial States were rocked by London's announcement that within just three years Britain would dismantle all of its bases and treaties east of Aden, in an effort to cut imperial expenditure and focus more resources on Britain's struggling domestic welfare system. The trucial sheikhs were so alarmed by the prospect of their protector's departure that they even offered to subsidise the deployment of British troops in the region after independence was granted. Britain's solution, however, was to encourage the trucial sheikhs to form a cohesive federation that would provide the lower Gulf sheikhdoms, along with nearby Qatar and Bahrain—which had also been part of the trucial system—with at least some degree of collective security. Various meetings and negotiations took place, but it quickly became apparent that Qatar and Bahrain were unwilling to form a state with their less developed neighbours. To make matters worse, Ra's al-Khaimah was also balking at joining the federation, as it still held ambitions to become an independent state, and on 1 December 1971—the day before Britain's official withdrawal—Iran seized the contested islands. Nonetheless, the following day a six-member federation of United Arab Emirates was inaugurated,[7] and the following month Ra's al-Khaimah reluctantly agreed to join. Given that Abu Dhabi commanded the bulk of the UAE's oil reserves it became the capital city, and its ruler—Sheikh Zayed bin Sultan Al-Nahyan—was installed as the UAE's first President.[8]

The 1970s was a decade of consolidation, as the wealthier emirates built up their oil industries and began to install the necessary socio-economic infrastructure for their rapidly expanding populations, most of which were made up of immigrant workers. Importantly, the UAE avoided conflict, and Abu Dhabi judiciously used a portion of its wealth to support Arab and Muslim causes elsewhere in the region, while also co-operating in the oil embargos against international buyers orchestrated by the Organisation of Petroleum Exporting Countries. With the 1979 Islamic Revolution in Iran, however, the tension of the 1960s returned, as the UAE feared that Ayatollah Khomeini's new theocracy would seek to export revolution to the Gulf monarchies, which many Iranians viewed as illegitimate British creations. When Iraq invaded Iran the following year the UAE duly offered public support to its Arab brothers, although the ruler of Dubai was reluctant to distance his emirate from Iran, given the city's long history of trade with the southern Iranian ports. This led to divided loyalties within the UAE, and at one point during the Iran-Iraq War it was believed that four of the emirates were siding with Iraq while three sided with Iran. Nonetheless, in 1981 the UAE joined the new Gulf Cooperation Council as a federal entity, in an effort to form another layer of collective security—this time with the other Gulf monarchies.[9]

Any optimism that the GCC could serve as a military shield was short-lived, as the UAE and its partners were unable to prevent or repel Iraq's invasion of Kuwait, a fellow GCC member, in 1990. Gas masks were issued to UAE residents and the families of expatriates left Abu Dhabi and Dubai, as it was feared that Iraqi forces would press through Saudi Arabia and invade the UAE. Much of the concern was due to the UAE's overproduction of oil at this time—exceeding their OPEC quota, which Baghdad had already condemned Kuwait for.[10] The remainder of the decade was relatively peaceful, as the eventual US-led liberation of Kuwait and subsequent US deployments in the region allowed the UAE's rulers to enjoy a similar sense of protection to that of the old trucial system.

The 9/11 attacks on New York's World Trade Center nonetheless brought the UAE back to the front line, as it soon emerged that two of the al-Qaeda hijackers were UAE nationals and that most of the funding for the US-based terror cell had been laundered and wired through Dubai's banks. International accusations that the UAE was turning a blind eye to terror organisations within its territory were seemingly supported by a consensus view among UAE residents that there was some form of unspoken deal in place between the country's rulers and such groups, especially given that the UAE—despite being much more moderate and liberal than neighbouring states—had not been the target of any major terror strikes.[11]

Political structures and personalities

On the same day that the UAE was formed—2 December 1971—a provisional constitution was signed by the rulers of the participating sheikhdoms. The UAE was envisaged as a loose confederation, with limited powers being transferred to federal ministries, most of which were to be based in Abu Dhabi which commanded the greatest oil reserves. Significantly, neither defence nor control over oil industries was transferred to the federal government, as it was felt that centralisation of such key matters would harm the status of the emirate-level governments and the various rulers' courts, leading to friction and instability. Indeed, when Abu Dhabi attempted to unify the different emirate-level armed forces in the late 1970s both Dubai and Ra's al-Khaimah threatened their withdrawal from the union, prompting a constitutional crisis. Eventually, by 1996 unified UAE Armed Forces were established, with the ruler of Abu Dhabi serving as supreme commander, and the constitution was finally made permanent. By this stage Dubai and most of the other emirates were pressing ahead with costly infrastructure projects in efforts to build up more diverse economic bases, and preferred to transfer as many costly services as possible to Abu Dhabi and the federal government.[12]

Overseeing the federal government since 1971 has been the Supreme Council of Rulers, which is made up of the seven hereditary rulers of each emirate and, on occasion, their respective crown princes. While the provisional constitution allows for an SCR presidential election to take place every five years,[13] in practice the rulership of Abu Dhabi remains synonymous with the presidency of the UAE, not least because of Abu Dhabi's almost single-handed financing of most federal development projects. The SCR also reflects Dubai's elevated status in the UAE by awarding only the rulers of Abu Dhabi and Dubai veto power in its meetings—as per an article of the constitution[14]—and by always appointing the ruler of Dubai as the vice president. In support of the SCR, or more specifically the president, there exists a presidential office and a presidential court with its own staff. However, given the ruler of Abu Dhabi's similar emirate-level institutions it is unclear if the two function independently.

Responsible for most of the federal government's decision-making is the Council of Ministers. Since its establishment in 1972 its composition has always reflected the relative power and influence of the member emirates. Although originally made up of eleven ministers in addition to a prime minister, the COM soon expanded to nineteen positions as the other emirates began to supply their contingents of appointees.[15] The premiership was transferred to the crown prince of Dubai, before the above-mentioned constitutional crisis persuaded the ruler of Dubai to become prime minister as well as vice president. Abu Dhabi has always held the lion's share of COM positions including the deputy premiership, the Ministry for the Interior, the Ministry for Higher Education, and the Ministry for Public Works. Today, the COM's membership has increased to twenty ministers and five ministers of state, including four women. But it remains equally in favour of Abu Dhabi, with members of the Abu Dhabi ruling family controlling the Ministry for Foreign Affairs and the Ministry for Presidential Affairs. In total, there are now seven members of the Al-Nahyan family serving as ministers. Abu Dhabi nationals are also serving as the ministers for Justice, the Economy,[16] and Energy,[17] with at least two further ministers also being de facto members of the Abu Dhabi contingent given their close ties to the emirate.

Operating underneath the COM, the Federal National Council is a consultative body made up of contingents from each emirate. Comprising forty members, including an internally elected speaker and two deputies, this chamber sits for sessions of two years at a time, and has a number of subcommittees. Much as in the COM, the more powerful emirates dominate, as per Article 72 of the provisional federal constitution,[18] with Abu Dhabi and Dubai each supplying eight members while Sharjah and Ra's al-Khaimah supply six and the other three emirates just four.[19] These contingents, which were originally all appointed, were often made up of senior representatives of non-ruling tribes or sections, and they now include women. In recent years there has been mounting criticism of the FNC, with many of its members and other citizens claiming that it is largely ineffective. While it has been successful in petitioning ministers on some rather banal subjects,[20] it has been incapable of making more substantive interventions,[21] and has often been unable to elicit responses from ministers.[22] In 2006 elections were held for half of the FNC positions, but these were widely vilified as only a few thousand UAE nationals were eligible to vote. A second round of elections should have taken place in late 2010, but it has been delayed until late 2011.

At the apex of the emirate-level governments are the private offices and courts of both the rulers and crown princes. These have their own staff and, especially in the wealthier emirates, an appointment as a chamberlain or director to one of these bodies confers a high status position that allows an individual to serve as an intermediary between the supreme, traditional power and the regular government and citizenry. Given Abu Dhabi's much greater geographical size, it also has ruler's representatives in both its eastern and western regions, and these also have their own private offices and courts. While it remains possible for unilateral decisions to be made by the rulers' offices and then issued as 'emiri decrees', in practise only Abu Dhabi's and Dubai's rulers still exercise this privilege, with most legislation now being crafted by the federal COM. Abu Dhabi, Dubai, and Sharjah all have emirate-level executive councils, which tend to deal with most domestic matters in their respective emirates. In many ways the Abu Dhabi Executive Council—founded in early 1971, before the creation of the UAE—is more powerful than the COM as it presides over several Abu Dhabi-specific government entities including the influential Supreme Petroleum Council, three municipalities and three police forces (one for the capital and one for each of its two outlying regions), along with a score of recently established bodies including the Abu Dhabi Education Council, the Abu Dhabi Tourism Authority and its Office of the Brand of Abu Dhabi, the Abu Dhabi Authority for Culture and Heritage, the Urban Planning Council, the Environmental Agency of Abu Dhabi, and the Executive Affairs Authority.

Sharjah's executive council, although much smaller, operates along similar lines, but it is noteworthy that Dubai's executive council is far less formal, with its meetings arranged on a more ad hoc basis, often in the conference suites of business hotels. In some ways, the nature of the Dubai Executive Council is supposed to reflect the emirate's history as a dynamic business hub (it is often referred to as 'Dubai Inc.'). Also at the emirate level, at least in Abu Dhabi and Sharjah, are national consultative councils. These are supposed to operate in a similar manner to the FNC and have faced similar criticisms. The Abu Dhabi National Consultative Council's usefulness is particularly questionable given that the Abu Dhabi Executive Council is not required to consider the recommendations that it receives. Moreover, after thirty-nine years of operation the NCC remains entirely appointive, and—incredibly—only three of the current members were first appointed in the last eighteen years.

None of the members are female, in contrast with the Sharjah council which now has 17 per cent female membership.[23]

The key figures in UAE politics have, unsurprisingly, been the rulers of Abu Dhabi and Dubai, along with their crown princes, brothers, and sons. The UAE's first president, Sheikh Zayed, succeeded as ruler of Abu Dhabi in 1966, having deftly removed his elder brother with British assistance.[24] Zayed's reign was uninterrupted until his death in late 2004 and he has been credited personally with strengthening the federation and shielding the UAE from regional conflicts. Following his death, his eldest son and Crown Prince, Sheikh Khalifa bin Zayed Al-Nahyan, was simultaneously appointed ruler of Abu Dhabi and UAE president, and he remains in place today.[25] Although he is firmly in control of Abu Dhabi's oil revenue, its largest sovereign wealth fund, and the federal budget, Khalifa's power is much more limited than his father's, as Zayed's third eldest son, Sheikh Muhammad bin Zayed Al-Nahyan, has assumed a prominent leadership role. As part of a secret agreement dating back to 1999, Muhammad was promised the position of deputy crown prince and then—following their father's death—the position of crown prince, despite Khalifa having two adult sons. Today, Muhammad serves as Crown Prince, chairman of the Abu Dhabi Executive Council, and deputy Supreme Commander of the UAE Armed Forces. In many ways he acts as Abu Dhabi's prime minister and is in de facto control of the military and many aspects of federal foreign policy.[26]

Significantly, Muhammad is the eldest of six 'Bani Fatima'—the sons of Sheikha Fatima bint Mubarak Al-Qitbi, who was Zayed's most prominent wife and still plays a discreet role in the emirate's politics. Given that Zayed had nineteen legitimate sons, the Bani Fatima form the largest and most powerful grouping of full brothers and thus function as a key faction within the ruling family. Under Muhammad, other Bani Fatima include Sheikh Hamdan bin Zayed Al-Nahyan, who was formerly Minister of State for Foreign Affairs and is now Governor of the Western Region. The third of the Bani Fatima is Sheikh Hazza bin Zayed Al-Nahyan, who serves as Abu Dhabi's Chief of Security and Intelligence Services, while the fourth is Sheikh Tahnun bin Zayed Al-Nahyan, who serves as director of the ruler's private office. Of the six, it is actually the two youngest who have gained the most seniority. Notably, Sheikh Mansur bin Zayed Al-Nahyan has enjoyed a meteoric rise in recent years, and now controls the emirate's second largest sovereign wealth fund in addition to serving as one of two federal deputy prime ministers; while Sheikh Abdullah bin Zayed Al-Nahyan, formerly the Minister for Information and Culture, is now the UAE's Minister for Foreign Affairs.[27] Almost in parallel to Zayed's reign, Sheikh Rashid bin Said Al-Maktoum became ruler of Dubai in 1958. Referred to as the 'Father of Dubai', he was credited with building much of Dubai's impressive transport and communications infrastructure, including the two deep water ports and the international airport. In something of a rehearsal for Abu Dhabi's 2004 succession arrangements, Rashid's death in 1990 led to the eldest of his sons, Sheikh Maktoum bin Rashid Al-Maktoum, becoming ruler, but with his ambitious third eldest son, Sheikh Muhammad bin Rashid Al-Maktoum, becoming the de facto ruler. Formally installed as Crown Prince in 1995, Muhammad headed Dubai's executive council and oversaw Dubai's forays into tourism and real estate from his vantage point on the top floor of the city's tallest skyscraper.[28] In 2006, at the height of Dubai's real estate boom, Maktoum died on holiday in Australia, thus clearing the way for Muhammad's succession as ruler.[29] With simultaneous appointments as the UAE's Vice President and Prime Minister, Muhammad was temporarily the second most powerful figure in UAE politics, and during this period any visiting heads of state—including US presidents—were obliged to visit his palace separately from their visits to Abu Dhabi. Since the crash of Dubai's economy in late 2009 and the emirate's increasing reliance on Abu Dhabi's assistance, Muhammad's influence has been greatly reduced. However, he still enjoys powerful regional and international connections, and his Crown Prince, Sheikh Hamdan bin Muhammad Al-Maktoum, is well regarded across the UAE. Among other members of Dubai's ruling family, Muhammad's surviving elder brother, Sheikh Hamdan bin Rashid Al-Maktoum, remains prominent as the federal Minister for Finance, while Muhammad's uncle, Sheikh Ahmed bin Said Al-Maktoum, serves both as chairman of the successful Emirates airline and as deputy chairman of the Dubai Executive Council.

Beyond Abu Dhabi and Dubai, few of the other emirates rulers now have significant influence in UAE politics. However, the long-serving ruler of Sharjah—Sheikh Sultan bin Muhammad Al-Qasimi—is well respected as a champion of culture and local history. Having served as the first federal Minister for Education, he unexpectedly became ruler in 1973 and remains in power today, having reasserted himself following a short-lived coup d'état in 1987. In 1989, Sharjah's banking sector was close to collapse, prompting Sultan to seek a rescue package from Saudi Arabia. The rescue came with strings attached, obliging Sultan to adopt more conservative rules, including a ban on alcohol and the introduction of more stringent 'decency laws'.[30]

The ruler of Ra's al-Khaimah until his death in 2010—Sheikh Saqr bin Muhammad Al-Qasimi—was similarly well regarded. He had ruled since 1948 and was the last sitting ruler to have been a party to the 1971 establishment of the federation. In 1987 he defused a coup attempt that was being planned in parallel to the Sharjah coup, and he ruled unopposed from then on.[31] However, for a decade a bitter struggle took place between Saqr's eldest son and former Crown Prince, Sheikh Khalid bin Saqr Al-Qasimi, and his third eldest son and more recent Crown Prince, Sheikh Saud bin Saqr Al-Qasimi. Having been exiled in 2003 in favour of Saud, Khalid launched an international media campaign to highlight his brother's Iranian business connections, and hoped that Abu Dhabi would intervene upon Saqr's death, installing him as the next ruler. However, when Khalid returned to Ra's al-Khaimah in 2010 to attend his father's funeral, he and his guards were arrested and he was forced to relinquish his claim.[32]

Economic development and diversification

The UAE's economic development is best understood by considering the contrasting macroeconomic environments of its two wealthiest constituent emirates—Abu Dhabi and Dubai—and the different diversification strategies they have pursued. With several further oil discoveries since the 1970s, the former's share of global reserves has continued to grow, and now stands at about 8 per cent, which represents nearly 95 per cent of the UAE's total. Following major investments, the emirate's output capacity will increase by over 30 per cent in the next few years, with most of the excess expected to be sold to the hydrocarbon-hungry economies of Pacific Asia, notably China, Japan, and South Korea.[33] Abu Dhabi also controls about 3.5 per cent of global gas reserves, and in the near future several developments will boost daily gas production by about 25 per cent. Despite these increases, however, Abu Dhabi will still face gas shortages, as some 85 per cent of the emirate's power plants are gas fuelled.[34] Hopes for a solution were earlier pinned on the massive Dolphin Gas project, which established Qatar as a co-supplier and committed Abu Dhabi to the large-scale transport and marketing of Dolphin gas to Dubai, Oman, and other net gas importers in the region.[35] However, despite two billion cubic feet per day of Dolphin gas now being piped in from Qatar,[36] the problem has not yet been solved. The long-term plan is the development of a number of nuclear power plants in the emirate, and an agreement was finalised in late 2009 with a South Korean consortium winning a bid to construct four such plants by 2030.[37]

Abu Dhabi has also established state-owned, export-oriented heavy industries. Most of these have concentrated on the production and export of metals, plastics, fertilisers and petrochemicals. These all require abundant energy to manufacture, and therefore capitalise best on Abu Dhabi's competitive advantages. The most prominent of these downstream industrial companies are Fertil,[38] the Abu Dhabi Polymers Company (also known as Borouge),[39] and Emirates Aluminium, the last-named of which operates the world's largest aluminium processing facility. Most of these exports are destined for India, Bangladesh, Sri Lanka and Malaysia.[40] Over the next few years the sector will continue to expand—gas shortages notwithstanding—with both the Crown Prince's Mubadala Development Corporation and the Abu Dhabi Basic Industries Corporation planning to build massive new aluminium plants.[41] The government has put its full weight behind these developments, having increased spending on industrial infrastructure by over 400 per cent since 2001.[42] Soon it promises completion of the $10 billion Khalifa Port and Industrial Zone, and it has committed a further $8 billion for other sector-specific infrastructure projects.[43]

Of equal if not greater importance to Abu Dhabi's economy has been the channelling of surplus oil revenue into long-term overseas investments. Conceived as a means of buffering the domestic economy should the international oil industry falter, most of these investments have been made through a handful of government-owned authorities or government backed companies. Of the latter, most simply state that their sole shareholder is 'the Government of Abu Dhabi'. Today, their combined assets are thought to be in excess of $1 trillion, and up until 2009 they were generating some 6–7 per cent in annualised returns.[44] The most prominent of Abu Dhabi's sovereign wealth funds is the Abu Dhabi investment Authority, now symbolically housed in the tallest building in Abu Dhabi;[45] it was estimated that ADIA reached nearly $630 billion

17

in early 2008.[46] Although this figure has certainly dropped since the onset of the global recession,[47] ADIA is still by far the world's largest sovereign wealth fund. Housing teams of foreign experts that scour the globe for investment opportunities, ADIA has historically favoured index-linked blue chip investments in the developed world. About 40–50 per cent of the portfolio is in North American markets, with 25–30 per cent in Europe, 10–15 per cent in developed Asia, and 10–15 per cent in emerging markets.[48] Other prominent Abu Dhabi sovereign wealth funds include the Abu Dhabi Investment Company, which is believed to manage over $15 billion in overseas investments, and the International Petroleum Investment Company, which now has an oil-related investment portfolio of nearly $14 billion.[49]

The centrepiece of Abu Dhabi's new economy and its diversification efforts has been a select range of high technology heavy industries. In most cases, these have involved the setting up of specialist subsidiary companies under the umbrella of the fast expanding Mubadala or other big parastatals. The new companies have then been turned into joint ventures as international partners have been brought on board. The latter provide the technology, the market contacts, and credibility, while the parastatals provide the capitalisation and ensure easy access to the necessary skilled labour by offering high, tax free salaries. Moreover, in some instances the parastatals have then strengthened the ventures by making direct investments in the foreign companies. Thus, the sovereign wealth component of the old economy has been reinvigorated and applied to the new, post-oil sectors.

One of the most prominent examples of the new industries is Abu Dhabi's aerospace sector,[50] led by Abu Dhabi Aircraft Technologies. While maintenance remains at the core of its business strategy, ADAT has recently won contracts to manufacture wing parts and other components for the European Aeronautic Defence and Space Company's flagship A380 Superjumbo. Also, ADAT has been approved by EADS as the only company in the Middle East permitted to service A380 engines.[51] Over the next five years ADAT plans to increase its annual revenue to $1 billion, expanding its maintenance operations from existing Gulf customers into the Indian market;[52] and by 2013 it hopes to win contracts to manufacture parts for EADS' forthcoming A350. In the long term ADAT intends to export its components to other buyers, and it has said it eventually intends to assemble entire aircraft in Abu Dhabi.[53] Abu

Dhabi has now also moved into the manufacture of computer microprocessors, with Mubadala's stake in Advanced Micro Devices having led to a new joint venture in the emirate between AMD and a new Mubadala subsidiary: the Advanced Technology Investment Company. The venture will produce video cards, mobile phones, and consumer electronics, in addition to processors.[54] Shipbuilding has been identified as another priority area, with the Abu Dhabi Shipbuilding Company having recently begun manufacturing entire ships in cooperation with joint venture partners. It is unlikely there will be an overseas market for the ADSB, but its production will at least contribute towards import substitution, and it has already begun to supply the UAE Navy.[55]

There has also been an effort to build up 'future energy' and other green industries. In 2006 Mubadala established a subsidiary to pioneer these developments—the Abu Dhabi Future Energy Company, AFDEC. ADFEC's first major project has been Masdar City, a large carbon-neutral development in Abu Dhabi's hinterland. The original aim was for ADFEC to provide the infrastructure for a 'free zone' that would allow up to 1,500 renewable energy and other environment-related international companies to base themselves in Masdar, or at least have their regional headquarters there. Some of these will be focused on carbon capture technologies and it is expected that they will export their services to nearby countries still relying on outdated hydrocarbon extraction technologies.[56] In early 2010 the Masdar plans were downsized, as they had originally discussed a sizeable real estate development. But the renewable energy free zone initiative remains in place.

Without sizeable hydrocarbon reserves, Dubai's economic development has had to focus on much more urgent diversification from oil exports and oil-backed investments than Abu Dhabi's. Although Dubai's manufacturing sector grew in the 1970s and 1980s, most of the activity was on a fairly small scale, and primarily geared to the production of basic goods that would otherwise be costly and inefficient to import, rather than exports. The greater emphasis was placed on reinforcing the emirate's historic role as a regional trade hub by building up transport and communications infrastructure. As a result, its two deep water ports and its international airport are now among the busiest in the world, shifting over 15 million metric tons of non-oil related traded goods per year, and accounting for nearly $31 billion in trade receipts per year.[57]

Since the mid-1980s Dubai also began to seek foreign direct investment, initially by setting up 'free zone' industrial parks that would allow foreign companies to relocate to Dubai and enjoy 100 per cent ownership without need of local business partners. The first of these parks, the Jebel Ali Free Zone, soon mushroomed to over 2,000 companies, many of which were European or North American. By 2001 a plethora of high-profile multinationals and other foreign companies, including Microsoft, Dell, Reuters and the BBC, were locating themselves in new sector-specific free zones such as Dubai Internet City and Dubai Media City. Since then many other free zones have opened, including entire 'villages' for branch campuses of foreign universities and health clinics, and even a Dubai International Financial Centre for foreign financial companies, which operates under English common law and attempts to bridge the time zones of European and Asian stock exchanges.[58]

In parallel to the free zone strategy, Dubai was also committed to building up a luxury international tourist industry. The Jumeirah International Group, established in 1997, was responsible for building a number of iconic resorts, including the Jumeirah Beach Hotel and the Burj al-Arab—the world's only seven-star hotel. So strong was the emphasis on high end tourism that in the late 1990s it was estimated that 10 per cent of the emirate's GDP was spent on developing this sector. By 2008, with hundreds of hotels including several dozen with five stars, the emirate was hosting over six million tourists a year. Backed by a successful airline, two annual shopping festivals, over forty shopping malls, and a host of international sporting and music events, the number of tourists was predicted to climb to ten million or more by 2012.[59]

To attract investment from wealthy individuals, a real estate sector was introduced in the late 1990s. This was controversial, given that it was against UAE law for foreigners to own property at that time, but Dubai bypassed the complication by initially allowing foreigners to buy renewable ninety-nine year leases. Real estate demand accelerated when the Nakheel property company began constructing two separate 'Palm Islands' off the coast of Jumeirah and Jebel Ali featuring villas, apartments and several five-star hotels. Following Sheikh Muhammad's succession in 2006, he promptly decreed that foreigners could own real estate in 'some parts of Dubai, as designated by the ruler' and would be entitled to residency visas from the Dubai government, thus altering the previous rule restricting residency visas to those with proof of employment. To further alleviate investors' risk-averse concerns, a law was passed establishing a Lands Department that would provide a centralised registry capable of issuing deeds. Demand for Dubai's real estate projects soared, and additional developments were launched. Emaar Properties, which became a 67 per cent publicly owned company following its flotation on the Dubai stock exchange, pressed ahead with its magnificent Burj Dubai: a mixed residential, commercial and hotel complex boasting some 165 or more storeys and a dynamic design so as to guarantee it would be the world's tallest structure.[60]

By the summer of 2008 Dubai had succeeded in diversifying its economy, at least on paper. With the non-oil sectors accounting for more than 95 per cent of the emirate's GDP, the hydrocarbon industry was pushed further into the background. An estimated $3 billion in annual foreign direct investment flows underscored Dubai's reputation as the most vibrant economy in the region, and UN reports ranked the emirate as the seventeenth most attractive economy in the world for foreign investment.[61]

In September 2008, with the global credit crunch entering its second year, Dubai appeared to have been spared the toxicity spreading throughout economies in the West. In early October at Cityscape 2008, the emirate's premier real estate convention, plans for a one kilometre-tall tower were announced, even as the Burj Dubai stood unfinished. Jumeirah Gardens and Waterfront City, projects that would lead to a new residential area the size of Manhattan Island, were being promoted aggressively. However, behind this façade Dubai's economy was already experiencing difficulty. Foreign investors' interest in real estate was declining markedly and hotel occupancy rates began to falter as tourists turned to cheaper destinations. Most seriously, Dubai's banks and mortgage lenders were struggling to find credit on the international market. Loans dried up, speculators began to disappear, and the first major wave of resale properties began to hit the market as investors decided to pull out. Dubai stock markets went into free fall, with share prices for erstwhile government-backed blue-chips such as Emaar Properties shedding over 80 per cent of their value by December. The two biggest mortgage lenders, Tamweel and Amlak, even had to be merged under a new federal authority.[62] Most awkwardly for Dubai, it was revealed that state-backed companies had accumulated a debt of more than $80 billion, most of which was due for re-servicing over the next few years. To allay fears, officials stated that the government's various assets, estimated at some $85 billion, would be enough to cover this.[63] But such claims were greeted with scepticism because the international media were reporting that most of Dubai's overseas assets were inaccessible or else had been eroded significantly by recessions in their host economies.

By the end of February 2009, Dubai was effectively bankrupt as it struggled to service even the first of 2009's major debt renewals. The Dubai stock exchange, which had earlier taken out loans to buy the Norwegian stock exchange, OMX, needed to refinance $3.8 billion of debt. A last-minute deal was reported in the domestic press as proof that Dubai could keep going, but it soon became apparent that only $2.5 billion of credit had been acquired on the international market, and that other Dubai entities had had to step in to make up for the shortfall.[64] Rumours resurfaced that the emirate would have no option but to seek assistance from oil-rich Abu Dhabi, no matter how unpalatable such a move might be, given the history of the federation described above. Up to this point, Abu Dhabi had remained aloof from Dubai's problems, having only injected $19 billion of liquidity into federal entities in November 2008, and in February having only guaranteed banks in Abu Dhabi, rather than across the whole of the UAE.[65]

By the end of the month, Dubai finally had to turn to Abu Dhabi, with the latter channelling a $10 billion five-year bond for Dubai via the UAE Central Bank. With interest rates set at 4 per cent, this was a lifeline for Dubai, as the emirate had little chance of acquiring such credit elsewhere.[66] In late 2009, with little improvement in the global economy and with one of Dubai's biggest state-backed conglomerates—Dubai World—unable to re-service more than $23 billion of debt, Dubai was obliged to turn to Abu Dhabi for further assistance.[67] While an additional bailout was provided, most analysts agreed this represented the end of Dubai's economic autonomy within the UAE, as Abu Dhabi was able to assume the position of ultimate creditor to its struggling neighbour. In many ways, the shift of economic primacy to Abu Dhabi was underlined in January 2010, when the opening ceremony for the Burj Dubai skyscraper in January 2010 included the unexpected renaming of the tower as Burj Khalifa—in honour of Abu Dhabi's ruler.[68]

Foreign policy and security

Since the above-mentioned amalgamation of the various emirate-level military forces in 1996, the Abu Dhabi-led UAE Armed Forces have evolved into one of the most advanced militaries in the developing world. In the near future their technological sophistication will increase even further given an array of military-related joint ventures, including those involving the Abu Dhabi Shipbuilding Company and Abu Dhabi Aircraft Technologies, mentioned earlier.

With annual armed forces spending amounting to several billion dollars,[69] the UAE Armed Forces are now among the few non-NATO customers both able and eligible to purchase the latest Western armaments.[70] For years the UAE Air Force has relied upon French Mirage jets, and it has now taken delivery of another large order of Mirage 2000s, complete with laser-targeting pods.[71] An even bigger French purchase has been $3 billion worth of Leclerc main battle tanks—in preference to British Challengers.[72] In the near future French manufacturers will be supplying the UAE Armed Forces with modular infrared units that will allow, among other capabilities, night vision and live communication between soldiers and field commanders. Other major army acquisitions have included Turkish armoured personnel carriers and South African and Dutch howitzers. The UAE Air Force has also taken receipt of British Aerospace Hawk 128s, Sikorsky Black Hawk helicopters, Apache AH64 gunships,[73] and a large number of F16E Desert Falcons from Lockheed Martin.[74]

Abu Dhabi has recently placed a special emphasis on missiles and integrated defence systems, as ultimately the UAE Armed Forces lack manpower. Although it may claim to have about 60,000 personnel, it is an open secret that several thousand are Arab or South Asian expatriates,[75] and in May 2011 it was revealed that the founder of the US-based private military contractor Black Water had been training a mercenary army of several hundred Colombian and South African veterans on behalf of Abu Dhabi's Crown Prince. Among the many missile acquisitions have been British-manufactured precision guided missiles specially customised for desert conditions,[76] and similarly customised cruise missiles supplied by a multinational European manufacturer.[77] In 2008 the UAE purchased the Terminal High Altitude Area Defense system (THAAD) manufactured by Lockheed Martin, which is capable of destroying enemy missiles in the stratosphere.[78] Backing up this system are early warning equipment including a US-manufactured radar facility,[79] Boeing early warning and control aircraft, and a German submarine surveillance system.[80]

For the final line of its defence the UAE Armed Forces have also been promised immediate support from superpower militaries, some of which have committed to dispatching rapid reaction forces in the event of conflict. Unsurprisingly, given its history of lucrative arms deals with Abu Dhabi, France has made the firmest guarantees to the UAE. For the past nine years there has been some form of agreement in place,[81] and in 2009 a French base housing between 400 and 500 soldiers was established in Abu Dhabi, although the option of hosting permanent foreign bases on UAE soil had been repeatedly rejected during Sheikh Zayed's reign.[82] The US has been less forthcoming with promises, but it is widely acknowledged that US military and intelligence personnel have been stationed at Abu Dhabi's Dhafrah air base.[83] After the 2005 crash of a US spy drone embarking on a mission over Afghanistan it was revealed that its take-off base at Dhafrah had been used by the US Army Air Force since 2002.[84] More obviously, Dubai's Jebel Ali Port and International Airport are very heavily used by the US Navy and US military contractors,[85] while Abu Dhabi's Mina Zayed is the US Navy's second most used port in the Persian Gulf.[86]

On a policy level, the UAE has continuously positioned itself as a wealthy active neutral. Historically, it has tried to intervene in almost every regional dispute, with the UAE Armed Forces regularly dispatching gift-bearing peacekeeping forces to troubled neighbours and the ruling families of Abu Dhabi and Dubai frequently seeking to broker peace deals. This strategy has allowed the UAE to build upon its overseas aid programmes by strengthening its reputation as a concerned Arab intermediary, which has undoubtedly helped to deflect public Arab opinion away from the UAE military's heavy dependency on a Western superpower umbrella.

The first example of such diplomacy was in 1974 when Zayed mediated a territorial dispute between Egypt and Libya.[87] And in 1977 UAE soldiers were deployed for the first time, when a contingent was sent to join the Joint Arab Deterrent Force in Lebanon.[88] In 1991 Zayed attempted to save Iraq from full-scale invasion by meeting King Fahd of Saudi Arabia and President Mubarak of Egypt in an effort to forge an agreement between Saddam Hussein and the displaced ruler of Kuwait, Sheikh Jaber Al-Ahmad Al-Sabah.[89] The following year the UAE Armed Forces made their maiden intervention outside the Middle East by sending a peacekeeping force to assist US operations in Somalia.[90] During the mid-1990s more UAE troops arrived in Somalia, in addition to Rwanda and Mozambique.[91] Significantly, in 1995 the UAE Armed

Forces became the first Arab military to intervene in a modern European conflict when they began to airlift wounded Muslims out of Bosnia. By 1999 Abu Dhabi was again proactive in the Balkans, sending a force to help protect the embattled Muslim Kosovars.[92]

In an echo of his 1991 negotiations, in early 2003 Zayed proposed an emergency summit with the aim of diverting the US from attacking Iraq. A meeting was held in Sharm el-Sheikh and presided over by the Arab League Secretary-General.[93] Zayed was reported to have offered Saddam Hussein and his family sanctuary in Abu Dhabi if he complied with US demands to leave Iraq.[94] Since Sheikh Khalifa's succession in 2004, Abu Dhabi's actively neutral foreign policy has remained unchanged. In early 2007 the UAE's Minister for Foreign Affairs, Sheikh Abdullah, flew to Iran to meet that country's leaders,[95] and later in the year (and within the space of just one week) Khalifa separately hosted both President Mahmoud Ahmadinejad of Iran and the US Vice President Dick Cheney, presumably with the intention of defusing the Iran-US nuclear standoff.[96]

In 2008 Abu Dhabi was, if anything a more energetic peacekeeper and middleman than ever before. Early in the year it was revealed by the BBC that several hundred UAE Armed Forces troops and armoured cars had been deployed to Afghanistan to maintain supply line security and deliver humanitarian aid. On occasion the contingent had to fend off Taliban attacks, which made it the only Arab force in Afghanistan that actually engaged the enemy.[97] Later in the year Condoleezza Rice, who was en route to East Asia, was invited to Abu Dhabi to debrief the US envoy William Burns on his Iran negotiations and also to meet Abdullah. Just one week before, Sheikh Muhammad bin Zayed had received Ali Rida Sheikh Attar, an envoy of Ahmadinejad and undersecretary to the Iranian Minister for Foreign Affairs.[98] Shortly afterwards Khalifa sent Abdullah to Baghdad—the first high-ranking Gulf Cooperation Council ministerial visit since the outbreak of war—and then appointed a UAE ambassador to Iraq for the first time in five years.[99] Combined, these actions earned Khalifa praise during United Nations Security Council meetings in August 2008.[100]

Nevertheless, despite the sophistication of the UAE's military build-up, its superpower support, and the skilful diplomacy, the country is still vulnerable to either an outright attack, or, more likely, collateral damage from a proximate conventional war—especially one that results in the blocking of key oil export arteries such as the Strait of Hormuz, or one that endangers the waters close to the UAE's offshore operations or the hinterland of its onshore operations. Of these threats the greatest is undoubtedly that of Iranian aggression, which will escalate if Iran is the object of Israeli or US interdiction and retaliates by threatening to strike a pro-US Gulf state. This risk is compounded by the ongoing dispute over the islands occupied by Iran in 1971. An accommodation was reached shortly after the invasion between the Shah of Iran and the ruler of Sharjah, which was supposed to ensure that the only inhabited island would technically remain a municipality of Sharjah. However, in the early 1990s Iran reneged on the deal as Revolutionary Guards began to demand that all UAE national residents of Abu Musa obtained Iranian entry visas.[101] Since then, Iran has opened an airport and a town hall on Abu Musa,[102] and in 2008 Tehran began to build a coastguard station and a registration office for ships and sailors. Most worrying, in addition to conducting naval exercises close to the islands, it has been reported that Iran intends to deploy 200km range anti-ship missiles on Abu Musa: these would be capable of closing the Strait of Hormuz indefinitely.[103]

Future challenges

Among the numerous future challenges facing the UAE, the need for indigenisation of the labour force has for some years been particularly acute. Although a generous welfare state has clearly been a cornerstone of the country's stability, many of the structures it has created have limited the indigenous population's potential to participate fully in the UAE's extraordinary economic development. Notably, a citizenry has been cultivated over the past forty years that is accustomed to material benefits and to very few forms of extraction, and thus lacks motivation to seek meaningful employment. With the diversification programmes already described beginning to take shape, this problem will become increasingly urgent as many of the new sectors are being spearheaded by semi-governmental bodies or in some cases even private sector companies, and there is a real danger that the current generation of UAE nationals will fail to integrate. Conservative estimates are that nationals now make up only 9 per cent of the UAE's workforce[104] and there are currently 17,000 unemployed Emirati adults.[105] Other estimates have put the figure as high as 35,000,[106] many of these being degree holders.[107] More broadly, it is thought that well over 50 per cent of those nationals in receipt of the generous social security benefits are able-bodied and capable of work.[108]

The only long-term solution seems to be improved education at all levels. Nationals must acquire the qualifications demanded by employers and thereby meet directly the needs of the new economy. Unfortunately the education system in the UAE is still failing badly, with the Education Development Index having recently ranked the UAE ninetieth out of 125 surveyed countries for the quality of its education provision.[109] Moreover, in 2007 the World Bank indicated that the UAE's knowledge economy—that is, the sectors of the economy relating to the production of knowledge and requiring educated professionals—had actually shrunk since 2005, with the blame placed on a deterioration of the domestic education sector.[110]

Another key challenge for the UAE is how to develop some form of roadmap for political reform. This has become particularly pressing in the wake of the 2011 uprisings elsewhere in the Arab world and the UAE's perceived role as trying to defend the status quo. This was most apparent in Bahrain where the UAE joined Saudi Arabia in contributing several hundred armed policemen to help put down a revolt. Although the current blend of informal and formal political institutions, backed by generous transfers of wealth to citizens, seems to have kept protestors off the UAE's streets, the authorities have nonetheless begun to take political prisoners. In March 2011 five signatories of a 133-person petition that called for an elected parliament were arrested and imprisoned. These included a prominent academic[111] and a prominent blogger and human rights activist.[112] Moreover, the few genuine civil society organisations that did exist have since been dismantled, or have been taken over by the government, their elected board members being dismissed. The most prominent examples are the UAE Jurists Association and the UAE Teachers Association, both of which signed the petition as institutional actors.

There are also a number of other pressures building that may soon require revisions to the UAE's political system, especially as the indigenous population continues to grow[113] and as increasing urbanisation[114] and female economic participation[115] reduce large, extended families to more nuclear units, and old informal connections are placed under strain. Quite simply, nationals will find it more difficult to access directly sheikhs in their courts or to find suitable traditional intermediaries. In addition, in Abu Dhabi's and Dubai's keenness to integrate their economies into the international system, the UAE has duly joined several international organisations. Some of these, including the World Trade Organisation—which admitted the UAE in 1996—require all member states to have a roadmap towards good governance.[116] Thus there has to be some kind of plan in place. Given the mixed experiences with Western-style democratic implants in Iraq and given the UAE rulers' hostility to the Arab Spring 2011 movements elsewhere in the region, it is likely that those rulers will try carefully to readjust the existing polity in such a way that it remains connected to the country's anthropological reality.[117]

Closely connected to the need for such reform is the need for greater transparency across the establishment, especially given the stronger spotlight that is beginning to shine on the UAE as it becomes more closely engaged in international partnerships and ventures. Thus far, most government departments and authorities remain opaque and secretive. Often the private nature of Bedouin culture is used as a convenient explanatory device by establishment figures or long-serving expatriate advisers. However, when most male members of the ruling family occupy key positions in government and when government controlled entities are effectively in control of the country's natural resources, its overseas assets, and therefore its future prosperity, there is a growing feeling that these individuals and institutions must submit to more domestic scrutiny. With so much ostensible public wealth at stake it seems fair that the broader citizenry should at least have access to basic information, and should especially be assured of the ethical correctness of any sovereign wealth investments or other foreign linkages. Moreover, as Abu Dhabi's massive funds extend deeper into other countries institutions and companies, the UAE will also have to be prepared to submit to more thorough external investigations.

Should the opacity persist, it will frustrate the ambitions of UAE's infant new economic sectors. All of the high technology heavy industries, the real estate developers, and the tourism developers are reliant on the UAE having a sound international reputation. Most of the parastatals and companies pioneering these developments need to be respected by their global partners as credible corporations with boards of directors and transparent codes of practice. In 2009 a new Abu Dhabi Accountability Authority was set up. It was granted powers to investigate the financial reports of government-backed entities that it wishes to place under greater scrutiny. Unfortunately, an article of its enabling legislation states that the new authority can only examine entities in which the government share is less than 50 per cent,[118] thus effectively keeping the major sovereign wealth authorities above inspection. Moreover, its powers are limited to Abu Dhabi, and do not extend across the whole of the UAE. Although less conspicuous, another significant challenge for the UAE will be to address the increasing wealth gap between the two wealthiest emirates and the five poorest. Although Abu Dhabi has a long history of assisting its more indigent neighbours and Sheikh Zayed was instrumental in inserting an article[119] into the federal constitution that called for the federal ministries to ensure a commitment to uniform health, education and welfare across the UAE,[120] in relative terms the wealth has never been spread evenly, and this has hampered the poorer emirates from developing their own economies. Some have national populations living in poverty-stricken circumstances, and opponents have claimed that unemployment rates for nationals in Fujairah and Ra's al-Khaimah could be as high as 60 per cent. The earliest federal development initiatives earmarked several million Bahraini dinars for projects across the UAE, but this was little compared to the hundreds of millions of dinars being spent over the course of Abu Dhabi's first five year domestic plan.[121] Recently, it was announced that the federal budget had been raised to $7.7 billion[122] and that a 'rescue package' of $4.3 billion had been allocated to oversee physical infrastructure projects in the northern emirates. In early 2011 another emergency package of $1.5 billion was announced. But these remain small sums compared with the enormous amounts being spent on developments in Abu Dhabi and Dubai. Unsurprisingly, announcements of such rescue packages have often been greeted with scepticism by the recipient municipalities.[123]

There have been two major consequences of the growing divide between the rich and the poor. First, the share of the federation's total GDP accounted for by Abu Dhabi and Dubai has continued to increase.[124] Secondly, given that the bulk of job opportunities for aspiring nationals are in Abu Dhabi and Dubai, many nationals from the poorer emirates have had little choice but to commute to the two wealthiest emirates, and in some cases even relocate. Very often such commuters have to share rented apartments close to their workplaces and can only return home to their family residences at the weekends, thus making them labour migrants within their own country. It is no coincidence, perhaps, that many of the 2011 petition signatories and two of the political prisoners were members of the largest Ra's al-Khaimah tribe.[125]

BAHRAIN

Jane Kinninmont

State formation

Bahrain may be the smallest country in the Arab world, but it serves as an important intersection for a variety of transnational political movements and regional strategic interests, and Bahraini civil society activists like to say that virtually every Arab political current has been represented in their country at one time or another. While Bahrain has been economically dependent on Saudi Arabia for most of the past century, its position as a small archipelago of islands in the Persian Gulf has helped it develop an historical identity that is distinct from the mainland of the Arabian Peninsula. In particular, its capital, Manama, has elements in common with other port cities, as its history of openness to trade and migration means it has traditionally had a cosmopolitan society. The modern state of Bahrain is young, like most of the other Gulf states, having declared its independence in 1971 when Britain withdrew from the region. Previously, Bahrain was indirectly ruled by Britain, and for some decades it was the seat of Britain's imperial administration in the Gulf. Many of the institutions of the modern state—and some of the key elements of the economy—were formed during the period of British rule, which was also the beginning of the oil era.

Bahrain's[1] earlier history remains politically contentious, and is a rich resource for today's competing political narratives. Given its role as a strategically important nexus for trade routes, blessed with natural resources (abundant fresh water, dates and pearls), Bahrain was fought

31

over by various tribes and empires throughout its history. It was ruled at different times by Iran, Portugal and Oman, among others. Iranian politicians still sporadically express nostalgia for Bahrain's former role as Iran's 'fourteenth province', routinely outraging Bahrain's government. Although such diplomatic disputes are usually short-lived, there nonetheless remains an anxiety among Bahraini policy-makers over Iran's intentions, which is unsurprising given the relative infancy of the state and the memory of Iraq's invasion of Kuwait in 1990—which was based on the revival of an old territorial claim. Suspicion of Iran also has detrimental effects on the ruling family's relationship with Bahrain's Shia community, which is believed to make up a roughly 60 per cent majority of the population. The fact that many Shia Bahrainis look to clerics outside the country—mainly in Iraq and Iran—as religious references has stoked fears among some members of the ruling family and some other Sunni Bahrainis that their Shia compatriots are not fully loyal to the state, or even that they are 'fifth columnists' for Iran. The current ruling family came to power in 1783, but Bahrain's identity as a country with defined borders and nationality laws took considerably longer to solidify. Historical narratives by official, court-sponsored historians tend to focus on the tribal history of the Al-Khalifa on the Arabian mainland and the instability that Bahrain faced prior to the Al-Khalifa's conquest, thus positioning the family as the rulers who finally brought peace and security to Bahrain (with perhaps a little help from the Britain's Royal Navy). By contrast, opposition discourse frequently presents the Al-Khalifa as foreign usurpers oppressing the 'indigenous' people, called 'Baharna'—a term that usually refers to Shia Arab Bahrainis. Both sets of narratives have their blind spots, however, and these are exacerbated by a paucity of historical archives from this period.

The Al-Khalifa's authority has its roots in the family's conquest of the Bahrain archipelago from the Persian Empire in 1783. Originally from the mainland Arabian Peninsula, the family is part of a wider tribal grouping known as the Bani Utub, as is the Kuwaiti ruling family, the Al-Sabah. Given Bahrain's small size and its location sandwiched between much larger countries, the ruling family has historically sought security guarantees from larger powers. The Al-Khalifa rulers made overtures to the Ottoman Empire and even the Persian Empire before developing a closer relationship with Britain. Britain's protection was set out by a series of treaties from 1830 and onwards and kept the Al-Khalifa's rule from being seriously challenged by external powers, such as the Sultan of Muscat, who had briefly conquered Bahrain in 1800. Nevertheless there were also political costs for the Al-Khalifa. Notably, Britain prevented the Al-Khalifa from fighting to regain territories they had once held on the nearby Qatari peninsula.

Initially, Britain's main interest in Bahrain was the securing of maritime trade routes between the Gulf and India (containing the influence of rival empires, deterring tribes from fighting in the region, and quelling piracy) and, as more British Indians migrated to Bahrain, safeguarding British subjects in the country. During the 1920s, however, Britain's role in Bahrain expanded significantly from the original protectorate relationship that focused on foreign policy and external threats to a far deeper engagement in the way Bahrain was governed. This partly reflected Britain's changing role in the Gulf and its concerns about rival powers. The personalities and views of individual British administrators were also important: communications with London or Bombay were slow and the 'man on the ground' thus had considerable decision-making power. Two figures, Major Clive Daly (British Political Agent from 1921 to 1926) and Sir Charles Belgrave (the Bahraini ruler's 'adviser' from 1926 to 1957), were particularly important.

A turning point in the relationship came in 1923 when British officials in effect compelled the ageing ruler, Sheikh Issa bin Ali Al-Khalifa, to step down after fifty-four years in favour of his son and heir apparent, Sheikh Hamed bin Issa Al-Khalifa. British records from the time indicate that Daly had become increasingly concerned about domestic instability at a time when Sheikh Issa had become largely disengaged from ruling and his two sons were openly competing for power. Moreover, Britain had already played a role in extending some protection to the rights of Persian merchants, fearing that Persia might use the mistreatment of its subjects in Bahrain as a pretext to press its territorial claims. In 1920, an unknown number of Bahraini Shia petitioned the British agency to protect them also from mistreatment by the ruling family. This was an early example of a tradition of popular petitions that continues to this day. Indeed, current Bahraini opposition activists emphasise the long-term legacy of protest in Bahrain and have drawn on British imperial records from the British Library, as well as Belgrave's unpublished diaries,[2] to build up a historical narrative about the ruling family's repressive tactics.

In response to the 1920 petition, Daly convinced London that following the First World War concerns about German or other foreign ambitions in the Gulf had lessened, and that Britain had never before 'been in so unfettered a position for insisting upon the long delayed and necessary reforms to the internal administration of Bahrain'.[3] Within three years Sheikh Issa had, in Belgrave's words, 'very unwillingly been persuaded by the British to retire'[4] and appoint his son, Sheikh Hamed, as prince regent. Sheikh Hamed then appointed several British officials as administrators and advisers, including Belgrave, who became his financial adviser and state treasurer. Belgrave remained the power behind the throne until 1957, when his growing unpopularity with the public was exacerbated by widespread anger over Britain's role in the Suez war and he, in turn, was persuaded to retire.

Meanwhile, Daly took further steps to expand British power in several key areas of domestic politics and administration.[5] The 1920s saw the establishment of the modern court system and the first formal schools. In 1926 elections were established for half the seats on municipal councils. In the economic sphere, Daly took control over customs revenue, previously the Al-Khalifa's main source of income, and instead paid the sheikh a stipend. In 1924 he restructured the pearl industry, weakening the control of the Sunni pearl merchants and, at least in theory, giving more rights to the debt-bonded pearl-divers.[6] There was strong resistance from the merchants. Some moved to the mainland, where they would not be hampered by such regulations. Bahrain's pearl exports duly shrank. Meanwhile, Britain successfully co-opted other leading merchants as 'native agents'.[7]

The financial power of the merchants allowed them to check the power of the ruler, particularly in the first three decades of the twentieth century, when pearling was still lucrative. Before 1929, when passports and nationality laws were introduced, the merchants were free to move between different parts of the Gulf, taking their boats and divers with them. Competition between different Gulf ports for trade encouraged Bahrain to maintain a relatively laissez-faire attitude to trade, still evident today. The collapse of the pearling industry from the late 1920s—following Japan's invention of the cultured pearl—was a near-disaster for Bahrain, sharply reducing the country's export revenue and 'threatening to undermine the socio-political order'.[8] But in an immense stroke of fortune for Bahrain, a new resource was discovered very shortly afterwards.

The discovery of oil in 1932 by the Bahrain Petroleum Company (Bapco) marked another step change in Bahrain's twentieth-century development. Bapco was originally a subsidiary of Standard Oil of the United States; finding oil in Bahrain encouraged Standard Oil to explore for oil elsewhere in the Gulf, including Saudi Arabia, where it obtained a concession in 1933. Oil gradually altered the relationship between the merchants and the royal family, which now had an independent source of income. Officially, oil revenues were split three ways between the ruler, the administration run by Belgrave, and an oil reserve fund. The 1930s also saw the emergence of a modern labour movement at Bapco, which soon became the largest employer in the country. After completing several major construction projects, it laid off many manual workers, slashing the Bahraini workforce by more than half between 1937 and 1938.[9] Meanwhile, an increasing proportion of jobs were being filled by Indian workers, who—in stark contrast to today—were paid higher wages, being perceived as more efficient and being British subjects.

November 1938 saw the first organised strike at Bapco. The ideas of Arab nationalism were spreading across the increasingly well-educated Bahraini population, and reform movements were emerging in Kuwait and Dubai. Pan-Arab media from Egypt and Iraq were encouraging resistance to foreign (mostly British) interference.[10] In early November 1938, just before the Bapco strike, five prominent Bahrainis—Shia and Sunni—signed a petition calling for jobs, better education, and judicial reforms. Several campaigners for reform were arrested. The Bapco strikers sought their release, better working conditions and equal pay for Bahrainis and Indians. Some of their demands were granted, though not equal pay, but another strike in 1943 made more headway in securing workers' demands.

Arab nationalism remained a powerful force throughout the 1940s and 1950s, its ideas spreading partly through transnational networks as Arab teachers from Egypt and elsewhere came to work in Bahrain. From the 1950s, the messages of Egypt's pan-Arabist and anti-colonialist leader Gamel Abdel-Nasser became popular among Sunni and Shia Bahrainis alike. With literacy rates improving, a series of independent Bahraini newspapers launched in the 1950s began to promote pan-Arabism and a more leftist approach to social justice.[11] Particularly important was *Sawt al-Bahrain* (Voice of Bahrain), an independent monthly published between 1950 and 1954, whose editorial board included two prominent nationalists, Abdelrahman Al-Baker and Abdelaziz Shamlan. They were among the founders of the Higher Executive Committee (HEC, also known as Al-Hayah), a nationalist organisation established in 1954 that aimed to mobilise labour, oppose Britain's role in Bahrain, and campaign for a more representative government. In 1955, the HEC established the first trade union, with around 6,000 members, mainly drawn from Bapco and the civil service.

By 1956, anti-colonial sentiments were widespread and tensions were simmering. In March that year, a standoff between police and Shia villagers, triggered by the case of a Shia peddler ejected from the bazaar for trading without a permit, ended with five villagers being shot by policemen. The HEC called a general strike, during which roads were blocked and property damaged. By May the government had begun to negotiate with the HEC leaders, after they met several preconditions, including a change of name (to the Committee of National Unity, or CNU). However, progress was slow. Fuad Khury's analysis attributes this primarily to the opposition's lack of a clear structure and organisation—it was deeply divided over methods of resistance, and particularly the role of street unrest,[12] and its leaders feared that they would be outflanked by more militant oppositionists. In November that year the British occupation of the Suez Canal sparked further anger among Arab nationalists. The CNU leaders staged a rally in central Manama, which quickly got out of control and sparked two days of rioting and arson. The majority of participants were from the urban Sunni population, and the government calculated that it would be able to take advantage of a largely sect-based split in attitudes to the events. The authorities therefore cracked down severely. Three leaders of the HEC—Al-Baker, Al-Shamlan, and Abdelali Aliwat—were deported to St Helena and jailed there for five years, having been accused of plotting to assassinate the ruler.[13] Back in Bahrain, a state of emergency was declared.

Despite the divisions over the riots, the Arab nationalist leaders of the HEC had been more successful than most in downplaying sectarian differences and in creating a cross-sectarian political leadership based on conceptions of class and nationality, not sectarian communal identities. This was in contrast, for instance, to the representatives of the Shia community who had unilaterally petitioned the British in 1920. Most of the literature on this period agrees that the rapid economic changes wrought by the discovery of oil and the inflow of foreign labour, combined with the transnational ideas of Arab nationalism, created new forms of class consciousness and political identity. Oil workers were drawn from both Sunni and Shia communities and labour organisers focused on their common conditions. Nationalist agitators were also drawn from Manama's commercial classes, who had grown wealthier as the revenues from oil exports expanded and circulated.[14] Furthermore, from 1932 onwards, Sunni and Shia schools were amalgamated into a unified education system, allowing for greater social interaction.[15] Sectarianism remained a threat and HEC activists worked hard to spread the concept of cross-sectarian unity. The Arab nationalist and secularist groups of today often portray this period as a golden age for cross-sectarian co-operation. This view may be romanticised, but nonetheless the contrast with the present-day situation—where most political movements are Islamists of one sect or another—is stark.

The 1960s and early 1970s saw the emergence of other secularist movements, notably the pan-Gulf Popular Front for the Liberation of Oman and the Arabian Gulf. Its members were often Bahraini activists who had been influenced by the rebellion in Oman's Dhofar province, and some even went to Oman to help the Dhofaris with their campaign. Political Islam also began to become more influential as the Iraqi Dawa party also became an important influence on Shia Bahrainis. All of these groups operated underground.

Another key change in Bahraini politics followed the British government's 1968 decision to withdraw from its territories east of Suez by the end of 1971. Withdrawal from Bahrain required first resolving the territorial dispute with Iran, and in 1970 the United Nations sent a representative to carry out a plebiscite on whether Bahrainis would prefer to be ruled by the Al-Khalifa or Iran. While this made a gesture towards the UN principle of national self-determination, it was in fact based on a survey of selected Bahrainis, and not, as is sometimes thought, on a genuine nationwide referendum. The plebiscite unsurprisingly found that Al-Khalifa rule was the preferred option for the majority of the people surveyed. In turn, and following extensive talks with Britain and Saudi Arabia, the Shah of Iran agreed to give up the claim to Bahrain. Some accounts suggest there was a deal that allowed Iran to retain three islands also claimed by the UAE—Abu Musa and the two Tunbs—in exchange for relinquishing Bahrain, though this account is controversial. Prior to Britain's withdrawal, the Bahraini ruler, Sheikh Issa, also agreed to lease the soon-to-be-vacated British military facilities to the US Navy,[16] effectively giving the newly independent country a new external protector.[17]

Following independence, a new constitution was drafted, providing for a fully elected parliament, which was duly formed in December 1973.

The electorate was restricted to male citizens over twenty years old. The main blocs were the eight-strong Popular Bloc, a leftist grouping, and a six-strong Religious Bloc, the rest being independents. The experiment proved short-lived. The parliament quickly fell out with the ruler over the state budget, the US presence in Bahrain, internal security legislation, and its members' desire for land reform. Public finances had become particularly contentious because oil revenues had swollen after the 1973 oil crisis. In 1975 the ruler dissolved the parliament and the country was without a parliament until 2002, with a fully elected parliament never being reinstated.

The 1979 revolution in Iran, and the subsequent establishment of an Islamic republic with a stated goal of exporting the revolution, had seismic effects in Bahrain. Following the revolution, an influential ayatollah, Sadiq Rouhani, sought to revive Iran's claim to Bahrain, saying it had been relinquished unjustly by the illegitimate regime of the Shah and accusing the Bahraini government of mistreating its population. Iran's foreign ministry denied that this was official policy. Nonetheless, Bahrain, like other small Gulf states, was profoundly concerned by Iran's ambitions and the repercussions of the revolution. There were pro-Iran demonstrations in Bahrain and five Shia clerics called for greater application of Islamic law in Bahrain. In 1981 the Bahraini authorities arrested seventy-three people accused of plotting a coup on behalf of a pro-Iran organisation, the Islamic Front for the Liberation of Bahrain (IFLB), led by an Iraqi cleric, Hadi Modaressi. There is controversy over the extent of the threat the IFLB posed to the government, and the degree to which it was supported by the central Iranian government. Nonetheless, the affair greatly added to the Al-Khalifa's anxieties over Iran's intentions towards Bahrain, as well as suspicions over the loyalties of Persian-origin Bahrainis.

The political opposition was relatively subdued for much of the 1980s. Outside the country, a group of Bahrainis studying or exiled in Britain formed the main opposition-in-exile, the Bahrain Islamic Freedom Movement (BFM), which was then led by Saeed Al-Shehabi, Mansour Al-Jamri and Majid Al-Alawi. The BFM has remained a staunch critic of the ruling family, but in contrast to the IFLB—which continued to issue statements from offices in Damascus, Tehran and London—it called for reinstatement of the parliament and the introduction of a constitutional monarchy rather than for a revolution.[18] This was to remain the case until 2011, when the success of the uprisings in Tunisia and Egypt would change its calculations.

The US presence in Bahrain was expanded during the Iran-Iraq war and again after Iraq's invasion of Kuwait in 1990. US military records indicate that Bahrain's ruling family supported the 1991 Operation Desert Storm attacks on Iraq, fearing that if Iraq was simply allowed to pull out of Kuwait, its army could remain a serious threat to the smaller Gulf states. A few Bahraini pilots took part in US-led raids on Iraqi radar installations.[19] Following the war, the US strategy of 'dual containment' for Iraq and Iran led the US to bolster its defensive forces in the region and step up joint exercises with local militaries. The US Navy duly signed a defence co-operation agreement with Bahrain.

At the same time Bahrain faced economic challenges as the price of oil had declined significantly by comparison with the 1970s boom. From 1981 to 1985 the price of dated Brent blend averaged $31 per barrel; from 1986 to 1990 it averaged $18 per barrel, and from 1991 to 1995 only $17.8 per barrel. Government spending and real average incomes declined in the second half of the 1980s, and although the government increased spending in the mid-1990s, economic strains were clearly being felt, especially with a population growth of 3.5 per cent per year. In 1992 some 300 prominent Bahrainis, including senior Sunni and Shia clerics as well as leftists, petitioned the ruler by calling for reinstatement of the 1973 elected parliament and the release of political prisoners. As a gesture, the ruler agreed to establish an appointed advisory council and said that it would end the discussion on the subject of parliament. Meanwhile, several pro-parliament activists were detained.

In 1994 a combination of religious and secular opposition groups formed a 'popular committee' that drafted a second petition calling for the return of the parliament and for female suffrage. Opposition sources claim that over 20,000 signed the petition. However, the drive to collect signatures was overtaken by increasingly serious unrest on the streets and December 1994 saw the emergence of a loose and decentralised uprising that opposition activists call the Bahraini *intifada*,[20] driven by issues of political, economic and social exclusion. Protests were heavily concentrated in Shia villages but Shia protestors found common cause with Sunni leftists in calling for the reinstatement of parliament. A heavy-handed government response was largely coordinated by the director of public security, Ian Henderson, a former British official whose previous experience included the British colonial operations against the Mau Mau uprising in Kenya. Three Shia leaders, including Sheikh Ali Salman, a young and charismatic cleric, were deported in January 1995. After this, mass demonstrations eclipsed popular petitions[21] as the main form of protest. Several prominent Shia leaders, including the country's most senior Shia cleric, Sheikh Abdelamir Al-Jamri (the father of Mansour Al-Jamri), were jailed in 1995 but freed after a few months following a tacit agreement whereby they would calm the unrest while the government considered their demands. No progress was made on their demands, unrest continued, and several of the leaders were rearrested. Unrest gradually intensified, with petrol bombings and arson attacks. In June 1996 the authorities claimed to have uncovered a coup plot by an Iran-backed, Bahrain-based offshoot of Hezbollah.[22] Draconian state security laws permitted lengthy detention without trial and around forty activists are believed to have died or disappeared before 1999, when Sheikh Issa died and was succeeded by his son, Sheikh Hamad bin Isa Al-Khalifa, in a smooth and uncontested transition.

Political structures and personalities

The relations between the different branches of government are laid out in the 2002 constitution. This constitution was controversial, as it reinstated a parliament of sorts but ensured that the powers of elected MPs were significantly weaker than they had been in the 1970s. As in most pre-2011 Arab states, the executive is the dominant arm of government, while the legislature and the judiciary are significantly weaker and depend heavily on the executive. The most powerful members of the executive are the ruler, the prime minister, and the crown prince. Hence the lines between state, government and ruling family are very blurred. Until 2002 Bahrain was an emirate, but in 2002 the new constitution promulgated by the ruler, Sheikh Hamad bin Issa Al-Khalifa, redesignated the country as a kingdom. Hamad thus became unusual among Gulf monarchs by using the title 'king' (the Saudi ruler holds the title of king but more often uses the more religious style of 'Custodian of the Two Holy Mosques'). The constitution concentrates power heavily in the king's hands; he appoints the cabinet, half the MPs and the judges, and needs to approve all laws.

The premiership, as an institution, can hardly be disentangled from the individual who holds the role—Sheikh Khalifa bin Salman Al-Khalifa, the king's uncle—as he is the only prime minister that Bahrain has ever had, having taken office at independence in 1971. Under the rule of Sheikh Issa, Sheikh Khalifa was responsible for much of the day-to-day running of the country. Under the rule of King Hamad, there were initially some gradual steps to rein in his powers, though this process may now have halted. Sheikh Khalifa is a controversial figure: his supporters say he has done more than any other individual to develop Bahrain's economy and argue that other Gulf monarchies would be unhappy if there was any attempt to remove such a senior figure (which could potentially be seen as a precedent for the retirement of other senior royals in the Gulf). His critics accuse him of continued attempts to hinder political reforms. Indeed, for many in the opposition, he is a symbol of continuity with the pre-reform political system. Public criticism of the Prime Minister has proved dangerous. When Abdelhadi Al-Khawaja, president of the Bahrain Centre for Human Rights, gave a speech in 2004 calling for the Prime Minister's resignation, he was jailed and his centre was banned. More recently, in 2010, there was a somewhat stage-managed outcry when Sheikh Ali Salman of Al-Wefaq suggested that in order to advance towards democracy, Bahrain needed to have an elected prime minister. Sheikh Ali was immediately denounced by pro-government MPs and was accused of 'open sedition', calling for a coup, and conspiring with the British.[23] In March 2011, the opposition pushed for Sheikh Khalifa's removal as a precondition for dialogue with the government. This appeared to be the main sticking point in the attempts to establish negotiations, and it suggests that the Prime Minister had a personal interest in the failure of those attempts.

There is a widespread perception that there has been a decade-long power struggle between the Prime Minister, associated with a conservative camp, and the Crown Prince, who is associated with efforts to modernise the economy and the political system. From 2000 onwards, responsibility for economic policy-making gradually shifted towards the Economic Development Board (EDB), a state agency chaired by the Crown Prince. One of the Prime Minister's sons, Sheikh Salman bin Khalifa Al-Khalifa, was chairman of the board of the Bahrain Petroleum Company, but in 2007 he was replaced by the Oil Minister, Abdulhussain Ali Mirza, a Persian-speaking technocrat who had risen up through Bapco's ranks as an engineer. Similarly, another ally of the Prime Minister, Sheikh Issa bin Ali Al-Khalifa—a former Oil Minister—was removed as the chairman of the second most important state enterprise, Aluminium Bahrain.

The Crown Prince, Sheikh Salman bin Hamad Al-Khalifa, is the eldest of the King's sons. He is deputy commander-in-chief of the army but is better known for his role as chairman of the EDB. Sheikh Salman is seen as a relative reformist, but with more of a focus on economic modernisation than on further democratisation. In 2008 he took the unusual step of complaining openly to his father that some members of the government were blocking economic reforms. The king responded by reiterating that the EDB has overarching authority for all economic policy and that ministers must answer to it. The EDB's board of directors was also expanded to include almost all of the cabinet, in effect setting up a parallel cabinet answering to the Crown Prince, whereas the regular cabinet meets on a weekly basis with the Prime Minister. Al-Khalifa family members hold most of the important ministries, with the notable exception of the oil and gas authority.

In early 2011 it appeared that the balance of power within the government had tilted firmly in favour of the conservative and security-focused members of the royal family and government, and away from the more reformist and development-focused members. The minister of the royal court, Sheikh Khalid bin Ahmed Al-Khalifa, and the Minister of Defence, Sheikh Khalifa bin Ahmed Al-Khalifa, had become increasingly prominent. There had always been some debate about the depth and seriousness of the apparent reformist-conservative split in the family; after all, such apparent internal divisions can in practice be used to alleviate pressures for reform (for instance, by justifying failures to reform on the basis that good intentions were being thwarted by others). However, in early 2011, the indications of a split within the royal family were stronger than ever.

The current parliament, established in 2002, has limited powers. In February 2001, the ruler held a referendum on a National Action Charter (NAC), which promised sweeping political reforms. While it claimed that Bahrain had always been a 'direct democracy' based on traditions of consultation and dialogue, it nevertheless promised to establish a bicameral parliament with an elected chamber to enact laws and an appointed chamber to advise.[24]

The document was immensely popular. According to the official results, it was ratified by 98.4 per cent of voters with a 90 per cent turnout. A number of important political reforms took place as a result. Two days after the referendum, the ruler declared that he was abolishing the state security law, which had given the authorities wide-ranging emergency powers often used against opposition activists, and dissolving the special security courts that were used to sentence hundreds of activists under this law. He also declared an amnesty for citizens who had been found guilty of security crimes, as long as their crimes had not resulted in fatalities. Political prisoners were freed and many exiles returned to the country. Several thousand stateless Bahrainis—mostly people of Persian origin who had never received passports—were given full citizenship. According to Al-Jamri, this was a 'honeymoon period' for relations between the Bahraini Shia and the Al-Khalifa family, as many '...believed that at last the strained relations had become part of a troubled history'.[25]

However, the parliament that was eventually established by the 2002 constitution fell far short of the NAC commitment, as the appointed chamber shared legislative powers with the elected chamber. The ability of the opposition to make changes through parliament was further limited by an uneven distribution of constituencies which diluted the Shia vote, by short hours (as the body sits just one day per week), and by the strength of the executive. The opposition was thus deeply divided over whether to participate in the problematic parliamentary process. Another controversial change introduced in 2002 was the extension of the 2001 amnesty to include military and government employees, some of whom were accused of torture. Bahrain comes closer than most Gulf states to permitting formal political parties in the form of political societies, which are licensed under a 2006 law. However, the law places significant restrictions on their operations and as a result not all political groups are registered under the law.

Perhaps the most important political society in Bahrain is the Al-Wefaq National Islamic Society, headed by Sheikh Ali Salman. Al-Wefaq was formed as an umbrella group for a range of different Shia groups that were active in the opposition in the 1980s and 1990s. Its goals include better living standards for its mostly Shia constituents, particularly in terms of access to jobs and housing, an end to sectarian discrimination (in particular, more merit-based access to government jobs), fighting corruption, and amending the constitution to give more power to elected MPs. Its MPs have also co-operated with Sunni Islamist MPs on so-called 'morality issues' such as restricting the sale of alcohol. Over the past decade it has increasingly focused on the controversial issue of political naturalisation—an alleged unofficial government policy of giving citizenship to Sunnis from overseas in an attempt to doctor the sectarian balance. While it is primarily an opposition movement, it has sought to take a conciliatory approach towards the government, and after boycotting the first parliamentary elections under the new constitution in protest against the limits on parliamentary power, it took part in the elections of 2006 and 2010, winning every seat it fought (but failing to obtain a majority in parliament because of the gerrymandering of constituencies). Al-Wefaq has many female supporters and activists, but has yet to field any female candidates for election.

Sheikh Ali has repeatedly said that the party seeks to participate in politics in a democratic, secular constitutional monarchy. Nonetheless, officials periodically accuse Al-Wefaq of having a hidden agenda to establish an Iranian-style theocracy in Bahrain, regardless of what the group itself says. Sheikh Ali is more influenced by Iraqi clerics than by those in Iran, describing himself as a follower of Ayatollah Al-Khoei, who was not a proponent of Iranian-style *vilayet-e-faqih* (Guardianship of the Jurist, a doctrine invented by Iran's Ayatollah Ruhollah Khomeini). Nonetheless, he needs to take account of the views of the country's most prominent Shia cleric, Sheikh Issa Qassim, a former Dawa member and ex-MP from the 1973–75 parliaments, who is generally believed to be more sympathetic to the Iranian approach. Sheikh Issa does not favour co-operation with secular groups, but Al-Wefaq has nonetheless formed electoral alliances with a leftist party, Wa'ad. All eighteen Al-Wefaq MPs resigned their seats in parliament in early 2011 in protest against a violent clampdown on protests in which several people were killed, and the group joined seven opposition societies in calling for the King to meet several conditions, including dissolution of the existing cabinet and removal of the Prime Minister, before negotiations on political reform. The seven societies were encouraged by the overthrow of presidents by popular uprisings in Egypt and Tunisia, angered by the deaths of unarmed protestors, and worried about being outflanked by more radical opposition groups that had begun to call for an outright revolution to overthrow the royal family. However, the seven societies appear to have misjudged the government's willingness to reform (perhaps because they were in contact only with the more reformist elements) as well as its ability to rally support both domestically (particularly from Sunni Bahrainis and naturalised citizens who were alienated and alarmed by people calling for the overthrow of the Al-Khalifa and by increasingly disruptive protests in the central business district) and regionally (particularly from Saudi Arabia and the UAE). In mid-March, Bahraini security forces began a heavy-handed and wide-ranging clampdown on the opposition, with backing from Saudi and UAE security forces brought in under the umbrella of the 'Peninsula Shield'—a collective defence force for the Gulf Co-operation Council. Some Al-Wefaq MPs were arrested and the Justice Ministry threatened to ban the group, but its clear popularity may have prevented it from being targeted quite as much as some of the other 'seven societies'.

Another of the 'seven societies' was a smaller Shia group, the Islamic Action Society, which represents the Shirazi strain of Shi'ism, followers of the Shirazi family of clerics from Karbala in Iraq. The society includes former members of the Islamic Front for the Liberation of Bahrain. Subsequently, however, the Shiraziyyin, as they were called, became opponents of the Iranian system of government. The group's secretary-general, a Shia cleric, Sheikh Muhammed Ali Mafoudh, was arrested in March 2011 along with several other opposition leaders accused of trying to overthrow the government.

The Sunni Islamist vote has been split between two societies, Al-Menbar, an offshoot of the Muslim Brotherhood, and Al-Asala, a Salafi group, as well as a number of (mostly pro-government) independents. The leaders of both parties are broadly loyal to the government and although they may share common ground with Al-Wefaq on some issues, such as concerns over corruption and living standards, they appear to judge broadly that the status quo serves their interests better than a Shia-dominated democracy. In sharp contrast to Saudi Arabia, the Salafis of Al-Asala have tended to be more open to co-operation with the Shia Islamists than the Muslim Brotherhood. They have criticised the government on economic and religious issues, but have been far less critical on issues of political governance or democratic reform.[26] Al-Asala, which is believed to have more low-income constituents than Al-Menbar, needs to place emphasis on issues such as corruption, opaque land acquisition, and naturalisation. A newer Sunni grouping, the National Unity Gathering, led by a cleric, Sheikh Abdelatif Al-Mahood, emerged in early 2011 in response to the protests and the demands made by the 'seven societies'. Sheikh Abdelatif has acknowledged the need for some reforms, for instance on corruption, but portrayed the February 2011 protests as a sectarian Shia initiative. It appears that the fear of Shia activism—and the government's allegations that the protests were the result of an external plot, variously attributed to Iran, Hezbollah and Iraq—drew together many Sunni Bahrainis who were previously disunited or even apolitical.

The political scene is not entirely segmented along sectarian lines. Notably, Wa'ad, formerly the National Democratic Action Society, has its origins in the Arab nationalism of the 1950s and argues for cross-sectarian co-operation. It could be described as a secular leftist group; its 2010 election campaign focused heavily on the problem of corruption. According to Wa'ad's secretary-general, Ebrahim Sharif—a businessman, economist, and former investment banker—the group's membership is 'about 60 percent Shia and 40 percent Sunni, roughly in line with society'.[27] Seven of its eleven leaders have married someone from another sect. Prominent figures include Munira Fakhro—a professor of sociology at the University of Bahrain, and part of the wealthy, Sunni Fakhro family—who is one of the best-known female political activists in Bahrain. Wa'ad has made efforts to co-operate with Al-Wefaq in elections; Al-Wefaq MPs have spoken at Fakhro's election rallies, in an unusual display of support for a female candidate (who also happens not to wear the *hijab*). The society was suspended in March 2011 and Sharif was among the arrested opposition leaders charged with seeking to overthrow the government.

For decades, Bahrain has had a vibrant civil society that is among the most advanced in the region. Despite Bahrain's cycles of protest and repression, local civil society has managed to find a variety of different political spaces in which to remain active. In the 1940s and 1950s, when nationalist and leftist politics dominated, the key meeting places were clubs and associations.[28] However, owing to their political role, the clubs were gradually shut down. As in many other Arab countries, it can be argued that the systematic closure of political spaces—from the clubs to the parliament—helped to push politics into religious spaces instead, contributing to the Islamist turn in politics throughout the region since the 1970s.

In the 1980s and 1990s, the key spaces for political discussion were the *majali*s (similar to the *diwaniya*s of Kuwait) and, for Shia Bahrainis, the *mataam*s (literally, the mourning houses for Imam Hussain). Since 2006, political societies have been officially recognised and have their own premises. MPs also have spaces for political *majali*s, a cross between a traditional *majlis* and a constituency surgery. The Internet is also an important civil society space. Discussion forums abound, a format pioneered in Bahrain by www.BahrainOnline.org, a web forum founded by Ali Abdulemam, a blogger. Today most villages in Bahrain have their own web forum, with topics ranging from news on marriages and births and goods for sale to political news and details of demonstrations. By 2010, many were blocked by the authorities and Abdulemam was put in jail after being investigated for the alleged 'international terrorist funding' of his Internet forum.[29]

Blogs are also important, though they have lost some ground to social networking sites in recent years. Abdulemam is one of the few bloggers to use his real name. Another is Mahmood Al-Yousif, founder and author of www.mahmood.tv, Bahrain's best-known blog. Several bloggers were arrested in the 2011 crackdown and one web forum moderator, Zakariya Rashid Hassan Al-Ashiri, died in custody after being arrested for 'disseminating false news'. Numerous Internet sites are censored in Bahrain, but over the years Bahrainis have grown adept at bypassing official blocks on websites as well as using software to mask their IP addresses.

Bahrain had some of the first non-government organisations (NGOs) in the region, including the first women's NGO in the Gulf, established in 1955. This bore the genteel name of the Bahrain Young Ladies' Society and was patronised by the wife of the British Political Resident, thus beginning a long trend of not-exactly-independent NGOs.

The government places tight restrictions on the operation of NGOs and requires them to submit to extensive and intrusive monitoring by the Ministry for Social Affairs. Human rights NGOs have proved particularly controversial. In 2002, as part of the broader reforms, the government licensed two human rights NGOs. The first was the Bahrain Human Rights Society (BHRS), headed by Abdulla Derazi, whose core members were often secular liberals. The second was the Bahrain Centre for Human Rights (BCHR), headed by Abdulhadi Al-Khawaja, which sought to bring together Islamists, liberals and leftists. The two also differed in their attitude to co-operating with the government. The more combative BCHR was officially dissolved in 2004, but remains active. Despite the BHRS' more conciliatory approach, in 2010 its board of directors was dismissed by the government and replaced with pro-government appointees. This came after the Ministry for Social Affairs decided that the society was 'biased towards a segment of society', implying that it had been too sympathetic to more than 200 Shia activists who had been detained in a wide-ranging crackdown.

There are now no legally recognised, independent human rights NGOs in Bahrain. One small human rights group is operated by a member of the appointed upper chamber of parliament, while another is run by an adviser to the Bahrain embassy in London—but both appear to be one-man operations that cannot be regarded as fully independent from the state. Another unrecognised human rights organization is the Bahrain Youth Society for Human Rights, which has applied repeatedly for a licence without success. Its president, Muhammed Maskati, was fined in 2010 for running an 'illegal organization'. The government has also set up a state-run human rights commission, the National Institute for Human Rights.

Economic development and diversification

Bahrain is one of the more diversified economies amongst the Gulf states. It was the first to discover oil, in 1932, had the first oil refinery, in 1936, and had the first aluminium smelter, in 1971. It has also been the first to face the problem of declining domestic oil production and therefore has had to move faster when it comes to economic diversification. Its limited oil wealth also means it is more dependent than most Gulf states on foreign investment, and it has one of the most open legal environments for foreign direct investment in the region, with full foreign ownership permitted in most sectors of the economy. Unusually for a Gulf state, Bahrain now obtains a greater share of its GDP from financial services than from hydrocarbon exports. However, much like its neighbours, the government still generates most of its revenue from oil, which still accounts for the bulk of all goods exports. These exports have a greater degree of value added than most Gulf oil exports as Bahrain is a net importer of crude and an exporter of refined oil. Similarly, instead of exporting natural gas, Bahrain uses its gas as feedstock for Aluminium Bahrain's smelter, turning it into a more value-added—and employment-generating—product.

This export base is facing challenges as the country's oil and gas production is stagnating. Bahrain is seeking to increase production and to start importing natural gas. Bahrain's National Oil and Gas Authority (NOGA), a state agency that oversees the sector, aims to more than double its current oil production through a programme of advanced oil recovery with investment from Occidental Oil of the US. NOGA says this will increase total recoverable reserves, not just speed up the rate of extraction.

If so, this would reduce Bahrain's economic dependence on Saudi Arabia, which is one of the major strategic issues that the country faces. The bulk of Bahrain's oil production is supplied not by the single onshore field, Awali, but rather from an offshore field, Abu Saafa, which Saudi Arabia has shared with Bahrain since the 1950s, and which is administered by Saudi Aramco. In 2004 Saudi Arabia decided not to proceed with a plan to increase Bahrain's share of production after the latter signed a unilateral Free Trade Agreement with the US, a move that went against Saudi Arabia's view that the Gulf Cooperation Council should only negotiate free trade deals as a bloc (which is inevitably a slower process). Officials denied any connection but the oil decision was generally seen as a reminder to Bahrain of its need for Saudi goodwill. In addition to dependence on Saudi-supplied oil, the country depends on Saudi Arabia for the majority of its tourists, for its sole land link to the Arabian Peninsula, and for extensive foreign aid (which contributes more to government revenue than all taxes, fees, and duties put together).

The financial services sector has been a key part of the country's diversification away from oil, but there are also concerns about dependency in this sector, which is dominated by foreign investment in offshore activities. The vast majority of the 133 banks[30] in Bahrain operate offshore, with only three large banks (National Bank of Bahrain, Bank of Bahrain and Kuwait, and Ahli United Bank) accounting for most of the domestic retail market. Thus the majority of Bahrain-registered banks, along with some 270 non-bank financial institutions such as insurers and fund management companies, are not deeply tied to Bahrain's domestic economy and may migrate elsewhere over time depending on the competitiveness of Bahrain's investment climate (for tax, regulation, lifestyle for expatriate staff and so on).

Competition from rival financial hubs in the Gulf, particularly Dubai, is therefore a significant risk to Bahrain's economy. Bahrain is very open to foreign investors, who can own up to 100 per cent of both onshore and offshore financial institutions, whereas the UAE does not permit majority foreign ownership except in specific export-oriented free zones (such as the Dubai International Financial Centre). However, Bahrain's onshore market is small and well-served by existing banks, and thus does not appear to be a major factor in location decisions for financial institutions.

Also in Bahrain's favour is the fact that its regulator, the Central Bank of Bahrain (formerly the Bahrain Monetary Agency), is generally well regarded. Some Bahrainis quietly hoped that the financial troubles experienced in Dubai following the collapse of the emirate's overheated property market in 2009 would encourage financial services institutions to look towards Bahrain as a more stable investment destination. However, Dubai still has several advantages: a critical mass of institutions and companies, a greater number of direct international flights, and a perceived lifestyle appeal that makes it easier to attract expatriate talent to relocate there. The cost differential between Dubai and Bahrain was also reduced by Dubai's recession and the subsequent fall in rents. In addition, the unrest and the heavy-handed government clampdown in early 2011 are generally seen as having damaged Bahrain's international reputation, making it harder to attract investors and talented professionals.

Trade has been Bahrain's historical economic strength. Bahrain has always positioned itself as an entry point for trade with Saudi Arabia, especially since the building of the causeway between the two countries. Its advantage is largely based on the difficulties of the operating environment in Saudi Arabia. Bahrain has a much more liberal investment climate and is more open to business travel; even National Commercial Bank, the biggest bank in Saudi Arabia, chose Bahrain as the base for its new investment banking offshoot, NBC Capital, citing the greater availability of visas for staff and for business visas. Also, Bahrain's more liberal social environment, from the availability of alcohol to the existence of places of worship for non-Muslim religions, means it is easier—and cheaper—to persuade expatriate staff to move there than to Saudi Arabia. The EDB has cited what it claims is a 'liberal' and 'progressive' culture as one of six key attractions for foreign investors.[31] Bahrain promotes investment in export-oriented sectors based in economic clusters, including the Bahrain International Investment Park and the Bahrain Logistics Zone, positioned near the causeway to Saudi. A major new port, Mina Khalifa bin Salman, opened in 2009.

Tourism is another important sector, and is heavily dependent on weekend traffic from Saudi Arabia as some 80 per cent of tourist arrivals come over the Bahrain-Saudi causeway. Saudi Arabian 'weekend tourism' has caused some social and political controversies and the elected MPs in the 2006–10 parliament voted unanimously to ban alcohol—a plan quietly dropped by the upper house.

At present no data on income distribution are publicly available, but economic inequality is fairly visible in Bahrain. Access to jobs—especially government jobs—and the availability of affordable housing are key political issues, with an estimated 50,000 Bahrainis on the waiting list for state housing. The EDB's long-term strategy—'Vision 2030'—aims to reduce unemployment by boosting the skills base. It also seeks to gradually reduce the role of the state in favour of a more dynamic private sector economy, in preparation for a post-oil age where the state will no longer be able to play the role it has taken on since the discovery of oil.

Labour markets in the Gulf states tend to be fragmented, with nationals making up the majority of the public sector workforce, while foreign workers hold most of the private sector jobs. Being a relatively low income Gulf state, with some tradition of vocational training, Bahrain has a higher proportion of nationals in the private sector workforce than most of its neighbours. This means there is more competition between nationals and foreigners for the same jobs. However, a combination of wage differentials and unequal legal rights means that nationals and foreigners do not compete on a level playing field. The ease of recruiting low-paid foreign workers with few legal rights has helped businesses keep their costs down.[32] But it has reduced job opportunities for Bahraini nationals and this has led to some social tensions. Concerns about the social and political impact of unemployment have meant that, since 2006, Bahrain has gone further than any other Gulf state in reforming its labour market, a process that has been arduous and slow, but is being closely watched by other Gulf states. However, the sackings of hundreds of workers who had participated in strikes and protests in 2011, and their subsequent replacement by expatriate workers, have weakened the EDB-led drive to reduce dependence on foreign workers.

Until 2008, Bahrain employed the sponsorship (*kafala*) system that is common across the Gulf states. Under this system, foreign workers have to be sponsored by a local employer in order to obtain a work visa. This remains common in many countries. An unusual and pernicious aspect of the system in the Gulf states is that the worker is usually then unable to change jobs without his existing employer's permission, thus creating a relationship of extreme dependence on the employer, which leaves employees vulnerable to exploitation and abuse.[33] For instance, the Migrant Workers' Protection Society (a local NGO) and local journalists have documented many cases where companies simply fail to pay their employees' salaries. With little knowledge of their legal rights, and often no working knowledge of Arabic or English, the workers have little recourse. There are also widespread reports of employers withholding employees' passports so that they are unable to leave the country. The problems are compounded in some cases by dishonest labour agencies that lure workers to the Gulf states with false promises about their jobs and salaries, and then hold them responsible for large 'debts' for travel costs and agency fees incurred.

Some Bahraini economists have defended the system on the basis that it insulates nationals from too much global competition, arguing that if foreign workers were given more mobility in the labour market, wages would go down across the board. Yet this is a hard argument to defend. Rather, wages in Bahrain are kept down by the ease of securing new supplies of foreign labour from low-income (primarily South Asian) countries, owing to the country's considerable openness to foreign labour. There is a strong argument that greater freedom to change jobs would give foreign workers more options and allow them to negotiate higher wages.

Wages for foreign workers are generally far lower than those paid to Bahrainis, with a few exceptions for highly skilled employees in certain areas such as financial services or government consultancy. The lower wages reflect the fact that most foreign workers originate from low-income countries where their earning power is limited. Typically they remit part of their earnings to families in their country of origin, where their salaries have a higher purchasing power. Also, most foreign workers are single men, or are forced to live as bachelors while they work in Bahrain; they cannot bring their families to Bahrain unless they earn a professional salary. By contrast, Bahrainis have higher wage expectations because they are looking to support families in Bahrain, and because they see their compatriots enjoying higher salaries.

There are additional reasons why private sector employers prefer foreign workers. They are easier to hire and fire. They are also less likely to organise themselves into trade unions, for fear of being fired and summarily deported. In many sectors, employers also claim that foreign workers have a better work ethic and more market-relevant skills than Bahrainis—although the comparison is not nearly as pronounced as in richer countries such as the UAE and Qatar. Compared with people of most Gulf states, Bahrainis are relatively well-educated and are more willing to take on a wider range of private-sector jobs, including service jobs in hotels, pumping petrol, or, famously, driving taxis. Many first-time visitors accustomed to other Gulf states comment appreciatively about their airport taxi being driven by a Bahraini, without necessarily realising that this occupation is in fact reserved by law for Bahraini nationals. Bahrain, like other Gulf states, has put a number of 'nationalisation' policies in place to compel private sector firms to employ Bahraini nationals. Some occupations are entirely reserved for nationals. More often, there are quotas—varying by sector and by size of firm—requiring a certain proportion of jobs to be filled by Bahraini nationals. In some cases firms employ Bahraini 'ghost workers' simply to make up the numbers.

The EDB wants to replace the 'Bahrainisation' system with a more market-driven system. Its first step, in 2006, was to introduce new fees that a company has to pay for every foreign worker it employs. In addition, 80 per cent of the revenue obtained from the fees has been earmarked for a fund, Tamkeen, for training Bahraini nationals, in order to narrow the skills gap. However, the EDB has encountered stiff resistance from employers who objected to the increase in their wage costs. The labour fees, which were introduced in 2006, have so far been set at a fraction of those originally planned and have barely altered the pay gap; they were suspended for at least six months in 2011 after unrest damaged business confidence in Bahrain.

Since 2008 Bahrain has also reformed the sponsorship system, which a former Labour Minister, Majid Al-Alawi, described as being akin to 'slavery' and not suitable for a modern country. A state body, the Labour Market Regulatory Authority, is now responsible for sponsoring foreign workers. It has also taken steps to make recruitment more transparent and to provide workers with more information about their jobs and working conditions before they leave their home countries—although there is a long way to go before this is fully implemented. Furthermore, the law was changed in 2008 to state that foreign workers do have the right to change their employers. However, this caused an outcry among businesses and MPs, who were completely unaccustomed to such a system, and expressed fears that employees would abscond with trade secrets. New conditions were attached, for instance one requiring foreign workers to complete a year's employment before changing jobs. In practice, many workers are not aware of their rights and it is not clear how many have taken up the right to change jobs as yet.

As foreign workers are still significantly cheaper, and as the country remains very open to foreign labour, many of the new jobs created in Bahrain have gone to new immigrants. The proportion of nationals in the total resident population has gradually fallen to just under 50 per cent as of 2008 (the latest data available).[34]

Foreign policy and security

Bahrain navigates a complex set of relationships in a region where most of the important political dynamics are beyond its control. Shifts in relations between its main allies and Iran—with which relations are officially friendly but unofficially wary—can have a marked impact on Bahrain. As in other Gulf states, the government also needs to balance its own relations with the US and support for Arab-Israeli peace by publicly opposing US and Israeli policies in the region; and it needs to balance its relations with the other Sunni monarchies in the Gulf with the sympathies of its large Shia population, many of whom look to their co-religionists in the Shia-led republics of Iran and Iraq. Despite its small size, Bahrain tries to punch above its weight in regional diplomacy, which years of conflict combined with significant external attention have made almost an industry in itself. Its officials have made some strong statements on the key issues of inter-state politics in the region including the Arab-Israeli conflict and the tensions over Iran's nuclear programme.

Saudi Arabia is Bahrain's key regional ally. Bahrain is highly dependent on Saudi economic support and susceptible to Saudi political pressure. From the Saudi point of view, Bahrain is a useful friend in the region, a key destination for Saudi tourists wanting to let off steam, and a useful offshore banking centre. Bahrain's gains from the alliance are political support from one of the region's diplomatic heavyweights, a steady stream of crude oil, tourist revenue, inward investment, and the benefits of having few barriers to trade with the region's largest economy.

Moreover, Saudi Arabia explicitly supports Bahrain as a fellow Sunni monarchy. This was made abundantly clear in 2011, especially following the Gulf Cooperation Council's Peninsula Shield deployment in Bahrain to support the government as it put down protests. Most accounts agree that this was a Saudi-led initiative, and Saudi troops made up the bulk of the personnel involved. Shia unrest in Bahrain is of particular concern for Saudi Arabia, which fears its own Shia minority may be infected; this community which is concentrated in the oil-rich Eastern Province, just across the causeway from Bahrain.

Ties with Kuwait are close given the links between the Al-Sabah and Al-Khalifa ruling families, and there are important transnational networks between different political groups in Bahrain and Kuwait. Relations with the UAE were strengthened by the marriage of one of King Hamad's sons to one of the daughters of Sheikh Muhammed bin Rashid Al-Maktoum, the ruler of Dubai, in 2009. Relations with Qatar have traditionally been tense owing to a history of conflict between the Al-Thani and the Al-Khalifa over the mainland fort of Zubara. The maritime border was finally delineated in 2001, giving Qatar control over Zubara in exchange for Bahrain keeping control over the Hawar Islands. The two countries have since tried to improve their relations with various gestures, the most lavish being a longstanding but much-delayed plan to build a causeway between them, dubbed 'The Friendship Bridge'. But the maritime border clearly remains sensitive, as dozens of Bahraini fishermen have been jailed in Qatar after wandering into Qatari waters.

The relationship with Iran is Bahrain's most difficult and complex. Tensions over Iran's claim to Bahrain, and possible linkages between Iran and Bahrain's Shia population, have existed for more than a century. The claim has been renewed at different periods, partly as a function of Iran's domestic politics and partly out of a sense of strength in the region. In 1927 Reza Shah demanded the return of Bahrain, and in 1957 the Iranian parliament passed a law that declared Bahrain to be Iran's fourteenth province. The degree to which Iranian comments about Bahrain are taken seriously usually depends on the broader state of Iran-Arab relations.

Since the Islamic revolution, there have been allegations that Iran finances and manipulates the opposition in Bahrain, whether out of Shia religious solidarity or as a card to play in its dealings with the other Gulf states. The Bahraini government has several times accused Iran of backing plots to overthrow the ruling family, most recently in 2011. Such allegations are notoriously difficult to verify as evidence tends not to be produced. The Bahraini government has an interest in alleging that the more hard-line elements of the opposition are supported by Iran, as part of its efforts to discredit these groups. Arguably the government also has an interest in portraying the Shia majority as loyal to Iran in order to forestall Western pressure for further democratisation. At the same time the government has maintained its diplomatic relations with Iran, perhaps not wanting to alienate such a powerful neighbour too greatly. In 2011 the King claimed that Bahrain had been the victim of a thirty year-long 'external plot' but stopped short of explicitly accusing Iran, although other officials made the reference abundantly clear. Iran protests whenever it is directly accused of interference, but the Iranian government seems to permit a degree of ambiguity, allowing Bahrain and the other Gulf states to believe that it does have loyal assets on their territory that it could call on in the event of any conflict. Iran also wants to pose as a defender of transnational Shia interests and its media organisations are very supportive of the Bahraini opposition, although it is not clear that they provide anything other than moral support.

Iranian clerics are widely revered in Bahrain, and many Bahraini Shia hold a romantic view of Iran as a defender of Shia rights. But support for Iran's political model of *vilayet-e-faqih* is believed to be limited in Bahrain, as is the case in other Shia communities outside Iran. Whatever the exact status of Iranian support for Shia opposition groups in Bahrain, the fundamental drivers of opposition and unrest in Bahrain appear to be domestic political and economic issues, which are not unique to the Shia community and predate the Islamic revolution.

The relationship with Iraq is complex as the Al-Khalifa are suspicious about the impact that the elected, Shia-dominated government in Iraq has on Bahrain's own Shia population. From the Iraqi government's point of view, its relations with Bahrain are vulnerable to tension resulting from Bahrain's mistreatment of its Shia population. Members of the Bahraini opposition claim that their country has recruited former Saddam-era loyalists from Iraq into the security forces, and it is feared that sectarian and intra-sectarian tensions in Iraq may also spill over into Bahrain. These political anxieties have constrained otherwise promising potential for trade. In 2010 Bahrain's national carrier, Gulf Air, was operating more routes into Iraq than any other Gulf airline, but in 2011 the Bahraini authorities suspended all flights to Iraq, Iran, and Lebanon amid accusations that Shia parties overseas had orchestrated the mass protests in Bahrain that year. Yet Iraq's experience should make it clear that Shia politics are in fact highly factionalised and not monolithic. Indeed, some commentators have even described Bahrain as a 'microcosm of the internal Shia divisions in Iraq'.[35]

Ties with the former protecting power, Britain, generally remain close. As of 2008, some 8,000 British nationals were living in Bahrain, according to the British embassy in Manama, with the most popular occupations being in finance and government consultancy. Despite the generally strong relationship, there can be occasional tensions over the activities of the Bahraini opposition in London. Britain is home to many Arab and Muslim dissidents and a small number of Bahrainis have sought and received political asylum in the past ten years despite the Bahraini King's much-heralded 'reform era'. The Bahraini government has objected to each of these cases, given the obvious implication that there is still political persecution in Bahrain.

The US is Bahrain's main security guarantor, Washington's primary interest in Bahrain being to maintain its naval base for the Fifth Fleet base. Also, as already mentioned, the two countries now have a free trade agreement, the first that the US signed with any Gulf state, although direct trade flows are still low. The former US President George W. Bush was an enthusiastic supporter of King Hamad's reforms and praised the country as a model of democracy, but more recently US government officials have been relatively quiet on issues of democracy and human rights.

Future challenges

The events of early 2011 have greatly exacerbated the challenges Bahrain will face in the future. Bahrain's small society has been deeply divided in its understanding of the protests that began on 14 February 2011, of the intentions of the opposition, and of the nature and intentions of the government's subsequent crackdown. Moreover, political polarisation has taken on an increasingly sectarian hue.

The unrest of 2011 demonstrates the failures and limitations of the previous decade's 'reform project', a process that was largely controlled by the government but did not meet the aims of either the government or the opposition. By mid-2010 the political reform process had stalled and had begun to undergo some reversals. There was significant public frustration with the parliamentary experiment, after generally positive expectations at earlier stages. The opposition had already been deeply disappointed by the failure to implement the promise of a parliament in which legislative power would lie with elected MPs. Moreover—and unsurprisingly given the parliament's limited powers—Al-Wefaq's participation in parliament yielded few results for the group's constituents. The group was unable to reach agreement with the Sunni Islamist MPs, who held the majority of seats, on many issues other than morality laws and MPs' pay rises. There was a widespread feeling among the opposition that they had been tricked into taking part in a parliament that was largely a public relations stunt.

Meanwhile, not all of the public saw democracy as desirable; although many democratisation theorists have focused on the role of the middle class in challenging authoritarian power structures, it is also true that in many contexts the middle class has proved to be primarily concerned with defending its own interests and not with extending democracy further down. In the Bahraini context, those that remained uncertain about the desirability of democracy included some businesspeople and liberals who were troubled by the fact that the parliament was dominated by Islamists complaining loudly about alcohol and tourism. These groups would tend to argue that the public was not educated or mature enough to deserve a meaningful vote. This group is an important constituency for the government.

From the government's point of view, the parliament had failed to contain the opposition; unrest continued on the streets and occasionally led to violent clashes between police and protestors. Even reformists in the government tend to portray reforms as a privilege or a gift from a magnanimous leadership, rather than as a right.

The large scale of the protests of February 2011 took most of the established political players by surprise. Protests had been a frequent occurrence in Bahrain since well before the uprisings in Egypt and Tunisia, but demonstrators were given an added impetus by the events in both those countries, where largely peaceful protests achieved rapid change. The first demonstrations were called on 14 February because it was the tenth anniversary of the referendum on the National Action Charter. They began on a relatively small scale but quickly gathered momentum after a protestor was shot dead by police on the first day of the protests, and another was shot dead the following day in clashes around the first protestor's funeral. Violence escalated dramatically that week after protestors occupied Lulu Roundabout, a traffic intersection in central Manama, and were dispersed forcibly by troops.

A month-long standoff ensued, during which protestors continued to occupy the roundabout and the disparate opposition groups sought to form a united front. While representatives of Al-Wefaq and the Crown Prince argued about the ground rules for negotiations, both were outflanked. Protestors calling for outright revolution marched on the royal court, blocked the central business district and prevented bankers from reaching offices in the iconic Bahrain Financial Harbour. And within days Saudi Arabian and UAE troops entered the country to bolster the government's beleaguered security forces as they dispersed and then arrested hundreds of protestors. The government also summoned its supporters to hold large-scale pro-government rallies and staged a campaign to gather 'loyalty pledges' from workplaces, universities and public places. By May 2011 at least twenty-three protestors or suspected opposition supporters, two policemen, and six bystanders had been killed—large numbers in a country with little more than half a million citizens.

The government has managed to entrench its support among much of the Sunni population, some of whom sympathised with calls for reform but not for revolution. Government narratives—especially on state television—have greatly inflated the role of the minority of opposition groups that called for revolution. Although a few voices, including the Crown Prince, acknowledged that most of the protestors had legitimate demands, government hardliners sought to portray all protestors as foreign agents with a purely sectarian agenda, who had brought the country to the brink of anarchy in order to establish an Iran-style theocracy through violent means. Several violent attacks on policemen and foreign workers provided fuel for the government to portray the opposition as malicious, although the vast majority of protestors were peaceful and unarmed. Four men were sentenced to death and three to life imprisonment for killing a policeman after a military trial, but one of the accused never made it to court because he died in custody, his body covered in torture marks. His video-taped 'confession' was aired on Bahrain Television, which said it would not rule out broadcasting the executions. The government has proved effective in discrediting the opposition among an important section of the population—a 'divide and rule' approach that serves the royal family's short-term interests but raises long-term worries about sectarian tensions and the potential for future violence.

Sectarian tensions have been stoked by narratives portraying Shia as disloyal and as foreign agents, creating distrust that will be hard to overcome. Moreover, in April 2011, the government began demolishing various Shia mosques (it said they had been built illegally, although some predated the system of permits and others claimed to have official registration documents). Historically, grievances among Bahrain's Shia population were primarily political and economic, and had less to do with religious freedom, which was previously well respected in Bahrain. The demolition of mosques appears to be a new element, and Iranian and Iraqi clerics have rushed to exploit this for their own reasons. The intensification and exploitation of sectarian tensions arouse deep concern, as divisions are harder to overcome when people believe they are distrusted or persecuted on the basis of their identity rather than their behaviour.

Any credible reform process will require major concessions, given the depth of distrust. There may also be a need for third-party mediation and for some form of truth and reconciliation process to address both the desire for justice and the sharply divergent narratives of what actually took place. However, there seems little indication that the government is willing to consider concessions. Reformists appear to have been greatly weakened, while hardliners appear to have gained in confidence, largely owing to Saudi support and a lack of serious international pressure on the Al-Khalifa. This has raised the prospect of a lengthy period of repression, loss of international reputation and investment, and an economy that will become increasingly dependent on Saudi aid.

Demographic and economic trends were among the key factors driving the 2011 unrest. Bahrain has undergone very rapid population growth over the past decade, putting severe pressure on resources and services. Land in particular is in short supply given the country's small size and already dense urban population, and the scarcity of land helps to explain the strength of popular feeling over perceived 'land grabs' by the ruling family (that is, the privatisation of public land and the giving of land to relatives and supporters as a form of patronage). Moreover, oil and gas resources are limited and domestic oil production may have peaked. Meanwhile, the country's industries and services face stiff competition from wealthier Gulf neighbours, notably the UAE.

The majority of new jobs created by the 2003–08 oil boom were taken up by migrant workers who, by 2008, comprised just over half of the population. Unemployment remains a key political and social issue. There are also deep tensions over the country's sectarian balance. For most of the twentieth century it was believed that 60 to 70 per cent of Bahraini nationals were Shia. There are no publicly available data on the breakdown of the population by sect. Some estimates were arrived at by counting the number of people in districts known to be mostly Shia or Sunni. In the first decade of this century, however, allegations emerged that the government was fast-tracking nationality applications for Sunnis from elsewhere in order to doctor the sectarian balance. Citizenship is normally very hard to obtain in the Gulf states because it usually brings significant economic benefits, intended to reflect a share in the country's natural resource wealth. However, there are longstanding claims that the government has fast-tracked citizenship for Sunni Muslims from Jordan, Yemen, Pakistan and Baluchistan, among other places. Some of these have been recruited into the security services in preference to local Shia. By law, a foreigner seeking Bahraini nationality should have lived in Bahrain for twenty-five years (or fifteen years for other Arabs), but the king reserves the legal prerogative to grant nationality to whomever he wishes.

The issue of 'political naturalisation' has heated up dramatically since 2006, when a British whistleblower, Salah Al-Bandar, published a controversial report alleging that a network within the government was seeking to undermine the Shia community by rigging the elections, fomenting sectarianism, and funding anti-Shia media. His report also implied that the group was trying to turn Bahrain's Shia into a minority within a few years. Al-Bandar's report was based on dozens of documents that he claimed to have obtained while working for the Central Informatics Organisation (CIO)—the state statistical body—and for the Ministry for Cabinet Affairs. The claims have never been fully refuted by the government, although Al-Bandar was expelled from the country and charged *in absentia* with treason, while the local press was banned from reporting on the affair, dubbed 'Bandargate'.

The allegations were given further fuel in 2008 when the CIO published new figures that showed the total resident population of Bahrain to be some 40 per cent higher than originally thought. This was partly because of a surge in the number of recorded foreign workers following an amnesty for illegal immigrants. However, the number of citizens also leaped, from 407,959 in 2002 to 527,433 in 2007—an increase of 119,474. The natural rate of population growth (based on the birth rate) would have yielded an increase of just over 47,000 in the Bahraini population over this period, so it appears that 72,000 persons were granted citizenship between 2002 and 2007. Some will have been formerly stateless Bahrainis, particularly those of Persian origin, but these are likely to be only a few thousand according to the US State Department's 2008 report on human rights in Bahrain. Moreover, Bahrain's Ministry for the Interior states that it has naturalised only 7,012 people, including formerly stateless children, since 2002.[36] There have been widespread media reports of an influx of new citizens. This has caused complaints among low-income Sunnis as well as Shia, as newly naturalised Sunnis are more likely to live in mostly Sunni areas and are seen as competitors for land and housing. However, the value of the naturalisation policy to the government was made abundantly clear in 2011. First, Bahrain's security forces proved readier to fire on Bahraini protestors than their counterparts had been in Egypt and Tunisia, where there was a greater solidarity between the soldiers and their fellow citizens on the street. Secondly, thousands of naturalised citizens bolstered the numbers at pro-government rallies.

SAUDI ARABIA

Kristian Coates Ulrichsen

State formation

The contemporary Kingdom of Saudi Arabia that was established in 1932 was actually the third attempt to establish a Saudi state in the Arabian Peninsula. The first incarnation was formed in 1744 after an alliance between the tribal leader Muhammad bin Saud and the preacher Muhammad bin Abd Al-Wahhab. This historic agreement laid the basis for the Saudi-Wahhabi partnership that continues to play a central, if sometimes uneasy, role in the contemporary Saudi polity. This initial proto-state expanded across parts of the Arabian Peninsula during the eighteenth century owing to the spread and application of Islamic law (*Sharia*), before being defeated militarily by an Egyptian force operating under Ottoman patronage at Dir'iyyah in 1818.[1] Nevertheless, the Al-Saud dynasty managed to return to power in 1824 in central and eastern Arabia, and establish a second Saudi state. This lasted until 1891 when it was defeated by forces belonging to the Al-Rashid dynasty of the northern province of Ha'il, after the two families had been engaged in a protracted struggle for supremacy over Najd in central Arabia. In 1902, the conflict took a decisive turn when Abdul Aziz bin Saud recaptured the key town of Riyadh and set in motion a series of conquests of the Al-Hasa province along with the rest of Najd, and finally of the Hejaz province (the home of the powerful British-supported Al-Hussein dynasty). These victories culminated in the creation of the present-day state of Saudi Arabia in 1932, two years after Abdul Aziz crushed the power of his Islamic militia force

63

(the Ikhwan) and decisively established the political primacy of the Al-Saud over the religious authority of the Wahhabi movement.[2]

State formation in Saudi Arabia therefore reflected an agglomeration of competing narratives and socio-cultural diversity within the kingdom. The persistence of religious, regional, tribal and factional sub-loyalties complicated early efforts to graft an integrative framework onto the new, proto-modern state. Considerable religious and cultural pluralism existed between the predominantly Salafi Najdis,[3] the more cosmopolitan and externally-oriented Sunni Hejazis, the Shia communities in the eastern province of Al-Hasa, and the Ismaili tribes in 'Asir and Najran that maintained close cross-border tribal and social links with Yemen.[4] These manifestations of diversity frequently clashed with state-led visions of Saudi homogeneity. They became stratified over time as the redistribution of oil revenue followed and widened existing fissures and created new networks of inclusion in, or exclusion from, new state-business networks and alliances.[5]

The accrual and redistribution of oil rents played a pivotal role in the processes of state formation in Saudi Arabia during the twentieth century. As late as the 1940s the political economy of the young state was still based upon rudimentary and subsistence-based techniques and traditional modes of production located within the boundaries of the village or tribe. The major sources of economic livelihood remained pastoral agriculture and trade, alongside small-scale artisanal and commercial activities in the towns.[6] A minimal state operated within strict financial constraints and considerable resource poverty, with little distinction between royal and state resources as the state initially appeared little more than an extension of the ruling family. The Saudi scholar 'Abd Al-Aziz ibn 'Abd Allah al-Khwaiter described this formative period of Saudi Arabian history as one in which:

...the king was the source of power. He had the final word, which was bound solely by the power of the *Shari'a*. He relied on no systematic administrative bodies other than the employees in his council, whose job was to submit to him the various matters that were raised in council, then to carry out his orders in addressing those matters. The King decided on administrative, political, military, economic and social matters, and referred what concerned the *Shari'a* to the relevant authorities.[7]

After 1948, a haphazard process of institution-building commenced in order to provide an administrative framework to oversee the extraction of oil. This was necessary to demarcate national boundaries and determine property rights for oil concession-holders, channel the incoming revenue into material development and the acquisition of support of tribal, merchant and Bedouin allies, and link the economy into world markets through oil exports. Yet substantive progress only gathered pace following Abdul Aziz's death in 1953, at which time there was no state apparatus capable of administering the country's principal resource. Hence the processes of modern state-formation were intricately connected to the receipt and redistribution of revenue generated by the export of oil.[8]

Classical rentier state theory was developed further in the 1970s and 1980s to examine the impact of external rents such as oil on the nature of states such as Saudi Arabia and their interaction with society. Beblawi argued that a rentier economy developed when the creation of wealth was centred on a small fraction of society, while in a rentier state the government is the principal recipient of the external rent, and plays the central role in redistributing this wealth to its population.[9] Luciani extended this analysis of rentierism by distinguishing between *allocation* and *production* states, in which the external origin of income derived from the export of oil frees allocation states from their domestic economic base.[10] State autonomy from domestic taxation and societal extraction was expected to change the political rules of the game, as the absence of the taxation/representation linkage would lessen the incentive for mobilisation around programmes designed to change political institutions or policy.[11] With its petroleum sector accounting for 89.29 per cent of budget revenue and 41.5 per cent of GDP at the end of the first oil-price boom in 1981, yet a mere 1.5 per cent of civilian employment (in 1980), Saudi Arabia came to represent an example of an oil state par excellence.[12]

Yet since the 1990s, a number of critiques of rentier theory moved beyond the structurally deterministic 'no representation without taxation' axis to emphasise the importance of local agency and decision-making in the creation of the contemporary Saudi state. These provide a nuanced and multi-causal approach to the study of the formative period of state-building in the 1950s and 1960s. Hertog examined the dynamic interplay between elite politics, factionalism and patronage networks, and the growth of administrative structures. He described a period of considerable institutional fluidity in which competing centres of power led to the construction of a segmented bureaucracy featuring numerous and often-overlapping states within a state. Over time, bureaucratic stasis ossified these bureaucratic fiefdoms into rigid administrative structures, although well-managed technocratic enclaves also emerged within this apparatus. These 'islands of efficiency' included Saudi Aramco, the Saudi Arabian Monetary Agency (SAMA), the Saudi Arabian Basic Industries Company (SABIC) and the Central Bank.[13]

Patterns of competitive institutionalisation and proliferating bureaucracies reflected the multiple circles of influence and power within the ruling Al-Saud family. These intensified after the death of its patriarch in 1953 and remain important to this day.[14] Okruhlik has emphasised the significance of political choice and the interaction between structural rentier theory and personal rule in explaining the political economy of oil states. She argued that rentier theory alone could not explain the rise of oppositional dissent in Saudi Arabia (as well as Bahrain and Kuwait), and that consequently the state's financial autonomy did not translate into immunity from civil pressures or societal contestation.[15] The reign of King Saud (1953–64), in particular, witnessed prolonged periods of labour unrest emanating from oil workers protesting over conditions at Aramco (Arabian American Oil Company) camps. In addition, progressive Saudi technocrats rose to positions of prominence during Saud's rule, the most notable being the first Oil Minister (and co-founder of the Organisation of Petroleum Exporting Countries), Abdullah Al-Tariki, whose views on the need to transform the Aramco oil concession earned him the nickname the 'Red Sheikh'.[16]

Profound differences over political and fiscal responsibilities between Saud and his Crown Prince and half-brother, Faisal, framed an internal power struggle that culminated in Saud's abdication in 1964. As the new King, Faisal embarked on an extensive modernisation programme that encompassed the creation of a judicial system and public sector reform. Moreover, his conservative financial policies differed markedly from the era of profligate spending under Saud, while the quadrupling of oil prices following the 1973 oil embargo provided a financial windfall that set in motion the 'oil decade', which lasted until 1982.[17] During this first boom in prices, Saudi Arabia, in common with the other oil-producing Gulf states, developed unique labour markets heavily reliant on foreign migrant workers. Between 1973 and 2002, the number of foreign workers in the Saudi labour force rose from 773,000 (42.9 per cent of the total) to 5,500,000 (60 per cent of the total workforce).[18]

The influx of oil revenue also facilitated the construction of a network of international Islamic institutions that extended Saudi Arabia's 'soft power' trans-nationally. These included the creation of the Muslim World League (1962), the Organisation of the Islamic Conference (1972), the World Assembly of Muslim Youth (1972), and the International Islamic Relief Organisation (1975).[19] Faisal also played an instrumental role in orchestrating the Arab oil embargo against the United States and selected European countries between October 1973 and March 1974. Both trends formed part of a stitching together of regime and religious legitimacy, a trend that continued after Faisal's assassination in 1975, and accelerated during the prolonged period of low oil prices in the 1980s.[20] Moreover, they established the Saudi state's credentials in the Arab and Islamic world following the inter-Arab rifts of the 1950s and 1960s and the region's division into 'conservative' and 'radical' states.[21]

Nevertheless, the use of religion as a legitimising tool proved a double-edged sword that left the Al-Saud vulnerable to contestation both in 1979 and again after 1991. In November 1979 Islamist dissidents led by Juhayman Al-Otaibi seized the Grand Mosque in Mecca and held it for fourteen days. Al-Otaibi came from a powerful Najdi family and his grandfather had been a member of the tribal force that fought alongside Abdul-Aziz in the 1920s. The dramatic assault on the holiest shrine in Islam was directed at the core of the regime's legitimacy by opponents calling for its overthrow and a return to pure Islamic beliefs. Although the siege ended with the (violent) retaking of the Mosque, the regime's use of French special operations forces in the operation further sapped its credibility in the eyes of its detractors.[22]

The seizure of the Grand Mosque overlapped with seven days of bloody street violence between state security forces and Shia protestors in the oil-rich Eastern Province. The unrest was motivated by currents of grievance regarding the perceived marginalisation of Shia communities in Saudi Arabia and the politics of uneven development, which was blamed for the denial of basic services to towns and villages in the Eastern Province.[23] This contemporaneous Sunni- and Shia-led opposition to the Al-Saud represented a grave political crisis for a regime already facing fallout from the Islamic Revolution in Iran. It stimulated a political and social response targeted at the socio-economic roots of the violence and eventually culminated in the National Reconciliation Accord between the government and the Shia opposition in 1993.[24]

Iraq's invasion of Kuwait in August 1990 and the massing of more than 700,000 American-led forces in Saudi Arabia prior to Operation Desert Storm posed similar questions about the regime. Despite heavy military expenditure throughout the 1980s, the Saudi military was unable to ward off the threat from Iraq without requesting US military intervention.[25] Five thousand American troops remained in the Kingdom following the liberation of Kuwait and their presence became a lightning-rod for Islamist opposition and dissent. It caused a rupture in relations with Osama bin Laden, himself a Saudi national, and a mobilising tool for al-Qaeda in the 1990s. Indeed, it featured prominently in bin Laden's February 1998 declaration of 'Jihad against Jews and Crusaders', in which he alleged that:

...for over seven years the United States has been occupying the lands of Islam in the holiest of places, the Arabian Peninsula, plundering its riches, dictating to its rulers, humiliating its peoples, terrorising its neighbours, and turning its bases on the Peninsula into a spearhead with which to fight the neighbouring Muslim peoples.[26]

Significantly, only three years later, fifteen of the nineteen hijackers who took part in the September 11 2001 attacks were Saudi Arabian nationals.

Political structures and personalities

Saudi Arabia is an absolute monarchy in which the king is the head of state as well as the head of government (as the prime minister of the Council of Ministers). Power and control is thus vested in the ruling Al-Saud family, and the Basic Law of 1992 narrowed this further by restricting succession to male descendents of Abdul Aziz. To date, every ruler since Abdul Aziz's death in 1953 has been drawn from the first generation of sons. However, the advancing age of the eighteen surviving sons (as of 2010, the youngest was sixty-five year old Prince Muqrin, head of the General Intelligence Directorate) means that positions of leadership and (eventually) succession will increasingly devolve to the grandsons of Abdul Aziz. This may inject a new momentum into competing factions within the Al-Saud, as vertical axes of patrilineal inheritance may join with existing horizontal divisions between coalitions of brothers and half-brothers of Abdul Aziz.[27]

The two decades since the Gulf War have witnessed an updating and modernisation (though not a transformation) of political structures in

Saudi Arabia. Procedural reforms institutionalised channels of state-society interaction but did not amount to a paradigmatic shift in the location of the source, distribution and power within the Saudi polity.[28] Periodic cycles of societal demands for political reform were rooted both in exogenous events (the aftermath of Operation Desert Storm in 1990–91 and the September 11 2001 terrorist attacks) and in changing internal calculations (the lengthy period of low oil prices in the late 1990s, and the outbreak of domestic terrorism in 2003). In each instance, the response of the ruling family was a pragmatic mixture of co-optation and adaptation followed by consolidation of the new status quo. Nevertheless, the state remains extremely powerful as the recipient of oil revenue, as well as the adjudicator of their redistribution within society.

The challenge to the legitimacy of the Al-Saud posed by the Gulf War became clear when a series of petitions were presented to King Fahd in its immediate aftermath. These marked a major shift in the articulation of societal demands for reform as a public (and printed) discourse emerged in place of hitherto private and informal channels of communication made directly to senior princes. Between 1990 and 1992, high-profile petitions for reform emanated from the business community (for example, in November 1990), as well as from religious scholars calling for the restoration of Islamic values (for instance, a 'Letter of Demands' in May 1991 and a subsequent and more assertive 'Memorandum of Advice' in July 1992), while between fifty and seventy-five Saudi women drove through Riyadh in November 1990 in an unprecedented display of defiance against the religious police or *mutawwa'in*. Although their demands for change differed substantively (and ranged against each other to a significant degree), they represented an influential mobilisation of elite groupings in favour of a formalised, accountable and rules-based system of governance.[29]

Taken together, the legacy of the Gulf War and the emergence of reformist impulses triggered a major reorganisation of the governing system. In 1992, King Fahd issued three royal decrees that collectively amounted to a 'Basic System of Governance' and laid down the aforementioned Basic Law (a constitution-like document) to regularise the political system in Saudi Arabia. This stated that the government drew its authority from the Qur'an and the *sunna* or traditions of the Prophet Muhammed, and reaffirmed Islamic law as the basis of the Kingdom. It also established oversight bodies to monitor the performance of government ministries and agencies, and defined the judiciary as an independent branch of government but subject to the appointment of judges by the King. These reforms were followed by four more decrees in 1993 which established a new Consultative Assembly (*Majlis al-Shura*) and a system of regional government. The charter of the Council of Ministers (founded in 1953) was also updated to enhance its accountability as both the legislative and executive organ of the Saudi state, although its members continued to be appointed by royal decree and all legislative proposals need royal assent and must be compatible with *Shari'a* law.[30]

These changes to the governing system in Saudi Arabia formed part of the ruling family's strategy to re-link religious and regime legitimacy in the turbulent aftermath of the Gulf War. The formalisation of the Islamic principle of *shura* or consultation represented an attempt to widen the basis of decision-making in accordance with Islamic practice. Although the principle of consultation was an embedded feature of Al-Saud decision-making, Fahd's decision to call on US military assistance in 1990 constituted a rare instance of a decision being taken without extensive prior discussion.[31] The Consultative Assembly began with sixty members representing a broad cross-section of merchants, technocrats, civil servants, religious elites, retired military personnel and academics. All were appointed by the King for four-year terms. Membership has since expanded to 150 and public debates have now replaced the original closed-door meetings and visibly enhanced the Assembly's role within the Saudi political structure.[32] However, it remains a consultative rather than legislative body, and the centre of decision-making power has stayed in the hands of the king and a circle of senior members of the ruling family.

A new demand for reform emerged after the September 11 2001 terrorist attacks on the US and in the prelude to the US-led invasion of Iraq in 2003. Its timing also reflected the lengthy period of lower oil revenues during the 1990s. Prices bottomed out in 1999, and this complicated the regime's strategy of anticipating or nullifying potential opposition by co-opting support through the redistribution of wealth.[33] The impact on the political economy of oil-producing states became clear in the contemporaneous liberalisation of political systems throughout all of the Gulf Cooperation Council (GCC) states in the late 1990s and early 2000s.[34] To this domestic disequilibrium was added the Bush administration's policy response to the attacks of September 11 2001, when the US and its international partners began to (briefly) promote reform in the Middle East through initiatives such as the Greater Middle East Initiative, its objective being the political, economic and social transformation of the region. In December 2001 these internal and external factors converged around a reformist coalition of educated Saudi professionals. Their initial demands included greater government accountability and regulation over the religious establishment, an independent judiciary, a more equitable distribution of resources, and enhanced civil and political rights in a constitutional monarchical system.[35]

Reformist pressures accelerated in January 2003, when 104 representatives of the business, academic and religious communities presented a petition entitled 'Vision for the Present and Future of the Nation' to the then Crown Prince Abdullah. This petition was noteworthy as the different strands of reform (Islamist and business) coalesced around a short-lived platform, instead of submitting rival and competing petitions as in 1990–92. Their joint influence was demonstrated when Abdullah met the petitioners and sparked a national debate over the process of reform in the Kingdom. However, the nascent alliance between liberals and Islamists remained vulnerable to differing interpretations regarding the rapidity and direction of further change. Hence a follow-up petition in September 2003 was entitled 'In Defence of the Nation' and gathered 306 predominantly liberal signatories, including fifty women but few Islamists, although a third petition in December 2003 was signed by Sunni and Shia Islamist leaders calling for implementation of the reforms outlined in the January 'Vision'.[36]

These pressures notwithstanding, the extended incapacitation of King Fahd due to poor health delayed meaningful reform until Abdullah's formal accession to power in August 2005. The decade of political sclerosis between Fahd's debilitating stroke in 1995 and his eventual death highlighted the continued interlinking of political and personal power in contemporary Saudi Arabia. Indeed, subsequent reforms to the judicial and educational systems became identified with Abdullah's leadership and vulnerable to any potential reversal in the future. Most notable was the 2007 Law of the Judiciary, which took practical steps toward judicial independence and established a new Supreme Court separate from the Ministry of Justice.[37] This was followed by a cabinet reshuffle in February 2009 that included the appointment of the first female deputy minister (of Education). The same year also saw the opening of the King Abdullah University of Science and Technology (KAUST) outside Jeddah. Its mixed-gender campus was intended to push social boundaries concern-

ing the role of women and education, and connect scientific and technological innovation to economic and social progress in the Kingdom.[38]

KAUST itself constituted one (albeit high-profile) dimension of an
ambitious project to overhaul and reform the system of higher education
in Saudi Arabia. More than 100 new universities and colleges opened
between 2003 and 2007 alone as part of a strategy to align education
reforms with the labour market and projects of economic diversification.[39] As an enclave located eighty kilometres outside Jeddah, and with
tight entry controls and few Saudis among its student body, KAUST is
an example of a carefully-managed and incremental step toward reform
consistent with Abdullah's initiatives elsewhere. Nevertheless, its strong
association with (and financial support from) King Abdullah highlight
an ongoing tension between processes of institutionalisation and the
ongoing personalisation of reform initiatives. Hassan Al-Husseini, a former administrator at the King Fahd University of Petroleum and Min-
erals, warned that 'when something is established by royal edict, then
that same thing can be reversed by another royal edict. It's not like you
have legal protection for such things in Saudi Arabia'.[40]

In addition to the judicial and educational reforms unveiled since 2005,
the experience of Saudi Arabia's first municipal elections in February 2005
further demonstrated the innate caution of reform processes. Voting was
restricted to males only, turnout was low at about 30 per cent in many
precincts, the elected councillors wielded little influence in practice, and
the follow-up round of elections which should have been held in 2009
has been postponed indefinitely. Nor did the exercise in electoral accountability shift any meaningful authority over (or influence within) the
municipalities away from the central government's Ministry of Municipal and Rural Affairs.[41] As with the experience of judicial reform, in which
judges are still appointed (and dismissed) by royal decree, the dominant
picture that emerges is one of considerable care in applying top-down
and controlled reforms that are unlikely to develop an autonomous trajectory of their own. Moreover, their attachment to a particular ruler (in
this case Abdullah) renders them fragile and vulnerable to contestation
should a new ruler decide to move in a different direction.[42]

Reforms within the Saudi political system are thus insufficiently
embedded within institutional structures. Patterns of personalisation are
not unique to Saudi Arabia, as the Dubai debt crisis in 2009 powerfully
demonstrated. Even in Kuwait, with its longer history of political struc-

tures, personal networks cut across formal boundaries between the political and economic (or state-business) spheres. Consequently, prominent and powerful political figures retain the ability to reconfigure policy and shape the structures of governance in their own image. For this reason, both political structures and policy-making are intertwined around the need to construct consensual coalitions and balance princely factions that can coalesce around a particular policy. The study of leading personalities is therefore a legitimate part of the process of political analysis and forecasting of possible future trends, as well as the likely evolution of policy-making and coalition-building within Saudi Arabia.

Despite comprising nearly 5,000 members, the Al-Saud family has consistently demonstrated an ability to control the broad pace of domestic (and transformational) change. Its pragmatic strategies of survival eased the regime through the period of intense transition that marked the entry into the oil era. These depended on the mixture of pragmatic adaptability and carefully-controlled reforms outlined above. Nevertheless the ruling family was far from being a monolithic entity with one official view. Rather sub-groups, often consisting of full brothers or alliances of half-brothers, formed powerful alliances that play a role in the direction of policy-making. Of these alliances, the most powerful consists of the sons of Abdul-Aziz and Princess Hassa bint Ahmed Al-Sudairi. Known as the 'Sudairi Seven', they have comprised the late King Fahd (who reigned from 1982 to 2005) and his six prominent full brothers, among them the current Crown Prince (and Defence Minister), Sultan, his designated successor (as second Deputy Prime Minister and Interior Minister), Prince Nayef, and the long-serving Governor of Riyadh province, Prince Salman. In contrast, King Abdullah always lacked a comparable power base and consequently built an alternative constituency comprising strategic alliances with the influential sons of King Faisal (including the current Foreign Minister, Prince Saud) and key tribal partners through his control of the National Guard.[43]

The advancing age of the surviving sons of Abdul Aziz and the looming transition to the second generation of princes inject new dynamics into intra-familial balancing. The creation of an Allegiance Council (*Hay'at al-Bay'ah*) in October 2006, consisting of thirty-five senior sons and grandsons, aims to formalise the process of future successions and ensure that the Al-Saud reach a quiet consensus around a suitable candidate as in the Al-Sabah family council in Kuwait. Significantly, and echoing the mini-succession crisis in Kuwait when Sheikh Saad was deemed too ill to reign following the death of Sheikh Jabir in January 2006, the Allegiance Council may medically assess the ruler's capacity to continue in office, or the crown prince's capacity to assume power. This notwithstanding, its relevance was called into question in 2009 when the announcement of Prince Nayef as effectively the third in line appeared to bypass the Council and come directly from King Abdullah himself.[44]

In 2008–9 the issue of succession assumed greater urgency during Crown Prince Sultan's lengthy absence through illness from Saudi Arabia. As the designated successor to Abdullah and a member of the group of Sudairi brothers described above, Sultan wields a substantial domestic power base. This is augmented through his longstanding control of the Ministry of Defence and Aviation (as Minister since 1962), where he has deeply embedded networks of influence and support, including those of his powerful son, Khalid bin Sultan. In December 2009 Crown Prince Sultan's return to Saudi Arabia following medical treatment in the US signalled his desire to resume royal duties and re-enter the political arena. This was followed in October 2010 by the unexpected return to Saudi Arabia of another influential son, the former long-serving Ambassador to the United States, Bandar bin Sultan, after a two-year absence abroad; this added to external speculation over the internal politics within the ruling family.[45] In the meantime, Nayef's appointment as second Deputy Prime Minister and his effective positioning next in line after Sultan demonstrated the continuing influence of the Sudairi brothers to determine the path of succession, whether directly through Sultan or passing over to Nayef.[46]

Nayef's rise to second Deputy Prime Minister (bypassing six older princes to assume a position held by both Fahd and Abdullah before they became Crown Prince) reflected his prominent role in neutralising the domestic threat from al-Qaeda in the Arabian Peninsula. As Interior Minister, Nayef pioneered the concept of *intellectual security* as the central pillar of the Kingdom's approach to countering terrorism. His emphasis on a 'war of ideas' against the 'challenge from a deviant ideology' turned the mobilising tool of religious legitimacy against disaffected elements to knit them back into the Saudi polity.[47] Nayef was thus instrumental in restoring the link between regime and religious legitimacy, which he saw as crucial to the core legitimacy and survival of the Saudi state, following the difficult aftermath of the September 11 2001 attacks. Yet his conservative reputation has disappointed advocates of reform, who fear he will jeopardise the legacy of Abdullah's tentative initiatives, perhaps by clamping down on future openings for civil society associations and other non-state modes of organisation.[48]

Like Sultan, Nayef has added filial depth to his base of support within his Ministry by placing his son, Muhammed bin Nayef, in a high-profile position of responsibility as deputy minister overseeing counter-terrorism operations. He and Khalid bin Sultan (Deputy Defence Minister) and Mitab bin Abdullah (son of King Abdullah and Commander of the National Guard) have emerged as the leading second-generation princes. All three hold security portfolios courtesy of the vertical transmission of power within the bureaucratic enclaves carved out by their fathers. Muhammed bin Nayef's reputation as the architect of Saudi Arabia's fight against domestic terrorism was boosted after he survived an assassination attempt in August 2009. Khalid bin Sultan was already a national figure following his military leadership in the 1991 Gulf War. Beginning in November 2009, he oversaw the four-month campaign to roll back boundary incursions from militants based in Yemen, and emerged as the public and international representative on key military issues. Mitab bin Abdullah benefited from his father's consolidation of power as he assumed greater responsibilities for the National Guard and attained ministerial rank in 2009 before being promoted from deputy to Commander in November 2010. Other prominent second-generation groups of princes include the sons of the late King Faisal, notably the former Ambassador to the US and head of intelligence Turki Al-Faisal, and the Kingdom's long-serving Foreign Minister (since 1975), Saud Al-Faisal.[49]

Economic development and diversification

Saudi Arabia remains a hydrocarbon-based economy. In 2009 the petroleum sector represented 45 per cent of GDP and provided roughly 80 per cent of the Kingdom's budget revenue and 90 per cent of its export earnings.[50] Oil rents transformed the political economy of Saudi Arabia and the other Gulf states, reshaped state-society relations during the twentieth century, and distorted the economic development of the redistributive, rent-based ('rentier') states that emerged.[51] The 2010 *BP Statistical Review of World Energy* projects the Kingdom's reserves-to-production ratio to last a further 74.6 years.[52] This ratio may deplete more rapidly if the progressive drawdown of supplies elsewhere places additional pressure on Saudi oil reserves in the future. Alternatively, technological developments in the production and diversification of energy may lessen global demand for oil in a climate-aware environment. Both scenarios require Saudi Arabia, in common with other oil-producing states, to take steps to diversify the economy and expand its productive (and sustainable) non-oil base.

With exports beginning after the Second World War, oil tied Saudi Arabia firmly into the international economic system. Strong mutual interdependencies developed between the Kingdom and Western economies, creating powerful linkages between oil-producing and consuming states in the post-1945 era of industrial reconstruction. Saudi Arabia was thus integrated into the global economy long before the acceleration of globalising flows and processes of economic globalisation in the 1980s and 1990s.[53] However, the structure of the oil sector created the peculiar nature of 'rentier economies' marked by enclave-based development largely isolated from the non-oil economic sector. Moreover, its capital-intensity meant that hydrocarbons provided few opportunities for integration with labour markets, accounting for only 1.2 per cent of the total workforce in 2004, while the accrual of oil rents to Saudi nationals (via state redistributive and welfare policies) created strong disincentives towards economic productivity. Dual labour markets emerged as the public sector absorbed Saudi nationals (constituting 86 per cent of all public sector employees) while the private sector largely became the preserve of the burgeoning immigrant workforce (60 per cent of the private sector total in 2008).[54]

Saudi Arabia nevertheless differs significantly from the 'extreme rentier' economies of the smaller Arab Gulf monarchies (particularly Kuwait, Qatar, and the United Arab Emirates). Its much larger population (29,207,277, including 5,576,076 foreigners in 2010) and its rapid demographic growth complicate the continued transfer of wealth through the redistribution of oil revenues.[55] Together these trends have caused rising and visible disparities in income and wealth, and intra-societal inequalities. Income per capita more than halved between 1980 and 2000, a fall from $16,650 to $7,239, consistent with a general fall in the value of oil exports per capita (throughout the GCC) from $15,000 to $6000 over the same period.[56] A high birth rate of 29 per 1000 of total population (double that of the US's 14 per 1000) and a median age of just 21.6 years exacerbate the decline, and place added pressure on the economy to generate the jobs that will be required to accommodate the youth bulge. In 2000, the scale of the challenge became evident in estimates that 3,474,000 new jobs would be created by 2020, compared with a projected increase in the Saudi labour force of 5,091,000.[57]

Programmes of labour indigenisation ('Saudisation') and economic diversification therefore formed the cornerstone of successive five-year development plans. These date back to 1970, with the eighth development plan covering the 2005–9 period. Particularly in their early years, they provided an opportunity to outline a broad set of principles to oversee and steer Saudi economic development.[58] While initial plans during the 1970s oil boom were characterised by lavish expenditure on prestige projects (often of questionable enduring value) in the context of state-led development, more recent ones have demonstrated a considerable maturing of economic policy objectives. In particular, the seventh (2000–4) and eighth (2005–9) plans shifted the focus of policy-making to embrace the private sector as the engine of economic diversification and growth, embedded within sustainable development policies through investment in human resources and science, technology and IT.[59]

Yet the numbers of foreign labourers employed in Saudi Arabia rose rapidly, in both relative and absolute terms, from 28.3 per cent in 1975 to 59.8 per cent in 1985, before peaking at 67.2 per cent in 1989 and falling back (in proportion though not in number) to 57.3 per cent in 2004. Throughout this period (1975–2004) the rise in Saudi employment in the labour force (1,253,000 to 3,356,300) was outstripped by the increase in non-Saudi workers (494,000 to 4,745,500), with by far the greatest influx of foreign workers coming in the decade between 1975 and 1985. Hence, attempts to reduce the size of the non-Saudi workforce only marginally succeeded in raising the Saudi share of the labour force while failing to stem the continual rise in the absolute share of non-nationals.[60] This notwithstanding, the number of workers (both Saudi and non-Saudi) employed in non-oil (private, agricultural, manufacturing and service) sectors rose by more than one million between 1999 and 2004. This provided an indication that job creation and economic diversification programmes were beginning to have an effect, even if not at the desired pace.[61]

Economic diversification programmes in Saudi Arabia have followed a two-pronged approach. One dimension focuses on creating economic cities as hubs of agglomeration and the creation and diffusion of knowledge, while the other emphasises the development of a sophisticated downstream petrochemicals industry, in addition to investment in other energy-intensive industries (such as aluminium) and capital-intensive technological sectors. Within the first strand, the major series of initiatives involve the construction of six economic cities, including the showpiece King Abdullah Economic City on the Red Sea coast north of Jeddah, containing an integrated seaport, industrial centre and financial sector.[62] These form the core of the Kingdom's strategy of economic diversification and job creation, and they build on Saudi Arabia's long-delayed accession to the World Trade Organisation (WTO) in 2005 and the privatisation of key economic sectors by the Supreme Economic Council in order to attract foreign investment.[63] More important, the cities are also designed to bypass cumbersome and ossified bureaucratic structures by creating parallel economies based on regulatory frameworks conducive to private sector investment.[64]

Massive investment in and development of large-scale industrial projects is the second pillar of economic diversification in Saudi Arabia. Of these, the most significant is the expansion of downstream petrochemical products and capacity-building. By 2009, the Kingdom was the fastest growing market in the Middle East for the petrochemical, printing, plastics and packaging industries, and accounted for 70 per cent of petrochemical production in the GCC. During the year, Saudi officials announced plans to consolidate their position as one of the biggest players in the global petrochemicals industry through the launch of three of the most ambitious petrochemicals projects in the world: the Ras Tanura Integrated Project, the construction of the world's largest integrated petrochemicals facility in Jubail Industrial City, and an upgrading of the Petro Rabigh Refinery into one of the most sophisticated integrated oil refining and petrochemical facilities of its kind. The three initiatives aim to expand Saudi Arabia's range of petrochemical products and substantially increase its global market base, in addition to creating 150,000 skilled engineering and technical jobs.[65]

Interwoven into the job creation and economic diversification programmes described above was the emergence and growth in the 2000s of an incipient private sector bourgeoisie. This comprised individuals and businessmen involved in the production of value-added goods and services, and less dependent on the state for the receipt and redistribution of oil rents.[66] Moreover, the second oil boom witnessed a substantial increase in private liquidity and non-royal millionaires, giving the emerging bourgeoisie a degree of autonomy from state structures and actions.[67] Luciani went as far as labelling the appearance of an autonomous national bourgeoisie a 'silent transformation' indicative of a shift towards a post-rentier framework of governance.[68] Yet several factors continue to constrain the breadth and depth of Saudi diversification, notably the resilience of opaque networks of familial political-economic alliances. These complicate the transition to a market economy with high standards of corporate governance, and introduce a measure of conceptual uncertainty into the notion of a 'private' sector genuinely operating beyond the realm of the state.[69]

Saudi Arabia's relatively opaque business culture became evident in May 2009 when two of the most prominent family conglomerates in Saudi Arabia (the Saad Group and Ahmad Hamad Algosaibi and Brothers) unexpectedly announced a debt restructuring.[70] This affected more than eighty domestic, regional and international banks, including Citigroup and BNP Paribas. A general lack of transparency and inadequate disclosure of information to investors demonstrated the difficulty in overcoming older ways of conducting business on the basis of informal and familial connections.[71] Nonetheless, the Kingdom's delayed accession to the WTO in December 2005 did inject a new dynamic into the economic reform process by benchmarking domestic governance to international standards.[72] This enmeshment in rules-based frameworks of global governance is a comparatively new process requiring further assessment over an extended period of time. It is, however, an important new trajectory that should reformulate state-business relations in Saudi Arabia over the medium and the longer term.

Underlying this changing domestic and international backdrop is a qualitative difference in fiscal policies between the first (1973–82) oil boom, in which spending tended to follow increasing oil prices, and the second (2002–8) oil boom, in which more than half of the surplus was saved. These more cautious fiscal policies enabled Saudi Arabia (along with other GCC states) to build up substantial levels of overseas reserves. Unlike sovereign wealth funds in Kuwait, Qatar and the UAE that made high profile investments in leading Western companies, the major investment vehicles in Saudi Arabia invest locally to promote the development of domestic services and industrial ventures. Thus they are not standard sovereign wealth funds, nor do they acquire stakes in foreign companies or countries, and they tend to follow a more cautious approach to investment than their Gulf counterparts.[73] Nevertheless, external recognition of Saudi Arabia's financial reserves and its fiscal responsibility positioned the Kingdom as an important player in the reshaping of international financial governance following the global economic crisis of 2007–9.[74]

Debates over the post-crisis financial architecture demonstrated the possibilities open to Saudi Arabia in a realigning balance of geo-economic power. During 2008–9, Saudi officials received international praise for their role in stabilising world oil markets as prices plummeted from record highs of $147 per barrel in July 2008 to a low of $33 per barrel in January 2009. Moreover, its membership of the G20 and the board of governors of the International Monetary Fund (IMF) allows the Kingdom to represent the Arab and Islamic worlds at these global forums. It also provides a platform for cooperation with other emerging powers such as Brazil, China, India and Russia to increase the voting powers of developing countries in the IMF at the expense of 'overrepresented' developed states.[75] These form part of a transformative shift eastward in global economic power amid the emergence of multiple centres of gravity and the relative decline of Western-centric organisational frameworks of governance. *Forbes* magazine's annual ranking of the world's most powerful people reflected this polycentric shift in power, as its 2010 edition listed King Abdullah as the third most powerful man in the world after the Chinese President Hu Jintao and US President Barack Obama, with the citation referring to his leadership of the world's largest oil producer and the home of Islam's holiest sites.[76]

During 2009 an emblematic milestone was reached as Saudi oil exports to China exceeded those to the US for the first time. This occurred as surging Chinese demand intersected with a 50 per cent drop in US requirements during the global economic downturn.[77] It represented a visible indicator of the deepening political and commercial relations between the two countries, which only established official diplomatic relations in 1990. China began to import crude oil for the first time in 1993, and Saudi Arabia became its largest source of supplies by 2002. China's rapid energy-intensive industrialisation meant it alone accounted for nearly 40 per cent of the increase in global oil consumption between 2004 and 2007.[78] The 2000s also witnessed thickening Sino-Saudi interdependencies that moved the relationship beyond the mere supply of oil to encompass substantial investment projects and joint ventures in each other's upstream and downstream energy sectors. Major initiatives included a 2001 agreement between Saudi Aramco and Sinopec in which the former acquired a 25 per cent stake in the expansion of a refinery in Fujian province and the construction of a new ethylene-production facility. Simultaneously, SABIC developed a 'China Plan' involving three joint venture production bases in China, as part of a strategic goal to support China's economic development and meet its rapidly-growing demand.[79]

Foreign policy and Security

In January 2006 King Abdullah made his first visit outside the Middle East since becoming ruler in August 2005. His choice of destination, China, drew attention to the burgeoning ties between the two countries, as well as the diversification of Saudi Arabia's foreign policy.[80] Moreover, the visit came at a point of considerable tension in the relationship with the US, hitherto a cornerstone of Saudi Arabia's foreign policy and security. Mutual recriminations over the involvement of Saudis in the September 11 2001 terrorist attacks and the George W. Bush administration's invasion of Afghanistan and Iraq severely strained a pragmatic association dating back to 1945. Despite this temporary friction, however, certain clear continuities and trends have long underlain the conduct of foreign policy and security in Saudi Arabia, and continue to delineate its parameters today.

At the outset it is important to distinguish between Western and Saudi conceptions of regional interests and objectives, as these have not always been aligned. The common bond is an agreement on the importance of protecting the export of oil that provides the Kingdom's primary source of revenue and energy for Western economies. Accelerating rapidly in the 1990s, this has translated into the projection of Western military power as the external guarantor of the security of friendly states and regional interests. These range from defence cooperation agreements with Bahrain, Kuwait, Qatar and the UAE to an access to facilities agreement with Oman, and multiple military agreements that have underpinned Saudi Arabia's security since the 1940s. Yet local and Western interests have frequently diverged over the nature of particular threats, most particularly over post-revolutionary Iran. Whereas successive generations of political leadership in the US have depicted Tehran as a strategic rival and military threat to its regional interests, ruling elites and much public discourse in Saudi Arabia and the other GCC states have instead concentrated on the ideational and political challenge that Iran poses to the internal security of their polities.[81]

Nonneman developed the theory of *omni-balancing* to conceptualise the multiple dimensions within which Saudi foreign policy operates. This involves a delicate balancing between threats and resources between the domestic, regional and global arenas. It constitutes the core of a preference for managed multi-dependence and a polygamous approach to foreign affairs characteristic of Saudi Arabia's (and other Gulf states') policy-making for more than a century.[82] Gause also emphasised the consistency of regime attempts to maintain security both against conventional regional threats and against trans-national ideological challenges to domestic political stability and legitimacy. It is the pursuit of these objectives that has created tensions regionally and globally, through hegemonic designs over the Arabian Peninsula and the trans-national dissemination of Wahhabi interpretations of Islam.[83] Globalising processes also posed a 'security dilemma' for the Al-Saud by interlinking international and domestic sources of instability in an attempt to erode sources of regime stability and legitimacy.

Saudi foreign policy has been consistent in the range of soft power tools used to realise its objectives and counterbalance its relatively weak military strength. Particularly since the advent of significant oil revenues in the 1950s and 60s, it has rested on a mixture of financial assistance to regional allies (*'riyal-politik'*, named after the Saudi currency) and the trans-nationalisation of its Islamic legitimacy through the creation and sponsorship of organisations such as the Muslim World League and the Organisation of the Islamic Conference. This led Peterson to identify the pursuit of two foreign policies, one secular and the other Islamic, that link up on certain issues, such as support for threatened Muslim populations and communities in zones of conflict such as Afghanistan, Bosnia and Chechnya.[84] Notably, it was their divergence in the 1990s and early 2000s that provided much of the impetus behind the rise of al-Qaeda and the subsequent flow of Saudi fighters to Sunni insurgent movements in Iraq and Afghanistan. Speaking in 2005, one Saudi intelligence officer encapsulated the difficulty of reining in a force the Kingdom could no longer control:

We encouraged our young men to fight for Islam in Afghanistan. We encouraged our young men to fight for Islam in Bosnia and Chechnya. We encouraged our young men to fight for Islam in Palestine. Now we are telling them that you are forbidden to fight for Islam in Iraq, and they are confused.[85]

Underpinning this foreign policy stance is the strategic alliance with the US. This constitutes the foundational bedrock of Saudi Arabia's foreign and security policy. It revolves around (but is not limited to) the nexus between oil and security first established at the meeting between President Franklin D. Roosevelt and King Abdul Aziz aboard the USS *Quincy* in Egypt's Great Bitter Lake in February 1945. Relations reached an apogee in the 1970s as President Nixon's 'Twin Pillars' policy derogated regional leadership to Saudi Arabia and Iran. Working in close cooperation with the US, King Faisal and the Shah emerged as solid pillars of support for a conservative and pro-Western policy in the region. This helped secure their monarchical polities against the Arab socialist threat from Baathist Iraq and also met US interests in maintaining the geo-strategic status quo in the Gulf.[86] Substantial expenditure on military imports from the US to build up Saudi security and defence forces augmented this strategic partnership as arms transfers exceeded $53 billion in value between 1950 and 1990.[87]

The Iranian revolution in 1979 and the Iran-Iraq war (1980–88) caused a major shift in this regional equilibrium. Saudi Arabia and the US gravitated decisively towards Iraq as a bulwark against Iranian attempts to export its Islamic revolution to neighbouring states. Particularly during the immediate aftermath of the revolution, Iranian agents were implicated in plots to destabilise internal security in Saudi Arabia (1979 and 1984), Bahrain (1981), and Kuwait (1985 and 1987–88).[88] The unrest in the Eastern Province of Saudi Arabia primarily involved Shia protests at perceived inequalities in access to resources and services. It thus had domestic roots, although Iranian revolutionary fervour did inspire and galvanise some of the protests in Saudi Arabia. Notwithstanding the powerful symbolism that Ayatollah Khomeini's ascendancy had for Shia communities, it was notable that the majority of Shia organisations continued to regard the nation state as their primary point of reference when articulating demands for reform.[89]

During the 1980s, Saudi Shia organisations therefore remained embedded in their domestic context and held a far more nuanced attachment to trans-national loyalties than was supposed by suspicious ruling elites.

Nevertheless, the legacy of this intermeshing of the internal and external spheres of security carried profound implications for Shia political organisation in Saudi Arabia and the other Gulf states, as officials frequently conflated questions of Shia loyalty and external Iranian interference.[90] In 2005, these sentiments culminated in Saud Al-Faisal's blunt allegation that the US-led invasion of Iraq was 'handing the whole country over to Iran without reason', and they lie behind the Kingdom's deep distrust of Iraq's Shia-led post-2003 governing elite, which it views as an Iranian proxy and as a source of multiple physical and ideational threats.[91]

In August 1990 the Iraqi invasion of Kuwait transformed Saudi Arabia's foreign and security policy posture as the US's 'over-the-horizon' policy was superseded by a direct military footprint throughout the Gulf. The Kingdom provided bases and served as a logistical hub for the liberation of Kuwait. Furthermore, Saudi forces commanded by Khalid bin Sultan participated in the fighting. In January 1991 they dislodged an Iraqi assault that briefly occupied the town of Ras al-Khafiji (at the cost of more than fifty Saudi casualties in the most direct threat to Saudi Arabia's territorial integrity since the foundation of the modern state in 1932). However, the enduring legacy of the war was an ideational rather than material challenge to regime legitimacy. This arose from the retention of five thousand American soldiers in Saudi bases after 1991 as part of the Clinton administration's policy of 'Dual Containment' of Iraq and Iran. It posed an acute strategic dilemma for the Al-Saud as their external security guarantee paradoxically constituted a radicalising grievance and mobilising tool for internal opponents, allowing individuals such as Osama bin Laden to question the Saudi King's legitimacy and suitability to act as the proper guardian of the land of the two holy places.[92]

In addition to the emergence of al-Qaeda as an ideational rejection of the Al-Saud, the appearance of a body called al-Qaeda in the Arabian Peninsula in 2002–3 posed both an existential and a direct challenge to Saudi legitimacy. This occurred as the group publicly declared its objective to force the withdrawal of Western forces and influence from the Arabian Peninsula.[93] Security officials failed to anticipate the rise of this Sunni rejectionist movement. Neither did they foresee the potential danger that the return of several hundred Arab fighters from Afghanistan might present should they intersect with local networks of militants. Moreover, the introduction of the Internet in Saudi Arabia in 1999 and other advances in information and communications technologies further eroded boundaries between the domestic and external spheres, and facilitated the spread of jihadist propaganda within Saudi Arabia.[94] This enabled al-Qaeda in the Arabian Peninsula to tap into broader currents of discontent, the scale of which was revealed in two unpublished Saudi polls, one (in 2001) said to indicate that 95 per cent of young males (aged 25–41) sympathised with bin Laden in 2001, and the other (in 2003) that 97 per cent opposed any form of cooperation with the US-led attack on Iraq in 2003.[95]

The threat from al-Qaeda in the Arabian Peninsula lasted until its last major attack, against the oil-processing facility at Abqaiq in February 2006. This failed operation was directed against the social and commercial contract binding the Saudi state to its society and to the international system more generally, given that so many expatriates were being targeted.[96] Thereafter, a combination of hard and soft security countermeasures led to the operational and tactical rolling up of al-Qaeda's militant networks in the Kingdom. It coincided with measures targeting Saudi-based individuals and charities suspected of providing financing for terrorist organisations, following blunt and very vocal criticism from the US in the aftermath of September 11 2001.[97] These initiatives succeeded in restoring damaged US-Saudi relations and overcoming the unprecedented challenge to the maintenance of Saudi Arabia's hydrocarbons-based political economy. However, as the following section makes clear, success may prove temporary as the current crisis of governance and erosion of security in Yemen are providing a haven for the reconstitution of al-Qaeda in the Arabian Peninsula.

Future challenges

Saudi Arabia faces a range of immediate and longer-term challenges at multiple and increasingly interlocking levels. The sudden emergence of the 'Arab Spring' sent shockwaves throughout the Middle East and North Africa.

Although the unrest originated in North Africa, it rapidly spread to three of Saudi Arabia's closest neighbours, all comparatively resource-poor: Bahrain, Oman, and Yemen. All three countries share maritime or land boundaries with Saudi Arabia, and the Kingdom felt itself encircled by instability. The sectarian composition of Bahraini unrest was especially alarming to Saudi policy-makers, who feared it could spread to Saudi Shi'ites in the oil-rich Eastern Province.[98] King Abdullah returned to Saudi Arabia in February 2011, following three months' medical treatment abroad, with a promise to increase benefits in housing, education, and social services. Over the next month, forty-one royal decrees were announced, providing for a total spending package worth $129bn.[99] Saudi officials also played a leading role in the creation of a $20bn GCC aid package for Bahrain and Oman designed to ease the spiralling tensions in both those countries.[100]

Saudi Arabia faced its own 'Day of Rage' on 11 March 2011. This failed to ignite as a heavy security presence maintained order and prevented demonstrations. But just days later, a Saudi-led GCC Peninsula Shield Force intervened in Bahrain to quell the pro-democracy movement threatening the ruling Al-Khalifa family. More than a thousand soldiers from King Abdullah's Saudi Arabia National Guard crossed the King Fahd Causeway into Bahrain, ostensibly to protect critical national infrastructure and restore stability in the archipelago. Their deployment triggered solidarity protests by Saudi Shi'ites waving flags and chanting in support of the Bahraini opposition.[101] The security crackdown that followed was part of a general authoritarian turn that sought to narrow political space and close down oppositional dissent throughout the Gulf. Thus, the founders of what would have been Saudi Arabia's first political party (the Islamic Umma Party) were swiftly arrested in March 2011 on the orders of Prince Nayef, after refusing to drop their calls for change.[102]

The decision to suppress or prevent demonstrations rather than engage substantively with demands for reform leaves untouched the larger issues of political representation and socio-economic sustainability and reform. Across the GCC, ruling elites sought to attribute the basis of the unrest to external manipulation, rather than acknowledge their domestic causes.[103] Moreover, the emphasis on benefits and handouts indicated a clear preference for technocratic or technological solutions to the problems facing them. Yet these ignored the crucial social dimension of the Arab Spring, which has empowered people with notions of entitlement and a desire for justice and accountability in their rulers. Resolving this paradox in a manner that balances and accommodates societal demands for reform without posing a domestic threat to regime legitimacy will be the key determinant of how the Arab Spring ultimately affects the direction of political change in the Kingdom.

Other challenges arise from the regional and international context, and from the blurring of distinctions between the domestic and international domains. Examples include the reintegration of post-occupation Iraq into the regional fold, addressing any fallout from the dispute between Iran and the international community over its controversial nuclear programme, and the unravelling of political legitimacy and governance in Yemen. This last issue presents a direct and immediate challenge from al-Qaeda in the Arabian Peninsula, following its reconstitution in January 2009 after the merger of its Saudi and Yemeni wings. Saudi officials must also plan for a looming transfer of power away from Yemen's President Ali Abdullah Saleh without endangering or diluting their dense networks of patronage and influence that have long provided strategic depth in their unstable southern neighbour.[104]

Domestic contestation of the continuing legitimacy of the Al-Saud may arise from the changing dynamic of oil redistribution as demographic growth erodes mechanisms of redistribution and co-optation. This changing resources-demands balance will interact with the longer-term drawdown of Saudi reserves and make more urgent the eventual transition to a post-oil economy.[105] The 2002–8 oil boom paradoxically complicated the processes of change by temporarily offsetting domestically-challenging measures of restructuring (such as raising the levels of domestic taxation to replace public spending as the means of wealth redistribution) aimed at a productive and value-added political economy based on competitive rather than comparative advantage.[106] This transformative shift links the ambitious programmes of economic diversification and development to the reforms of political, judicial and educational structures described in this chapter.

For reforms to succeed, they need to address entrenched patterns of unproductive rent-seeking behaviour and embed strategies of human capital development in tackling distorted labour markets. Moreover, they will require officials to roll back progressively layers of subsidisation, to reflect more accurately the market value of goods and services. These will, in turn, place a greater onus on participatory mechanisms to replace older methods of political co-optation and rent redistribution. Underlying these trajectories is the fact that the welfare state consolidated during a period of seemingly limitless resources in the 1970s is no longer sustainable in the medium or longer term. Official acknowledgement of this need for change lies behind Abdullah's incremental reforms, but they have yet to reformulate the systemic imbalances to labour markets and economic structures that, if left unchecked or inadequately tackled, will undermine long-term solutions.

The looming transition to a new generation of leadership drawn from the grandsons of Abdul Aziz is the factor underlying all of these economic reforms. Political decisions, and the personalities that lie behind them, will determine their speed and depth. The reforms initiated by Abdullah are significant but have yet to be tested during the transition to a new ruler. In this regard, the example of KAUST may become a barometer for Saudi reform initiatives and processes. It confronts many of the socio-cultural taboos in Saudi society, such as the intermixing of men and women in a coeducational environment and allowing women to go unveiled and drive on campus. The creation and gradual widening of such enclaves of modernisation may be seen as a way of sensitising Saudi Arabia to the inducement of change in carefully-controlled environments before mainstreaming such reforms into Saudi society at large. Alternatively, KAUST may be marginalised under a successor regime, or maintained as a carefully-controlled environment with little if any overspill or linkage with wider society. Should this happen, it will question the institutional durability of educational reforms and their alignment with programmes of economic diversification and labour indigenisation.

These issues feed into a broader set of future challenges facing the Kingdom in the coming years and decades. At their core lie the reformulation of the social contract and mechanisms of state-society relations inherent in the gradual shift towards post-rentier structures of governance. The size of Saudi Arabia's oil reserves means it does not confront the problems of imminent depletion and transition to a post-oil economy, as in neighbouring Bahrain, Oman, and Yemen. Finding a sustainable balance between incremental yet substantive reforms to political and economic structures will ultimately determine whether the resulting changes are aggregated and consensual rather than abrupt and contested.

KUWAIT

David Roberts

State formation

A town in modern-day Kuwait first appeared on a map in 1765. Previously known as Grane, the town is thought to have been established in the mid-seventeenth century. The name Kuwait is likely to have been derived from the addition of a small fort, a *Kut*, to Grane's defences around 1680.[1] Kuwait's ruling family, the Al-Sabah, stem from the Bani Utub tribe which was expelled from the large Al-Anizah tribe in the late seventeenth century.[2] They migrated north, eventually residing in Grane under the protection of the Bani Khalid tribe. This migration separated the Bani Utub from their traditional lands and forced them to engage in new sea-based activities. From then on an independent identity began to emerge.

Most sources state that the Al-Sabah's rule, unbroken to this day, began in 1752.[3] The first Al-Sabah ruler of Kuwait, Sheikh Sabah bin Jabr bin Adhbi, operated in a consultative manner. He dealt with political and tribal relations whilst other Bani Utub families, such as the Al-Khalifa, controlled commercial activities.[4] Kuwait was soon prosperous. By 1760 a fleet of 800 small boats was exploiting fertile pearling beds, whilst the town's strategic location as a station for caravans from the south and east to Syria underwrote Sheikh Abdullah I's rule from 1756 to 1814. Also during Abdullah I's reign, Al-Sabah control was assured as the Al-Khalifa relocated to Qatar and Bahrain in 1766.

Throughout the nineteenth century Kuwait prospered under nominal Ottoman protection, which became further embedded as the century wore on. Kuwait's most revered ruler, Sheikh Mubarak the Great, who reigned from 1896 to 1915, reoriented Kuwait towards Britain. This culminated in the 1899 signing of an exclusive 'trucial' agreement.

During the First World War Kuwait hedged its bets. On the one hand Britain was allowed access to Kuwaiti docks. Yet Mubarak's successor, Sheikh Salem, facilitated regional trade with the Ottomans, thus breaking the British blockade of the Turkish army in Damascus. This was stopped only after strenuous British demands.[5] The inter-war years were a time of economic difficulty for Kuwait. The pearl industry, on which up to half of Kuwait's population depended, collapsed following the introduction of the Japanese cultured pearl. Although oil had been discovered, it could not be exported until the end of the Second World War.

These economic issues were compounded by an increased threat from Saudi forces, with the 1920 Battle of Jahra serving as a defining moment in Kuwait's history. On 10 October Salem intercepted Saudi forces about to invade, but after taking heavy losses he retreated to the Red Fort in Jahra and throughout the night managed to fend off the Saudis. The arrival of a British contingent convinced the Saudis to withdraw. This galvanised the Kuwaitis and emphatically enunciated their separate identity which had been emerging for generations. Additionally, it demonstrated that Kuwait was more than just a town and was capable of defending itself as a city state. Thus 1920 is used today as the 'cut off' date for claimants of Kuwaiti citizenship.

The fact that Britain saved Salim at Jahra was used to pressure his successor, Sheikh Ahmed, into signing the Uqair boundary agreement with Saudi Arabia in 1922. This gave Saudi Arabia nearly two thirds of Kuwaiti territory in reparation for its losses from an earlier treaty it had had to sign with Iraq.

The first oil shipment left Kuwait in June 1946. Revenue from these early exports fostered the rapid development of societal and civic institutions from the 1950s and onwards. Under the leadership of Sheikh Abdullah III, Kuwait's development was systematised in five year plans which led to 'new hospitals and clinics being built by the hundreds, and schools by the thousands'.[6] So successful was Abdullah III's management of Kuwait's transition to a rich, functioning, and modern state that his accession date—25 February—is now celebrated as Kuwait's national day.

Thus, by the time Kuwait became independent from Britain on 19 June 1961, the state was relatively well developed by comparison with its immediate neighbours. However, the one thing it clearly lacked—a meaningful defence force—was soon highlighted. After only a week of independence Iraq began to object vehemently, stating that Kuwait was a region of Iraq and not a sovereign state. British forces duly returned to Kuwait to deter any Iraqi aggression, but only after the accession of a new Iraqi government in 1963 were relations established between the two countries. Even then, Kuwait faced sporadic harassment on its border for much of the next two decades, including a massing of Iraqi troops on the border in 1973.

Whilst Britain's departure from the Gulf in 1971 forced Kuwait to diversify its security arrangements, it was the Iranian Revolution that most significantly changed Kuwait's predicament. No longer was Iraq the prime threat to Kuwait, as Iran was more explicitly anti-monarchical and implicitly anti-Sunni. Not coincidentally, the 1980s saw significant disturbances in Kuwait ranging from numerous terrorist attacks to an attempted assassination of the Emir in 1985.[7]

In reaction to the Iran-Iraq war Kuwait generously funded Iraq with an estimated $13 billion of aid. And at one point Kuwait even considered joining the United Arab Emirates federation in an effort to enhance security.[8] Instead, Kuwait took a leading role in the foundation of the Gulf Cooperation Council in May 1981. In turn this led to the establishment of the largely symbolic 'Peninsula Shield' coalition force, which was ostensibly made up of the GCC's six member militaries. Kuwait's support for Iraq was, however, not enough to deter or placate Saddam Hussein. Baghdad accused Kuwait of siphoning oil from the Iraqi side of the border and deliberately crashing the price of oil through overproduction.[9] On 1 August 1990 Iraq massed over 100,000 troops on the Kuwaiti border, and within thirty-six hours Kuwait was conquered.

With Saudi Arabia also under threat, the US-led Operation Desert Shield mobilised within five days, and early in 1991 Operation Desert Storm, comprising over a quarter of a million troops from the US and its allies, was ready. Combat operations began on 16 January and it took an estimated 100 hours to rout the Iraqi army from Kuwait,[10] with estimates of the Iraqi dead ranging from 82,500 to 250,000.[11] Although it was liberated, Kuwait's infrastructure, hospitals, oil fields, schools and other public buildings had been decimated. Estimates of the costs of repair were between $20 and $30 billion, with $60 billion in lost earnings.[12]

In the immediate aftermath the UN confirmed Kuwait's official borders (Security Council Resolution 833) and forced Iraq to give up its territorial claims on Kuwait. Iraq was also obliged to donate 5 per cent of its future oil revenue by way of reparation. By October 1992 Kuwait had signed defence cooperation agreements with the US, the UK and France. So close was Kuwait's relationship with the US that up to 60 per cent of its territory was devoted to the US military when required.[13] Nevertheless, Kuwait was well insulated from the US-led invasion of Iraq in 2003. Unlike Syria, for example, which had to cope with millions of Iraqi refugees, there were few signs of the war in Kuwait, aside from US troops in Kuwait International Airport and a handful of missile attacks.

The late 2000s saw continued bickering in Kuwait's Parliament, to the detriment of long-term planning and development. Aside from protests from Kuwait's *bidoon* population (long-term residents without citizenship) and smaller Shia protests at events in Bahrain, the Affects of the Arab Spring on Kuwait have been more subtle. The sectarian lens which has been explicitly foisted on the Arab Spring in Bahrain by the Gulf Cooperation Council (GCC) states has re-energised the Sunni-Shia dynamic in Kuwait, which has been, aside from sporadic flare-ups, historically restrained.

Political structures and personalities

The most powerful institution in Kuwait remains the Al-Sabah ruling family. Having ruled continuously since the mid-eighteenth century, it has been sewn into the fabric of Kuwait's politics and society not so much through dictatorial methods but rather by conciliation and wholesale cooption in the post-oil era.

Originally, the traditional ruling bargain in Kuwait was an accommodation between the Al-Sabah and the leading merchants. The former needed the latter's taxes, thus giving the merchant community great influence. However, the exclusive agreement of 1899 with Britain granted Sheikh Mubarak a stipend from London and assurances for the security of Al-Sabah date groves along the Shatt al-Arab waterway.[14] This was to make Mubarak 'the first Al-Sabah ruler leader to act at least partially independently of Kuwait's powerful merchants'.[15]

The merchants recognised the threat that this new development posed to their relative strength and influence. When Mubarak's successor and son, Sheikh Salim, died abruptly, the merchants sought to institutionalise their influence better. In 1921 the Consultative Council was formed and proposed three candidates to be the next ruler. Sheikh Ahmed was elected and was initially sympathetic to the merchants' desire for greater consultation. The Council was however soon crippled by bickering and dissolved by the ruler.[16]

With Ahmed's initial acquiescence, a new merchants' movement in the late 1930s codified its constitution and passed laws such as the banning of monopolies as well as outlawing the Al-Sabah's use of slave labour. However, when the merchants attempted to exercise control over the army and the state's oil revenue, Ahmed dissolved the body. He rewrote the constitution, changing the merchants' council from being a legislative body to an advisory body, but this was rejected. Instead, the merchants held a bigger election and continued to debate issues. The newly elected council was disbanded but still continued to meet and began to discuss ever more militant topics. The climax came when Ahmed had a speaker who questioned Al-Sabah rule arrested and executed.

In 1950 Sheikh Abdullah III ascended to the throne. He used exponentially increasing oil revenue to finance the building of a modern state structure complete with ministries and development committees. These were invariably headed by prominent members of the Al-Sabah who turned them into their own money-making fiefdoms at the expense of the merchants. Nevertheless, in the context of growing Arab nationalist sentiments in the region and anger at corruption within the elite, Abdullah III instigated some short-lived reforms. Advisers for government departments were elected, clubs were formed, and an active press was encouraged.[17] By the end of the decade most of these reforms had been curtailed, but by then the state's distributive mechanisms—including free health care and free education—were in place and actors began to be bought off, lessening the pressure on the ruling family.[18] Moreover, in return for institutionalised economic advantages, including a sponsorship system and exclusive import licenses, most of the merchant class tacitly agreed to leave governmental political decisions to the Al-Sabah.[19]

With independence came an immediate threat from Iraq. This prompted 'the populace to turn to the established leadership and the leadership to turn to popular support'.[20] To galvanise legitimacy a new assembly was set up and a new constitution was drawn up in 1961. Less than two years later elections were held for the new fifty-seat National Assembly, commonly referred to as the parliament. All literate male Kuwaitis were allowed to stand for election and around 210 ran in 1963.[21]

The new constitution affirmed the Al-Sabah as the hereditary and inviolable rulers of Kuwait with succession being limited to male descendants of Mubarak the Great. The parliament was to set the Emir's salary and vote on his choice of crown prince, who was also to serve as the prime minister. The selected prime minister was then to appoint sixteen cabinet members, only one of whom needed to have been elected to the parliament. This system allowed the Emir to install family members in key posts. Significantly, political parties were also not allowed and the Emir retained the power to dissolve the parliament at any time on the proviso that he would call for elections soon afterwards. It was also decided that whenever the parliament was not in session the Emir could pass 'urgent' laws. In lieu of members of parliament voting directly on the cabinet's proposals, they could instead call for votes of confidence if they gathered at least ten votes.[22]

Whilst the parliament was intended to act as a rubber stamp for the Al-Sabah's decisions, it proved to be considerably more vibrant and spirited than anticipated. Initially an Arab nationalist opposition bloc emerged led by Ahmed Al-Khatib. To counter this bloc the government pursued three policies. First, it made an alliance with pliant Islamists, promising them greater influence in return for their support.[23] Second, it engaged in widespread 'ballot stuffing, miscounts, and gerrymandering'.[24] Third, the government enfranchised local tribes, guaranteeing their loyalty, to further weaken the opposition.

Nevertheless in 1976 the Emir unconstitutionally dissolved the parliament.[25] Its ever more combative nature meant that it had effectively become paralysed, delaying the budget and other issues in 'endless debate'.[26] The Emir also feared that links were developing between the opposition and international supporters. Soon after the Iranian Revolution, hoping for more popular support the Emir chose to restart the parliament. Before doing so he passed a law increasing the number of districts from ten to twenty-five. This diluted the opposition power as many of the new districts were made up of recently nationalised stateless people, many of whom had resided in Kuwait for decades; they were grateful for enfranchisement and therefore staunch government supporters. It also helped the Islamists who, like the government, increased in power. In an effort to accommodate the growing Islamist element in Parliament, the government supported the banning of Christmas celebrations in 1982 and increasing controls on alcohol.[27]

In 1983 there was a series of bombings committed by Shia terrorists punishing Kuwait for supporting Iraq. Any government attempts to co-opt Islamists were swiftly ended. A crackdown including waves of arrests and the deportation of thousands ensued.

In the 1985 elections overtly religious candidates fared poorly, but the government still proved to be highly obstructionist. The near-assassination of the Emir in the same year and a spate of bombings led the Emir to dissolve the parliament in 1986. Many supported this decision, with the security situation seemingly getting out of control. But by the late 1980s there were fresh pro-democracy stirrings, and following the invasion by Iraq the exiled Emir and Crown Prince met opposition leaders, promising further democratisation for their support for the restoration of Al-Sabah rule after liberation.

After the Iraqi withdrawal the Emir did not return immediately even as disquiet was building in Kuwait. There was anger with the government at letting this occur, and there was impatience with the slow speed of restoring basic services. Social tension also emerged between the *al-samidoon* (those that stayed) versus the *al-hariboon* (those that fled).[28] When the Emir returned there was an immediate crackdown on the media and security amid growing domestic and international agitation for elections. Eventually a date was set for late 1992. Two thirds of the elected members of parliament ran in opposition to the government, leading to a split assembly. Moreover, a failed motion to give women the vote highlighted rifts between liberals and conservatives, while a failed motion to reframe Islam as 'the' not 'a' source of Kuwaiti law pitted Sunni members against Shia members.[29] The Emir's decision to push through debt forgiveness as a simple but effective way to buy off opposition was not enough.[30]

Throughout the acrimonious 1990s the opposition concentrated on government corruption as a way to stave off reforms that would financially impinge on the makeup of their constituencies. Egregious examples were highlighted, such as the Kuwait Oil Tankers Company incident.[31] The 1997 elections returned a nominally more pro-government parliament. Voters heard little but bickering for years and those elected ran mostly on a 'service' platform of promising increased benefits and subsidies. However, after the dissolution of parliament in May 1999 and the ensuing elections, it was the liberals who made the most gains. During the hiatus between governments the Emir tried to enfranchise women, but this was rejected when parliament returned. The Islamists rejected the reform on principle, while others argued on constitutional grounds and some asked who would look after the children if women went to vote.[32]

The intransigence that characterised Kuwait's parliament reached new levels in the 2000s. Despite fresh elections in 2003 the parliament was dissolved three times in quick succession: in 2006, 2008, and 2009. After elections in 2003, with the deteriorating health of the Crown Prince and Prime Minister Sheikh Saad Al-Sabah, the title of prime minister was ceded to Sheikh Sabah Al-Sabah (who had effectively been Acting Prime Minister for two years). This broke with tradition as the prime minister was no longer the direct heir to the throne as well. Significantly, this meant that it became theoretically possible for members of parliament to question their prime minister. Though Sabah was never questioned before he acceded to the throne in 2006, there have been repeated problems with his appointed Prime Minister, Sheikh Nasser Al-Sabah, ever since.

Initially the issue was the reorganisation of constituency boundaries. Constituency populations ranged from 3,000 to 11,000,[33] which left some areas vulnerable to vote-buying and other irregularities. As ruler, Sabah refused to acquiesce to the parliament's demands for a new delimitation. When members of parliament demanded to question the Prime Minister over this issue Sabah dissolved the assembly in 2006. On this occasion, when the parliament reconvened there was a sufficient majority amongst opposition members to force through the reorganisation, leaving Kuwait with just five electoral districts.

Yet opposition unity did not last long. Now that the taboo of questioning a prime minister was broken each faction 'used their new tools with abandon in pursuit of no coherent agenda'.[34]

Women ran for election in 2006 and 2008, having been enfranchised in May 2005, though they did not win any seats. It is interesting to note that in order to ensure emancipation the government approved a $377 million public sector pay increase 'as part of an attempt to woo wavering members of parliament'.[35]

Sabah's accession after the death of Sheikh Jabr III and the forced abdication of the gravely ill Saad after just 9 days on the throne in early 2006 broke an unwritten rule in Kuwaiti politics that power was to alternate between the Jabr and Salim branches of Mubarak's descendants. Sabah appointed his half-brother Sheikh Nawaf Al-Sabah as Crown Prince and his nephew Nasser Al-Sabah as Prime Minister, all from the Jabr side. Whilst this must have caused considerable tension within the family, it was well contained, though it has been suggested that some of the ensuing prime ministerial questioning problems were encouraged by disgruntled members of the Al-Sabah family.

The first elections with five constituencies took place in 2008 and gave Islamists a strong representation. Argumentative politics resumed with one member of parliament filing a motion to question Sheikh Nasser, which forced the cabinet to resign in November 2008. Another set of elections took place and Nasser was reappointed by the Emir. During his oath-taking ceremony a group of members of parliament ominously walked out. Despite Nasser reappointing his fifth cabinet in just three years, three new motions were immediately filed to 'grill' him. Two of these motions were filed by individual Islamist members. Unequivocally on this occasion members were seeking to question the prime minister over minor issues in an effort to force parliament's dissolution.

The 2009 elections reflected a general weariness with these tactics. Fewer candidates registered to stand for parliament, far fewer members were returned, far fewer people voted (58 per cent, compared with previous turnouts of over 65 per cent) and blocs—notably the Islamists—were soundly defeated. Change was due with four women being elected and with 40 per cent of the members being first-timers. The mood in parliament duly improved. When the Minister for the Interior was grilled, he became the first minister to face a vote of no confidence, as opposed to simply resigning beforehand. After he passed this test, the next one came in December 2009 when Nasser was petitioned to be questioned once more. Instead of prompting the cabinet to resign in protest, he agreed to sit and be one of four cabinet members questioned over a twenty hour marathon session which finished in the early hours of the morning. This fostered some goodwill and thwarted the minority who sought to further instability by forcing the parliament's dissolution. Soon after, desperately needed economic stimulus packages and privatisation laws—some eighteen years in the making—finally made it through the parliament.

Yet this amicable hiatus did not last. The Prime Minister sat for a nine-hour interpolation in late December 2010 over alleged repression of public freedoms, and only just survived the ensuing vote of no confidence (twenty-five votes to twenty-two). In March 2011 the Cabinet resigned over the number of interpellations filed by members of parliament against ministers. Without any issues being resolved amid rising acrimony, Sheikh Nasser delayed the formation of his seventh government until mid-May to try to make sure that the government made it to its four-month summer recess without another crisis.

The 'grillings' of the 2000s highlight an inherent weakness in the structure of Kuwait's parliament. They have evolved from being a straightforward parliamentary tool to becoming a partisan circus act. As they can be brought about by a single member over any matter (such as the destruction of a mosque), the parliament remains subject to the whims of any given member. Someone with a personal grudge or a desire for the limelight, or with deeply held but minority views, can effectively grind parliament to a halt. Until the Prime Minister sat in front of an interpolation, as they are formally known, one member could literally force the dissolution of the government.

Furthermore, it has been suggested that interpolations have two other important effects. First, royal family members and ministers will not be appointed if they have a chance of being grilled and voted out by the parliament. Hence those with good (or better) relations with the parliament will fill the seats again and again. Second, these appointees, if they want to remain in the cabinet, have an incentive to acquiesce in or agree with what the parliament wants, and in this way their careers are more likely to continue. A long-term-thinking Cabinet member looking to push through a piece of tough legislation is therefore structurally encumbered and unlikely to retain his place for very long under the current system.[36]

Economic development and diversification

British influence and the presence of British trading companies in Kuwait towards the end of the nineteenth century brought serious challenges for the established *asil* merchants.[37] As British influence became British protection, the Al-Sabah became less dependent on *asil* merchants' taxes. Lesser established second tier merchants who primarily traded goods from inland were less affected, as they still had a wide variety of goods to trade.

The First World War was a time of relative prosperity for Kuwait. The *asil* families benefited from the sudden absence of British competition and regained some of their influence, while the second tier merchants continued to act as conduits. However, the inter-war years were more difficult. Kuwait was hit hard by a combination of Ibn Saud's fourteen-year economic embargo of Kuwait and the development of the cheaper cultured pearl in Japan, which decimated the pearling industry. The effects of the Great Depression exacerbated these issues.

Oil soon changed Kuwait's fortunes once more. A British-US alliance between the Anglo-Persian Oil Company (APOC)[38] and Gulf Oil led to the establishment of the Kuwait Oil Company (KOC) in 1934. Four years later oil was discovered in commercial qualities in the Burgan field. The Second World War postponed the first shipment of oil until June 1946. Nevertheless, Sheikh Ahmed received $178,000 in 1934 and at least $35,000 per annum until oil was exported, then a minimum of $94,000 per annum.[39]

In 1946 Kuwait produced 5.9 million barrels of oil and within ten years this had increased nearly 70 times to 402.7 million barrels.[40] Oil quickly dominated Kuwait's economy, with traditional crafts and trades soon becoming economically unattractive.[41] In the 1950s and early 1960s Sheikh Abdullah III began to expand the Kuwaiti state, mostly by using oil-financed subsidies. First, to appease potential rivals he apportioned fiefdoms and stipends to senior Al-Sabah family members. Secondly, the staffing of new departments enabled Abdullah III to share some of the wealth with ordinary citizens, dovetailing perfectly with the traditional paternalistic notion of providing for one's tribe. Provision of free and relatively good health care; better quality and quantities of water; an exponential increase in free educational opportunities; and wider ranging subsidies and emerging job 'guarantees' for Kuwaitis constituted the birth of the cradle-to-grave Kuwaiti welfare system.

The concurrent boom in construction in Kuwait was fed, if not led, by *asil* merchants. When in 1953 Kuwait faced a budgetary crisis these traders found an opportunity to expand their influence by temporarily loaning money to Abdullah III, whose distributive policies had been corrupted. Various Al-Sabah sheikhs had been abusing their positions and siphoning off money. But even worse were the British companies that were carrying out the majority of construction, as their oligopoly was inefficient and massively expensive and took the majority of work (almost $30 million per year) away from the indigenous merchants.[42]

Throughout the 1950s and 1960s various mechanisms were set up to guarantee the merchants' wealth. First, the British companies were banned from submitting tenders. Secondly, merchants were granted monopolies and, later on, lent money by the Emir, often as start-up equity. The Kuwait Oil Tanker Company and Kuwait Airways were founded in this way. Thirdly, merchants were given legal advantages. Rules were introduced stating that all companies had to be at least 51 per cent Kuwait-owned.[43] Fourthly, the Al-Sabah tacitly promised to withdraw from commerce and trade. Fifthly, the land acquisition programmes of the 1950s and

1960s transferred huge amounts of wealth from the government to the merchant class, buying land from the merchants at inflated prices and then selling it back at bargain rates.

From an early stage, with oil accounting for well over 95 per cent of Kuwait's exports and a similarly high percentage of state income, it was recognised that the state needed to diversify. Thus the 1950s also saw the founding of Kuwait Investment Office (KIO), the forerunner of Kuwait's current sovereign wealth investment authority.[44] This institution and others like it initially invested in domestic industrial operations, for example aluminium casting and the bottling of oxygen.[45]

Large-scale operations began with the establishment of the Shuaiba Industrial Zone in 1962. After mixed initial progress a $3 billion development plan concieved by the World Bank launched in 1967. In 1971 this was followed by a $16 billion plan focusing on Kuwait's domestic industries. Nevertheless, by comparison with other oil-rich states, government support remained modest.[46] 'The government... essentially acknowledged that the prospects for non-oil based services industrialisation... [were] ...limited' and concentrated on delivering for Kuwaitis and investing abroad.[47]

Starting modestly in the 1950s, it was not until after independence and then again with the oil boom that Kuwait's role as international investor really began. The Fund for Future Generations (FFFG) was established in 1976 with $7 billion and 10 per cent of annual oil revenue. This was to be a ring-fenced foreign investment platform for Kuwait's future. For this and other investments, Kuwait preferred western European and US blue chip companies (such as Daimler Benz and Britain's Midland Bank). By the late 1980s Kuwait was earning more from its international investments than from oil ($6.3 billion in 1987).[48]

With regard to the oil industry, in 1951 the Kuwaiti government rearranged a fifty-fifty profit sharing deal with KOC. Subsequent lobbying from the Arab League prompted further concessions, but when the world's largest oil companies unilaterally reduced the price of oil with no consultation, five producer states including Kuwait (representing 85 per cent of the global oil market) met in Baghdad and formed the Organisation of the Petroleum Exporting Countries (OPEC). This cartel was not immediately effective, but by the early 1970s the market was changing to the seller's benefit. Growing nationalist sentiments in the parliament rejected two further renegotiations with KOC in 1965 and 1973.

The 1973 oil boycott—fully supported by both the government and the parliament—led to an immediate tripling of oil revenue. The next year the government sought a 60 per cent nationalisation of the oil industry, and in 1975 it was wholly nationalised.

In downstream diversification, refining oil into fuel began with the establishment of the Kuwait National Petroleum Company in 1960. After cornering the domestic market it began exporting abroad but only became profitable following the oil price hikes of the 1970s. By the late 1980s Kuwait had the third largest refining capacity in OPEC and was exporting almost 90 per cent of its oil as refined products.[49] Internationally, Kuwait bought and formed various companies across Europe to distribute their fuel (such as Q8). Kuwait thus controlled the production of its oil, its refining, its transport, its marketing and its downstream distribution to thousands of petrol stations in Europe.[50] For upstream diversification, in the early 1980s Kuwait set up the Kuwait Foreign Petroleum Exploration Company. Concessions in Morocco and Oman were secured in 1981 and soon investment was undertaken around the world. Additionally, Kuwait acquired the US company Santa Fe, a global drilling, engineering and construction company.[51]

The 1970s oil boom directly facilitated these investments. Whilst towards the end of the 1960s Kuwait was making roughly 270 million dinars per year from oil, by 1974 this had increased to over 2 billion dinars.[52] The underlying dynamics of the distribution-based ruling bargain were the same but the methods changed. Instead of land purchases, money was pumped into improving social services and the public sector, already a large employer, became even bigger and more unwieldy.

The extra liquidity and the prevailing sentiment enabled the government to nationalise industries (including oil in 1975, gas in 1971). Also, after the establishment of the Kuwaiti Stock Exchange in 1977, the government bought shares in numerous companies. The private sector shrank further with its share of GDP falling from 43 per cent to 30 per cent from 1970 to 1975.[53] Attempts were still made to encourage industrialisation in Kuwait but they largely failed, with manufacturing's contribution to GDP increasing from only 3.6 per cent in 1970 to 5 per cent by 1976.[54]

With Kuwait awash with cash in the 1970s a burgeoning industry of stocks, shares, securities, and other financial instruments boomed. The stock market of 1977 held stocks of Kuwaiti companies only, while quasi-illicit trade in foreign companies was banned from the institution. To fill this gap, in 1979 the technically illegal Suq Al Manakh was created. But fiscal conditions soon changed, with oil prices dropping 15 per cent from 1981 to 1983, prompting Kuwait to run a budget deficit in 1981 for the first time.[55] In 1982 Suq Al Manakh, built on postdated cheques, paper companies and a bullish attitude fostered in an era of easy money, crashed spectacularly, leaving more than 5,000 individual debts of some $92 billion, which was more than seventeen times the foreign reserves of Kuwait.[56] Curiously, the crash was advantageous for the established *asil* families who preferred the official stock exchange. The government sought their advice once more and the *asil* families vicariously benefited from government attempts to restart the economy. Yet despite their objections, the government ended up writing off most of the debts itself and invested heavily in order to prop up companies. Given the small size of Kuwait and the severity of the crash, debates and recriminations went on for years. Only following the Iraqi invasion in 1990 did they subside (though many were to pick up again afterwards).

Some estimates suggest that Kuwait lost as much as 30 per cent of its GDP in the wake of the invasion and occupation. But the policy of investing abroad meant that Kuwait could liquidate its assets to fund recovery. The primary goal post-liberation was the restoration of the oil industry, no easy task with 751 oil wells destroyed and the vast majority burning out of control.[57] But with foreign assets, foreign loans and a large deficit, progress was quickly made. Once economic life began to return to normal, the government adopted new policies for the 1990s. The stated goal was to reduce Kuwait's dependency on oil and its price fluctuations, to encourage the private sector, and to bolster the state's defence.

Even though the first two goals were mutually compatible, reforms in Kuwait proceeded at a glacial pace. The 1995–2000 five-year plan was partly inspired, partly mandated by Kuwait's World Trade Organisation accession on 1 January 1995. Private sector activity was to be encouraged by a WTO privatisation programme and the institution of taxes and a reduction in subsidies was to go towards paring down the deficit. Both plans were opposed in the parliament, particularly the latter which was bitterly resisted. Many if not all members of parliament understood that Kuwait's public sector was distended to an egregiously inefficient degree; 93 per cent of Kuwaitis worked in the public sector, 44 per cent of whom had no secondary schooling qualifications while only 20 per cent had a university degree.[58] Yet many members of parliament, accountable to their constituents, stubbornly refused to acquiesce in measures that would adversely affect Kuwaiti nationals. They defended their short-term stance by demanding that 'government waste' and corruption be tackled before ordinary Kuwaitis faced such adverse effects.

Nonetheless, privatisation was planned in two phases, the first of which is better described as divestment given that the Kuwait Investment Authority sold off the companies that the government had bought in the aftermath of the Suq Al Manakh debacle. These sales went ahead as the decade progressed with relatively little aggravation from the parliament. The second phase was the supposed selling off of telecoms and utilities. This was fought bitterly and some members of parliament criticised such plans as 'legalising theft'. Many feared that only an elite minority of Kuwaitis would benefit from such sales while the Kuwaitis who worked in these bloated companies would lose their jobs. Also, prices—frequently kept below cost by the government—would have to rise. But despite a general mistrust of privatisation, the Kuwaiti telecoms industry was successfully sold off. Annual growth in the sector has since averaged around 15 per cent and Zain and Wataniya, Kuwait's oldest operators, have become powerful and profitable global players. A new privatisation effort in mid-2010 called for the establishment of a Supreme Privatisation Council to oversee any projects and protect workers. Although it passed through parliament, seventeen members walked out in anger, one declaring that this was 'the sale of Kuwait'.[59]

Historically Kuwait has sought and received only limited amounts of foreign direct investment. From the mid-1990s the government sought to introduce various laws to make Kuwait more attractive to foreign investment. Up to a decade later, such laws eventually emerged from the parliament. For example, in 2007 a law was passed reducing corporate tax from 55 per cent to 15 per cent, and in 2001 a law permitting 100 per cent foreign ownership in certain sectors emerged. However, Kuwait's FDI remains pitifully low by comparison with other Gulf states. In 2008, for example, Kuwait received 32 times less FDI than Bahrain, 52 times less than Oman, 683 times less than Saudi Arabia and 235 times less than the UAE.[60]

Numerous multi-billion dollar projects to engage foreign firms have foundered in the parliament. These include the thirteen-year-long 'Project Kuwait' saga and the highly embarrassing Dow Chemicals joint-venture which the parliament spiked by threatening grillings of ministers.

Whilst some smaller projects have gone through, Kuwait's inability to complete these international prestige projects has been embarrassing and damaging for its reputation. The thaw in parliamentary relations in 2010 did allow for the passage of a four-year, $104 billion development plan (the first for decades), including a proposal to build a kilometre-high 'Silk' tower as part of a new city, but one must be sceptical as to whether it will ever be completed.

Foreign policy and security

Growing Saudi-Wahhabi power in central Arabia in the nineteenth century was beginning to threaten Kuwait, prompting a firming of Kuwait's nominal alliance with the Ottoman Empire. In addition to flying the Ottoman flag and paying tribute, Kuwait contributed men and logistical support to the 1871 Ottoman expedition against the Wahhabis.[61] Sheikh Abdullah Al-Sabah even accepted the Ottoman title of *kaymakam* (local governor) as a sign of his loyalty and Kuwait formally became a *kaza* (district) under the *vilayet* (province) of Basra in Iraq. Yet practically there was no interference in Kuwaiti affairs by the Ottomans.

Kuwait's most celebrated ruler, Sheikh Mubarak the Great, came to power after killing his brothers in 1896. Initially Mubarak assiduously attempted to court the Ottoman Empire's support and recognition as its legitimate governor of Kuwait, only to be consistently rebuffed.[62] In lieu of Ottoman support, he then sought good relations with the Wahhabis and requested British protection after an aborted Ottoman attack in 1897. An exclusive agreement was signed with Britain in 1899 which placed Kuwait's defence and foreign relations in British hands until independence in 1961.

Kuwait's good relations with Saudi Arabia effectively died along with Mubarak. Not only did Ibn Saud have a poor personal relationship with Mubarak's later successor, Sheikh Salim, but Kuwait's growing wealth made it an increasingly vulnerable target. After skirmishes earlier in the year, on 10 October 1920 Salim oversaw the legendary battle of Jahra. This not only marked a new low in Kuwaiti-Saudi relations, but also highlighted the role of ultimate guarantor that Britain was now playing, as it was British forces that saved Salim from likely defeat. This role came at a price, however, with roughly two thirds of Kuwait's territory being given to the Saudis as compensation for their losses from an earlier British-drafted border demarcation treaty.

Though relations with Saudi Arabia began to ease, they nonetheless remained fractious throughout the twentieth century. Exogenous factors sporadically pushed Kuwait closer to its neighbour, but rarely for very long. Fundamentally, Kuwait, as a small but rich country aware of Saudi Arabia's historically predatory actions, constantly sought out allies to counter any renewed threat from Riyadh. Such attempts often took the form of encouraging a 'federative alliance' with the other small Gulf sheikhdoms.[63] Kuwait sought to use its foreign aid and its status as an unthreatening and relatively advanced brotherly state to foster such ideas, particularly after Britain announced its coming departure from the Gulf in 1968. The formation of the United Arab Emirates federation in 1971 without Kuwait prompted the Al-Sabah to seek looser 'structured cooperation' with the UAE and its other small neighbours.[64] Saudi Arabia resisted such endeavours at every stage and no 'federative' notions were to come to fruition until 1981.

Iran's Islamic Revolution in 1979, as a serious external threat, nonetheless allowed Kuwait and Saudi Arabia to overcome some of their rivalries and helped to push the Arab Gulf states closer together. Despite Kuwait's initial attempts to retain cordial relations with Tehran, the gap proved insurmountable, particularly after the outbreak of the Iran-Iraq war in 1980, which effectively polarised the region. By October 1981 Iran had attacked Kuwaiti oil installations, and by December 1981 Kuwait had pledged over $2 billion of war aid to Iraq. This enraged Iran, and there followed numerous bomb attacks in Kuwait including the attempted assassination of the ruler by groups linked to Tehran.

In this context, intra-Arab cooperation was able to coalesce and the Gulf Cooperation Council (GCC) was formed in 1981 by Kuwait and the five other Arab Gulf monarchies. The GCC included notions of economic inter-cooperation along with the founding of an intra-GCC military force, but neither objective was realised to a meaningful, practical degree.

During the remainder of the war, Kuwait continued to use its wealth as a foreign policy tool, a long evident Kuwaiti foreign policy trait. In 1961 Kuwait established the Kuwait Fund for Arab Economic Development (KFAED), and it was soon used strategically as a political tool. Indeed, it has been noted that 'virtually every time a danger presented itself, Kuwait responded with foreign aid'.[65] For example, in 1961 when Kuwait sought Egyptian support against the burgeoning Iraqi threat, millions of dollars of aid were directed to Cairo, and since 1963 Kuwait has given Iraq hundreds of millions of dollars in aid to stave off threats from Baghdad.[66]

During the Iran-Iraq War, with Kuwait's tankers becoming increasingly targeted by Iran, Kuwait was prompted to seek assistance from superpowers with which it has had a complex relationship. Immediately after independence Kuwait needed British military support against Iraq. Since then, cognisant of its relative weakness, Kuwait has maintained relations with a number of great powers despite domestic opposition.

After independence, in addition to its British alliance, Kuwait sought relationships with both the US and the Soviet Union. Technical and economic agreements with the Soviet Union in 1964, followed by diplomatic recognition from the People's Republic of China and North Korea, aroused fears in the US that Kuwait was about to fall under the Communist umbrella. But in reality the Al-Sabah still needed regional Arab support for their legitimacy, and this required a foreign policy heeding the non-aligned, Arabist rhetoric during the Cold War. In 1965 formal (but discreet) overtures were made to the US for military protection. Though this was declined—as Washington judged Britain's guarantees to be sufficient—defence studies and trade between the US and Kuwait nevertheless began and the relationship was established.

Kuwait was thus able to contact both superpowers for shipping protection. Initially, Kuwait preferred to seek Soviet assistance, partly to avoid antagonising Iraq with its Soviet leanings, and partly to mollify the pro-Palestinian (and thus pro-Soviet) domestic opposition. After the Soviet Union reflagged three Kuwaiti tankers, the US—conscious that the Soviet Union might gain a stronger foothold—offered a more comprehensive solution by reflagging Kuwaiti tankers and escorting them with US warships.

When the Iran-Iraq war ended in 1988, Kuwait believed it had good relations with Iraq. For decades Kuwaitis had feared their larger, more powerful neighbour, and often with good reason. Since General Qassim's 1961 denial of Kuwait's independence, there had been a plethora of incidents between the two countries. Iraq occasionally recognised Kuwait but often reneged. Iraq also repeatedly demanded control of the Bubiyan and Warbah islands, and disagreed over its border with Kuwait, and it amassed troops on the border in 1973. Yet, after Iraq had received enormous financial and logistical support from Kuwait, not to mention being bloodied by their common Iranian enemy, Iraq's next move completely surprised Kuwait.

On 1 August 1990 over 100,000 Iraqi troops were amassed on the Kuwaiti border. At that point, Kuwait had all but forgiven Iraq its enormous debts and was offering more loans of up to $9 billion. However, the same day that the Al-Sabah were being reassured by Saudi Arabia that Iraq would not invade, the Iraqi negotiators left Jeddah and Kuwait fell within thirty-six hours.

An international coalition headed by the US was soon formed and deployed to the region, and on 7 August 1990 Operation Desert Shield was put in place to protect Saudi Arabia's oil rich eastern provinces from any further Iraqi aggression. The subsequent Operation Desert Storm in early 1991 easily routed the Iraqi army and liberated Kuwait.

After the liberation, the Al-Sabah ruling family did not immediately return to Kuwait. When they did, rumours spread that they were ordering chandeliers and electricity generators for palaces whilst most Kuwaitis were still living in darkness.[67] Given that law and order were barely functioning, with weapons being scattered around the city, strict security was prioritised above all else. Within hours of the Iraqi withdrawal martial law was declared, newspapers were temporarily banned, and even before electricity was working again Kuwait had placed an order with a US company for a new computer system for its internal security.[68] 'Collaborators' were hunted down by both vigilantes and the authorities. Kangaroo courts were established with little due process. Two thirds of Kuwait's expatriate population that had left Kuwait were not allowed back, and thousands of other foreigners were deported. In this way Kuwait was trying to redress its demographic imbalance which it saw as a security threat.

On the macro security level, the invasion unsurprisingly had many profound effects. Kuwait's relations with the US were wholly changed. Kuwait had long understood the potential necessity of close US relations but had, when faced with a choice, eschewed visible American support. The US did not have a particularly good reputation in the region, largely because of its uncompromising support of Israel. After the Iraqi invasion, however, it was deemed necessary that there should be a large and visible US presence to secure Kuwait's existential security. To secure this relationship, Kuwait fell back on a typical foreign policy trait: it used money and the award of lucrative construction contracts. $13.5 billion was paid to the US for the costs of the war, and soon after liberation some $90 billion worth of contracts were signed with the US Engineering Corps to rebuild Kuwait's infrastructure. The US also became the partner of choice when it came to rearming Kuwait.

Elsewhere, however, Kuwait's stature as a generous foreign aid donor was seen as ineffectual if not counterproductive: clearly loyalty could not always be bought. This was most notable with the Palestinians. Previously staunch and generous supporters of the cause, most Kuwaitis were bitterly angry to see the Palestinian leadership openly supportive of Iraq's invasion of their country. Kuwait responded by severing relations with the Palestinian Liberation Organisation, and Kuwait-based Palestinians were deported by the thousand.

Kuwait's foreign and security policy for the remainder of the 1990s was largely seen through the Iraqi prism. Maintaining a strong relationship with the US was the first priority, followed by encouraging the continued regional and international isolation of Iraq. It took nine years, for example, for Kuwait to resume relations with Jordan following its role in supporting Iraq. It was only with the impending US invasion of Iraq in 2003 that Kuwait and Iraq signed their first agreement: a guarantee of Kuwait's sovereignty from Baghdad which came decades too late.

Unsurprisingly, Kuwait was the only Arab state that readily and explicitly supported the 2003 invasion. Despite the difficulties that this caused domestically (including numerous attacks on Westerners) there was never any doubt that Kuwait would do anything but support the removal of Saddam Hussein. Hopes of a fresh start to the Iraq-Kuwait relationship have yet to materialise. In 2004 the question of the legality of Kuwait's borders was raised by an Iraqi official, and in 2011 Iraqi politicians have been seeking talks with Kuwait to discuss re-examining their borders and resolution 833. Despite Kuwait returning an Ambassador to Iraq in 2008, Kuwaitis and their parliament have been unwilling to drop the issue of Iraq's continued reparations to Kuwait, the question of the missing prisoners of war, and the return of Kuwait's missing archives and artefacts from 1990.

Future challenges

Whilst estimates vary, on average current oil reserve projections suggest that Kuwait will have ample oil resources for over a century. Despite some rhetoric to the contrary, this has been lulling Kuwaitis into a false sense of security. Feeling secure in its resources, Kuwait has not engaged meaningfully in any post-oil diversification. Egregious policies pushed by members of parliament, such as a 22 per cent annual public service pay increase, continue to entrench the rentier mentality in Kuwait.[69] Whilst in all rentier economies the link between the fruits of the resources and work needed to harness such fruits is broken, in Kuwait the link at times seems beyond repair. If members of parliament want to be elected, it takes a strong willed and highly principled politician not to resort to the low but effective politics of a service platform, promising greater subsidies, industry protection and resolutely no taxes. Such policies meet an electorate safe in the knowledge that Kuwait has 'loads of oil' and thus understandably feeling it has the right to receive some part of this wealth. Indeed, it can seem as though no appreciation has been made by anyone below the governmental level that such excess will have to stop sometime. The hard decisions that will need to be made—including introducing taxes, privatising industries, introducing electricity and water rates, and limiting wage increases—are simply not entertained.

The most damaging aspect of this phenomenon is that Kuwait is being woefully left behind. Other Gulf states have been competing fiercely—some for decades now—to establish world class financial centres, profitable non-oil industries, and industrial complexes. Some have built advanced shipyards, international airlines, and prominent cultural brands vying for international tourism and trade. Much of this has been done by attracting significant foreign investment and involvement. During this time Kuwait has, by comparison, done practically nothing apart from investing money abroad. There is a concern that by the time Kuwait realises it needs to diversify away from oil, the most obvious and viable routes will have already been explored and established by their GCC neighbours and the barriers to entry will be extremely high.

Nevertheless, even if such a future materialises, Kuwaitis will not be on the breadline. The state's foreign investments, if handled correctly, should be more than sufficient to provide for Kuwait's relatively small population. Yet it can only provide to a certain level and the rentier induced indulgences will have to go. Thus far there is a yawning chasm between the exigencies of Kuwait's post-oil realities and their current appreciation of their predicament. This is the central domestic challenge for future Kuwaiti leaders.

Inextricably aligned with this problem is the question of parliamentary reform. There appear to be two outstanding problems with Kuwait's

Parliamentary system. First, the lack of political parties means that '300 candidates have 300 policy priorities'.[70] Often lacking a simple, well-known party ideology behind them, candidates must appeal to their electorate individually. This often leads to prospective members of parliament offering a 'service' platform. Secondly, there is no positive onus or responsibility on individual members of parliament to face up to a difficult decision or accept any responsibility when things go wrong. This is primarily because parliamentarians do not have a say in the formation of the government.

Remedying these issues will be difficult. Legalising political parties and introducing a non-royal as the prime minister who must cooperate to form a government may sound like a possible solution, yet there are two immediate issues. First, fears that institutionalising political parties may lead to stronger Islamist platforms are rife. Second, the relative unity in the Al-Sabah ranks is significantly predicated on the ruler's ability to give plum cabinet appointments to key allies or placate would-be enemies. Moreover, the 'sovereign' posts are seen as 'core prerogatives' of the Al-Sabah and something they would be loath to give up without a struggle.[71] The ruler is however unlikely to be able to revert to a more typically Gulf-style parliament (where the parliament has essentially no power) as the notion of Kuwait as the region's most advanced democracy is now thoroughly embedded in Kuwaiti culture.

A central feature of Kuwait's future security discourse will continue to be Iraq, as the 1990 invasion will remain an indelible part of the Kuwaiti mindset for generations. The unforgiving nature of Kuwait's ire towards Iraq is building worrying levels of resentment in Iraq, and it is not hard to see why. It is now twenty years on and Iraq still owes Kuwait $25 billion which it continues to pay via a UN-mandated 5 per cent oil profits 'tax'. This continues despite the intervening time, the change of government in Iraq, the pervasive destruction and civil unrest wrought by the 2003 invasion, and the fact that Kuwait is, once again, one of the wealthiest countries on earth. 'Kuwait suffered for a few years from Saddam', goes a common Iraqi retort, 'but we suffered for decades'.

As Iraq slowly begins to resemble a functioning state, the Iraqi tone towards Kuwait is hardening. Nationalistic rhetoric and the occasional newspaper editorial can be found praising the 1990 invasion and stoking up anti-Kuwaiti sentiment. While such editorials are, for the moment, from the fringes of the Iraqi press, the danger is that Kuwait will become a rallying point for Iraqi nationalism; that Kuwait becomes 'the other' against which all Iraqis, both Shia and Sunni, can agree and focus their anger. It is in Kuwait's immediate interests to take the venom out of its relationship with Iraq as soon as possible, and the issues of missing prisoners of war, missing artefacts, and outstanding debts must be addressed and perhaps dropped for Kuwait's greater good. Yet Kuwait's populist parliament makes such accommodations exceedingly difficult.

Conversely, it must be noted that Kuwait's vibrant parliament has insulated the country from the worst effects of the Arab Spring, allowing all Kuwaitis ample voice for their views. Certainly, Kuwait's youth groups have increased in volume, but their existence predates the 2011 regional unrest by some time. Instead the key concern is that the polarising rhetoric (and actions) of other GCC states thus far could pollute Kuwait's domestic politics for some time to come. The decision on whether to send troops and police to Bahrain was a clear example of a decision pitting Sunni against Shia within the parliament. The arrest and conviction in March 2011 of an Iranian spying ring in Kuwait further added to tensions. Yet even in an increasingly febrile, sectarian and revolutionary era, Kuwait's intrinsic systems of rule appear fairly sound, and if unrest increases in Kuwait the focus is unlikely to be the political system itself but rather something specific, for example the embattled Prime Minister.

QATAR

Steven Wright

State formation

The history of the Qatari peninsula is rich, varied, and deep-rooted. In terms of the contemporary events leading up to the emergence of statehood, it is best to begin with a brief sketch of the history of Zubara, a town located on the west coast of the Qatari peninsula which in many ways symbolises how power shifted from the western side of the peninsula to the eastern side, helping the rise of the Al-Thani dynasty as the rulers of Qatar. In 1715 the Bani Utub tribe left the heartland of central Arabia and began its famous journey, which would over time shape the political structure of both Kuwait and Bahrain, while also forming a crucial chapter in modern Qatari history. The Bani Utub first settled near Zubara and remained there for around two years before continuing on their long journey to Kuwait. By 1766, disagreements within the tribe over the distribution of power and wealth saw its Al-Khalifa sub-section flee Kuwait and return to Zubara.

For generations Zubara has been under the control of the Al-Musallam tribe, and initially the Al-Khalifa were able to settle there without much difficulty.[1] But after only two years, a dispute over the payment of taxes to the Al-Musallam emerged. As a result, in 1768 the Al-Khalifa built a fort on the outskirts of Zubara in Al-Murair, and within a decade the Al-Khalifa were able to dominate Zubara from this strategic position and the wealth they were able to generate from their own taxes. With the Al-Khalifa having gained dominance over Zubara, they turned it into a free port which had significant ramifications in terms of customs receipts for other nearby ports such as Oqair and Al-Hasa, in addition to established regional ports such as Muscat and Basra.[2]

Zubara soon became a major and vibrant commercial town, yet its success also brought it into conflict with the families of rival ports. From 1777, forces under the Persian governor of Bahrain made repeated attacks on Zubara, but in 1783 a combined force of the Al-Khalifa and various local Qatari tribes were able to defeat the Persian garrison stationed on Bahrain in a counterattack.[3] Following this victory, however, the coalition abruptly broke apart as the Al-Khalifa were unwilling to share the spoils of war. In this way, the Al-Khalifa gained control over Bahrain, but lost any direct influence on the Qatari peninsula.

In 1800 Bahrain was overrun by the Imamate of Muscat's forces on the pretext of Bahraini ships having failed to pay tax for transiting through the Strait of Hormuz.[4] Given the relations of rivalry between Muscat and the Al-Saud of the Arabian interior, a second invasion was launched by Qatari tribes loyal to the Al-Saud, who began to occupy Zubara from 1793 in an effort to project their influence over Bahrain. This proved successful and thus Bahrain, along with Zubara, fell under the control of the Al-Saud. This situation lasted until 1811 when an invasion of the Saudi heartland of Najd by Ottoman-Egyptian forces commanded by Ibrahim Pasha forced the Al-Saud to withdraw their forces from Zubara. In another turn of events, the Al-Khalifa took advantage of this weakening of the Saudi position by crafting an unlikely agreement with the Imamate of Muscat for them to be a tributary if they were restored to power in Bahrain. With fresh troops from Muscat to back them, the Al-Khalifa's rule over Bahrain was thus restored by 1811.[5] The forces from Muscat then expanded their attack and targeted bases in Zubara, ostensibly to counter any possible threats against their newly reacquired dominion of Bahrain. As a consequence, the once prosperous town of Zubara was levelled and burned.

The effective destruction of Zubara in the pursuit of security for Bahrain by the Imamate of Muscat marked an unintended turning point in the historical development of the modern Qatari state. The distribution of power across the peninsula had fundamentally changed and commercial activities shifted to other localities, and in particular to the eastern side of the peninsula at Al-Bida. Al-Bida shared a bay with the small town of Doha al-Shaghir (little Doha).[6] However, it was not until 1849–

50 that Sheikh Muhammed bin Thani of the Bani Tamim moved to Doha from Fuwairet and was able to take advantage of the power vacuum that had arisen. Sheikh Muhammed was the leader of the Al-Maadhid tribe and chief of Fuwairet. He moved to Doha to develop further his pearling interests and was soon able to establish himself as the Chief of Doha in addition to Fuwairet.[7] Sheikh Muhammed thus emerged as the leading figure on the Qatari peninsula, and this was reinforced through an agreement he was able to sign with Emir Faisal bin Turki Al-Saud who had entered Qatar in 1851. Emir Faisal's entry into Qatar was rooted in an ambitious plan to invade Bahrain using Muhammed as an ally. Given the Qatari desire for security from the Al-Khalifa, such a relationship was of clear mutual benefit. Importantly, it was during this period of Saudi external protection that Muhammed was able to consolidate his power, and according to William Palgrave who visited Qatar in 1863, Muhammed had by this stage become ruler of the entire Qatari peninsula.[8]

Relations between Qatar and Bahrain became stable, but in 1867 a dispute occurred with Sheikh Ahmed bin Muhammed Al-Khalifa who was residing in Wakra as a representative of the ruler of Bahrain. Sheikh Jassim bin Muhammed Al-Thani, who was the eldest son of the Qatari ruler, travelled to Bahrain to resolve the issue but upon arrival was imprisoned by the ruler of Bahrain.[9] A counter-attack against Wakra, Al-Bida and Doha was then launched by Bahrain in alliance with Abu Dhabi in October 1867, and Lorimer describes the resulting damage as severe.[10] Qatari forces responded in June 1868 by invading Bahrain and were able to secure the release of Jassim. Despite the violence, the events of 1867 and 1868 were nonetheless turning points in the development of the Qatari state as the outbreak of hostilities led Britain to become involved in the crisis. Britain formulated a peace treaty which was signed by Muhammed in September 1868.[11] Of great significance, the treaty signalled Britain's formal recognition of Muhammed as the legitimate ruler of Qatar. Qatar had thus received important external support as an independent territorial state, and it also placed restrictions on the Al-Khalifa from further interfering in Qatari domestic affairs. Muhammed was thus in a strong position to consolidate his powerbase and promote development and trade across the peninsula. He remained ruler until his death in 1876, at which point his eldest son, Jassim, succeeded him.

Since the death of Emir Faisal bin Turki Al-Saud in 1865 and the opening of the Suez Canal in 1866, the Ottomans had become increasingly interested in the Gulf region. The Governor of Baghdad, Midhat Pasha, sent a contingent of troops to Qatar and they crafted an agreement with Jassim shortly after his accession. This led to the establishment of a small Ottoman military presence on the Qatari peninsula in exchange for Jassim receiving the title of *Qaim Muqam*—a provincial governor.[12] The Ottoman presence served the interests of Qatar well, as it offered protection from the myriad threats the peninsula was facing at the time. The trend of Qatar pragmatically using a foreign power as a guarantor of its security had thus become firmly established. It was however some years later, in the context of the First World War, that the Ottoman presence came to an end in 1915, with the small Turkish contingent abruptly abandoning its fortification in Doha as it feared an attack from Britain.

Following the Ottoman withdrawal Sheikh Abdullah bin Jassim Al-Thani, who had become ruler in 1913 following Jassim's retirement, made the decision to sign a fresh protection treaty with Britain only one year after the Ottoman withdrawal. Discussions had begun prior to the Ottoman departure and in many ways he had skilfully played Britain off against the Ottomans. With the Ottomans having departed, a closer security relationship with Britain thus made strategic sense. The resulting 1916 treaty of protection allowed Qatar to establish a more formal external security arrangement which allowed for a degree of security and autonomy in its domestic affairs. Indeed, for Qatar the price to pay for this was mainly confined to Qatar's foreign affairs which were ceded to Britain, but it retained autonomy in its domestic decision-making. The resulting British-protected status is vital to understanding how Qatar was then able to mature politically and economically on its own terms until Britain's withdrawal from the Gulf in 1971, as it cemented further the position of the Al-Thani dynasty as the rulers of Qatar.

Britain afforded Qatar both stability and security, and the announcement in 1968 of an impending British withdrawal was unwelcome to all of the Gulf rulers. Britain attempted to promote a union of the nine Gulf sheikhdoms it had treaties with, but after the withdrawal this proved unsuccessful owing to the incompatibility of the nine Gulf rulers' interests.[13] Qatar withdrew from the talks along with Bahrain and became a fully independent state on 3 September 1971. The quest to maintain the level of security and autonomy in its domestic affairs that it had enjoyed under its arrangements with the Ottomans and the British thus became a key post-independence goal for Qatar.

Political structures and personalities

To fully understand Qatar's political structures, one must first recall the history behind the formation of such institutions. In 1960 Sheikh Ahmed bin Ali Al-Thani came to power after the abdication of his father, Sheikh Ali bin Abdullah Al-Thani, and Ahmed thus became instrumental in the financial and political development of Qatar prior to the announcement of statehood in 1971. The policies he implemented were to lay the initial foundations for Qatar's constitutional, legal and institutional development, and so are necessary to an understanding of the contemporary system. Under Ahmed, Qatar enacted its first nationality and labour laws in 1960 and 1962, as well as establishing a trade registry and a chamber of commerce and regulations concerning trade with foreigners. The foundations were also laid for the future institutional development of the country. Whilst no ministries were established during this period, a number of key departments were set up with the help of British and Egyptian advisers, and these were to be the basis of future ministries. They included an agricultural department, a customs authority, an immigration service, a department for labour and social affairs, and a lands and registration department.

Yet perhaps even more important for understanding the move away from a traditional and personalised system of governance towards a more formal and codified system was the introduction of a constitution. This was known as the Basic Law and was enacted in 1970. It was subsequently revised in 1972 owing to another change in leadership, from Sheikh Ahmed to Sheikh Khalifa bin Hamad Al-Thani. The context in which the new provisional constitution of Qatar was drawn up is of particular significance as there were clear political and security maxims in the region. Prime among these was the impending British withdrawal from the region, announced in 1968. This was compounded by regional dynamics such as the renewal of Iranian claims to Bahrain, the Dhofar rebellion in Oman, and the 1958 revolution in Iraq which saw the overthrow of the British-backed Hashemite dynasty. Also significant was Kuwait's independence in 1961 which led to border disputes with Iraq, the Yemeni civil war which involved both Saudi Arabia and Egypt, and the rise of Arab nationalism across the region, which was leading to Arab-British clashes. As mentioned, the immediate response of the smaller Gulf sheikhdoms to British withdrawal was to push for political unity as a means of ensuring stability and countering the wide range of external forces that existed. This was something actively promoted by Britain, and negotiations were started for the formation of a federation of Arab emirates, which would include all nine of the small Gulf monarchies. However, Qatar objected to Bahrain's demand to be the capital of the new federation, given the Al-Khalifa family's longstanding security problems with Iran, while Bahrain's claims were supported by Abu Dhabi, with which it had a long history of ties.[14] Qatar received support from Dubai as the more suitable leader and base for the federation, not only because the two emirates had strong familial ties, but also because Dubai was objecting to Bahrain's position on Iran as it had a large resident Iranian population of its own, which it needed to appease. As with Bahrain, Abu Dhabi also had clear security problems, given that Saudi Arabia had renewed its claims to the Buraimi oasis. The formation of a nine-member union was thus an idealistic goal at best, given the early disagreements between the nine rulers.

Whilst four meetings took place and an agreement was reached on the formation of the United Arab Emirates, disagreement existed on who would be the vice-president, on the structure of and control over defence, and on whether the UAE should have a consultative or legislative assembly. This was further compounded by perceived British meddling in the details of the negotiations. For Qatar, joining a unified political system was not seen as being in the best interests of the country at the time, and so a provisional constitution was drawn up in 1970. This was enacted some days before Bahrain received recognition of its independence from the United Nations.

Given the troubled context of the UAE's formation, Qatar's 1970 provisional constitution reflected this reality. Although the provisional constitution did refer to Qatar becoming a constituent emirate of the UAE, it nevertheless clearly specified that Qatar was going through a transitional period. Therefore, it was more of a flexible initiative designed to leave open the possibility of joining the UAE should circumstances demonstrate that it was in Qatar's best interests to do so. The Basic Provisional Law of 1970 was also highly reflective of the new social and economic order that Qatar found itself in. Qatar had historically been ruled by an unwritten code of governance, but given a population boom and a rise in wealth following the granting of oil concessions, the system was proving to be inadequate. It was also, however, a means of keeping

Qatar's options open in the period of uncertainty during the negotiations with the other eight prospective members of the UAE, as it provided the basis for an option of having an independent state.

The provisional constitution declared Qatar to be a sovereign nation as it prohibited under Article 2 the relinquishing of control of any part of its territory or waters. This was mainly a revision to the 1916 treaty Sheikh Abdullah bin Jassim Al-Thani had signed with Britain, which required Qatar to seek the approval of the British government before any territory was ceded. Other key articles in the constitution stipulated a law on citizenship (Article 4), the rule of law, and the creation of a national flag and a national anthem (Article 3). The hereditary rule of the Al-Thani was also confirmed in the constitution and was given attention in an explanatory memorandum which stated that:

it naturally follows that he [the ruler] should be vested with authorities and powers, and should be bound by the duties arising out of the acceptance of such election by consensus, as prescribed under Islamic Sharia law, which imposes a duty on those who take part in the consensus formalities, and, through them, on the whole nation, to pledge their loyalty and absolute obedience to the Ruler in the fear of God.

Succession was governed by Article 22 which called for a consensus among key members of the ruling family. Given that the provision was not supplanted by any procedural specifics on how succession was to take place, this underlined how in this early stage of political development formal codified forms of political participation were supposed to work alongside the existing informal mechanisms.

The constitution also laid the foundations for a Council of Ministers, which would be formed by the creation of ten government ministries: Education and Culture, Finance and Petroleum, Justice, Interior, Public Works, Public Health, Industry and Agriculture, Electricity and Water, Communications and Transport, and Labour and Social Affairs. These were followed by the creation of a Ministry for Economics and Commerce in May 1970 and a Ministry for Foreign Affairs in 1971. In addition to the Council of Ministers, the constitution specified in Article 43 the formation of an Advisory Council or *Majlis al-Shura*. The Advisory Council was the first of its kind in Qatar and was to be composed of twenty regular members in addition to the Council of Ministers who were automatically members. The members of the Advisory Council were all appointed by the ruler, by then renamed the Emir. The selection criterion was based on the Emir receiving recommendations from key members of the ruling family in consultation with other tribal leaders. Selection was also representative of Qatar's ten electoral districts as a shortlist of four people for each district was made, but only two from each district were selected by the Emir to be in the Advisory Council. The size of the Advisory Council was increased by emiri decree in 1975 to thirty members. Whilst elections were required, the council members had their term of office extended by emiri decree on a periodic basis. Although a consultative mechanism was implemented, the ruler was permitted under Article 74 to carry out any 'amendment, deletion, or addition if he deemed such revision necessary in the public interest'. Moreover, all laws under the Amended Basic Provisional Law 1972 required the ratification of the Emir under Article 23, paragraph 3.

In April 2003 a permanent constitution was finally adopted following a referendum. This was to be the turning point in the political history of the country as it ushered in a number of reforms to the previous system that existed under the Amended Basic Provisional Law of 1972. After Sheikh Hamad bin Khalifa Al-Thani took power in 1995, there was a level of uncertainty over what the new leadership would bring to the country. However, a range of progressive reforms were quickly implemented. The most important was the establishment of a national committee in 1999 to draft a permanent constitution. The underlying reason for the move towards a permanent constitution was a need to bring clarity, transparency and stability to Qatar's political system. In many ways the reforms in Qatar were purely elite driven and a product of a fresh generational change in leadership.[15] Hence it is a mistake to assume that Qatar's reforms were a product of external forces or even internal pressure.

On close inspection, the current constitution can only be fully appreciated by consulting three separate documents: first, the actual document of 150 constitutional articles of April 2005 following its endorsement in a popular referendum in 2003; secondly, a law on political rule and succession which was passed after the introduction of the constitution; and thirdly, the law defining citizenship. These latter two laws are referred to in Articles 8 and 41 of the 2005 constitution respectively, and are thus listed as having 'constitutional validity'. In essence they are deemed to be special laws which are part of the constitution and thus carry an equal weight.

The law on political rule comprises 18 articles and thus greatly expands on the original text in the constitution of 2005. Under Article 148, no amendment is allowed within a period of ten years following the coming into force of the constitution. Under Article 146, the provisions of the law on political rule and succession are deemed ineligible for amendment, even under the procedure for constitutional amendments as laid out in Article 144. Yet the constitution can also be seen as highly progressive as it provides for a codified and transparent procedure for succession of monarchical rule to take place. Given that Qatar did not have a clear written rule of succession under the Basic Provisional Law of 1970 and the Amended Basic Provisional Law 1972, it can be understood as a reform which caters for a more legalistic and formal system of governance and more stability.

The second law which deals with nationality is also of key importance. It is directly referred to in, and specific articles of it are cited by, the law of succession, so it is questionable whether changes to the nationality law become invalid given that the constitution prohibits changes to the law of succession. The question of citizenship is dealt with in Article 41 and provisions on this are determined by the nationality law and have constitutional validity. A citizen is defined in the law as an individual whose father was resident in Qatar prior to 1930. This is similar to how citizenship is defined in Kuwait, as residence prior to 1920 is listed as a requirement for full Kuwaiti citizenship. The provision grants Qatari citizens specific privileges such as participating in the legislative affairs of the state. A second path to citizenship is through naturalisation, for which those individuals resident in Qatar after 1930 are eligible. The final form of citizenship is honorary, and is typically given to sports personalities or people who have done an exceptional service to the Qatari state. The key distinction between these three forms of citizenship is that only Qatari citizens whose ancestors were in Qatar prior to 1930 are eligible to stand for election to the Advisory Council.

A further key feature of the law on political rule and succession is that it required the establishment of a Ruling Family Council. Such a council already existed in Kuwait. For Qatar it comprises a minimum of five persons, with a maximum of nine. The Emir is the head of the Council and his heir apparent is also a member. Other members are drawn from senior sections of the Al-Thani family and are appointed by the Emir. The role of the Ruling Family Council in Qatar's mode of rule and succession is important as it is a constitutionally mandated procedure that becomes active in times of succession and provides for stability. Under Article 1 of the law on succession, the order of succession is listed as: sons of the Emir, then grandsons, brothers, and sons of brothers. This has added clarity to Qatar's political system and underlined the importance of the rule of law.

Before the 2005 constitution came into force, the structure of Qatar's legislature was governed by the Amended Basic Provisional Law of 1972. The structure of government comprised the aforementioned Council of Ministers and Advisory Council. Under the provisions of the revised 2005 constitution, Qatar's Advisory Council is now set to comprise 45 members, 30 of whom will be directly elected by the people while the remaining 15 will be appointed by the Emir from a pool of ministers and other key officials. Therefore, the key reform in contrast to the system under the 1972 Amended Basic Provisional Law is the wider enfranchisement of civil society, but the lack of distinction between the legislative and executive spheres has continued.

When examining the procedural mechanisms outlined in Qatar's constitution, it is instructive that under Articles 61 and 76 the Advisory Council is understood to have legislative competency. Article 61 states that '...the legislative authority shall be handled by the Advisory Council as stipulated in this Constitution', while Article 76 states: '...the Advisory Council shall handle the legislative authority, approve the general State budget and monitor the executive authority in a manner stipulated by this constitution'. In essence these two articles echo the same point, that the Advisory Council has a legislative capacity. An initial observation is that the source of legislation can come from both the legislative and the executive branches. Article 105 provides for members of the Advisory Council proposing laws for consideration by the relevant committee within the Council. Subject to it being accepted, a proposal can be drafted into a law and then discussed by the Council. An interesting requirement, however, is that the draft law then needs to be referred to the Council of Ministers for its consideration and approval. If approved, it will then be returned to the Advisory Council for its considered approval before being submitted to the Emir for consideration and signing into law. The procedure outlined highlights a clear input of the executive branch in legislation formation. Similarly, legislation can stem from Article 121 which gives the Cabinet the competency for 'proposing drafts of laws and decrees'.

With elections to the Advisory Council set to take place some time in 2011, it is important to consider the elections that have already taken place at the municipal level. Although not a constitutionally mandated organ of government, the Municipal Council is significant as it is the first formal and codified avenue for political participation through voting that the population has had. Qatar's municipality was originally founded in the early 1950s, but did not take on an institutional form until 1972 when there was a move towards the establishment of ministries following full independence. Those holding positions in municipalities were traditionally appointed until Sheikh Hamad bin Khalifa Al-Thani issued a decree in 1998 that set in motion the formation of a Municipal Council to be constituted through direct elections. In tandem with this initiative a preparatory committee was established under the direction of the Emir's wife, Sheikha Moza bint Nasser Al-Misnad, to begin a campaign for women's awareness, encouraging women to vote and participate as candidates. For Qatar this was a clear and progressive break from the past as it was not only challenging the very conception of the role of women, but also introducing clear paths for women to participate actively in political life.

In 1999, some 248 candidates contested the 29 seats available for a four-year term of office. The campaign to promote women did enjoy some success as six women stood for election. Voting took place in March 1999 and the eligible electorate was 21,995.[16] The electorate comprised all those over 18, including both Qatari citizens and those naturalised citizens who had been resident for more than 15 years. Moreover, the election was monitored by 35 Arab parliamentarians from across the region. Voting was done through an open rather than secret ballot, and voter turnout was 55 per cent. This compares with a disappointing 40 per cent turnout for the April 2003 elections, which was compounded by a reduced field of candidates, amounting to 88. The most recent elections held in April 2007 saw a larger turnout of 51.1 per cent, and were hotly contested as billboard adverts for the candidates were a common sight on roadsides in the time leading up to the elections. Although turnout was higher than in the 2003 election, only slightly more candidates (116) put themselves forward for election. Either way, voter turnout and the number of candidates were still less than in the first election held in 1999. But an interesting observation is that upwards of 70 per cent of voters for these elections were women.[17]

Economic development and diversification

Efforts geared towards economic diversification in Qatar remain a priority in national economic policy. As with the other Gulf states, Qatar has historically derived the majority of its GDP from the energy sector. Indeed, Qatar's natural gas sector has been the focus of the greatest attention. The vast North gas field was discovered in 1971 and is the largest non-associated gas field in the world. Its estimated reserves stand at over 900 trillion cubic feet, which amounts to over 160 billion barrels of oil, and the field spans an area of around 6,000 square kilometres. This translates to Qatar having just slightly less than 14 per cent of the world's total natural gas deposits. Within the region, Iran has higher reserves of natural gas, but they are spread over a much greater area and are thus more costly to exploit.

Qatar has become the largest global supplier of Liquefied Natural Gas (LNG) products in addition to Gas to Liquid Fuels (GTL). By 2014, the largest consumer block on Qatari gas exports will be the European Union member countries which will account for around 40 per cent of Qatar's 77 million tons per annum (mtpa) of gas exports from the state-owned companies RasGas and QatarGas. This is followed by around 23 per cent going to the US. The trend of increased exports to EU countries and the US breaks from the past where the majority of Qatar's gas exports were being sold to Asian buyers such as Japan, Korea and India. The benefit of engaging with Qatar for the EU countries is that it allows them to diversify their energy imports away from Russian dependency. Yet it is important to recognise that Qatar has increasingly incorporated diversion clauses into its supply agreements. This is important as it gives Qatar the ability to redirect gas shipments in order to take advantage of opportunity costs. Moreover, as investment is being directed towards tanker supply, Qatar's ability to direct shipping to the most attractive market is only limited by the need for a suitable port facility to unload the gas cargo.

In addition to tanker based supply, Qatar's economy has benefited from revenue generated from pipeline supply and consumption. The Dolphin project was the first gas export based project within the Gulf Cooperation Council and is likely to be the precursor to any GCC gas grid, with supply coming from Qatar. The UAE imports upwards of 2 billion cubic feet per day from Qatar (15mtpa), supplied to Abu Dhabi and Dubai, through the Dolphin Energy Company.[18] By 2014, this will make the

UAE the largest importer of Qatar gas after the US. Yet it should not be forgotten that the price agreed between Qatar and the UAE was well below its potential opportunity cost, and future contract renewals may reflect this.[19]

In terms of how the growth of the oil and gas sector has impacted on the economy, it is clear that an economic boom has been taking place. Qatar's real GDP growth is indicative; from 2005 to 2009, growth averaged 17.4 per cent per annum. Even in the midst of the global economic downturn, real GDP growth in 2009 still achieved 8.7 per cent and was projected to be 14.5 per cent in 2010. But on closer inspection, Qatar's non-hydrocarbon sector only managed to achieve a growth rate of 2.8 per cent in 2008, and shows that the country was not completely immune from the global downturn. However, strong real GDP growth was still achieved as this was buttressed by the confidence generated by the oil and gas sectors in addition to targeted inward investment by the government. In 2009 the non-hydrocarbon sector amounted to 53.8 per cent of overall GDP. The gas sector alone accounted for 24.5 per cent, and oil amounted to 21.7 per cent of GDP.[20] This is highly significant as it indicates that Qatar did have a degree of success in diversifying its economy away from the oil and gas sectors, despite expanding gas production and export during this period. Nevertheless, oil and gas revenue still formed the primary source of income for the government.

Part of the economic growth and indications of diversification in Qatar can be attributed to the construction sector, as although there was a slowdown in 2009 after several years of rapid growth, and also the knock-on effect from the crisis that engulfed Dubai's economy, continued public investment has helped keep this sector vibrant. Indeed, government investment in major infrastructure projects has helped maintain the performance of this sector. A good example of such investment is the Dohaland project, which will involve a targeted $5.496 billion being invested over five phases from 2010 to 2012 to redevelop the Musheireb district of Doha.[21] Similar so-called megaprojects such as the new Doha International Airport and the facilities at the Qatar Foundation's education city have also played a key role in maintaining a healthy construction sector; however, public investment remains the primary vehicle driving such growth. This underlines a key difference from Dubai's experience as projects there were primarily funded by foreign direct investment followed by units being offered for sale to private investors. Given the long-term revenue Qatar can expect to generate from its gas sector alone, continuation of such inward investment seems likely.

As can be expected with such high levels of GDP growth and public sector investment, this has had an impact on consumer prices, resulting in inflation. From 2005 to 2009, inflation averaged 8.9 per cent, whilst in the 2000–2004 period a more healthy average of 2.5 per cent was recorded.[22] As shown, the scale of growth in the construction sector has been considerable, and this has been the primary driver of such high levels. According to data published by the Qatar Statistics Authority, inflation in the housing sector reached 29.3 per cent in 2007, 19.6 per cent in 2008, and following the global economic downturn in 2009 there was reported deflation of 12 per cent.[23] Inflation brings with it risks in project tendering, especially in the construction sector, affected as it is by the prices of raw materials. In addition to this, given the volatility in the housing sector, it also elevates the risk of defaulting on loans by expatriates, as occurred in Dubai. Although the majority of Qatar's inflation increases were concentrated in the housing sector through rents, they had a wider impact on other sectors of the economy and raised the unit cost level of services or products, thus making it more difficult to attract foreign direct investment for key sectors. Indeed, in 2009 the rate of inflation reported on food, beverages and tobacco averaged 19.9 per cent.[24]

A Further area that has witnessed strong growth has been the financial sector, which is another part of Qatar's diversification policy. The Qatar Financial Centre (QFC) is at the heart of the sector and was established in 2005 as a way of attracting international financial institutions to Qatar. The QFC was established to operate within a separate legal and commercial system, which was achieved through the establishment of its own independent commercial and regulatory authority. An advantage of this is that it provided a framework that ran separately from the domestic economy, which meant that it would not be affected by any new rules or regulations applying to the domestic economy, whilst also assuring foreign commercial organisations that they would be able to conduct business through a regulated system modelled on practices in London. There is potential for the QFC to take on a more prominent and larger role in Qatar's economic diversification strategy, given the likelihood of continued inward public investment within Qatar that it will be called on to manage. Yet the real test will be the extent to which it can attract business away from Dubai given the latter's status as the preferred financial hub of the region.

Also of note are the various arms of Qatar's sovereign wealth fund. Established in 2005, the Qatar Investment Authority has since been linked with large scale investments on a global level. The driving force behind the sovereign wealth investment strategy is to allocate the budget surpluses income to projects able to yield income for the future. Indeed, the logic is for a continued rent income to exist once revenue from oil and gas declines. Bahrain, for example did not undertake such a strategy, and has experienced significant economic problems since its oil revenue depleted. For Qatar, the strategy of sovereign wealth investment is a sound one as holding offshore assets reinforces confidence in the economy, and over the long term the revenue stream from profits are likely to form a valuable source of revenue. However, it must be recognised that although this is evidence of diversification away from oil and gas revenue, it is nevertheless still another source of rent income, when what is really needed is more added value and sustainable economic development within the state itself. Overall, the conclusions that can be drawn on Qatar's economic status and its efforts towards diversification are that there is great potential for continued economic growth given the confidence and security instilled by the revenue generated and potential from the hydrocarbon sector. The willingness of the government to undertake large-scale inward investment has allowed for rapid economic development, yet it has also brought with it inflation and a growing urgency for the improvement of the human capital to best take advantage of this economic growth. Moreover, whilst economic diversification is taking place, it is apparent that sustainable development and a reducing reliance on public investment are also needed for the economy.

Foreign policy and security

Qatar's foreign policy has emerged as a fascinating example of a small state achieving an international presence far beyond its size. Much of this can be attributed to Qatar's desire to become a global foreign policy player, but it is equally important to recognise that achievement of this vision has been possible because of Qatar's economic capacity. Qatar is a special case in international relations on account of its massive gas reserves, most of which are exported globally, and an intercontinental basis which enmeshes them in energy security calculations on a global level. Importantly, this translates to consumer countries having a vested interest in Qatar's security. Although it is not an overstatement to claim that Qatar has emerged as an energy superpower and that this has brought with it particular dynamics in its foreign affairs, for us to have a clear understanding of Qatar's, it is important in the first instance to consider Qatar's geopolitical position and how this factors into foreign policy construction.

Qatar's geopolitical position underlines a systemic insecurity problem, which mirrors the historical experience of the other small Gulf states. Within the region, both Iran and Saudi Arabia can be understood as regional superpowers, and have posed varying degrees of threat and assistance to all of the smaller Gulf states. In addition to this, the overlapping nature of tribal areas, tributaries and loyalty has also been a crosscurrent theme in the Gulf, which has factored into elite decision-making. Given these factors and the geopolitical perceptions of threat, it is understandable that Qatar has displayed a tendency to seek protective alliances or security umbrellas from external powers. Such security perceptions and motivations may be unstated, yet they explain why Qatar has entered into historical relationships with the Al-Saud, the Ottomans, the British, and in the contemporary period the US. In terms of the US relationship, it has been argued that the security and autonomy of action Qatar achieves through this relationship cater for its aspirations on a global stage.[25] Therefore, the contemporary manifestation of Qatari foreign policy can be attributed not only to the aspiring vision and economic capacity to fulfil it, but also to the ability to have a sufficient level of national security which enables autonomy and independence of action in its foreign affairs.

Qatar's contemporary foreign policy began to take shape following Sheikh Hamad bin Khalifa Al-Thani's succession in 1995. Yet it is telling to look at the 2005 constitution, as Article 7 states that

...the foreign policy of the State is based on the principle of strengthening international peace and security by means of encouraging peaceful resolution of international disputes; and shall support the right of peoples to self-determination; and shall not interfere in the domestic affairs of states; and shall cooperate with peace-loving nations.[1]

This article underlines the vision of a wide-ranging foreign policy which would work towards supporting international peace and includes the idealist goal of supporting self-determination. Yet it also made clear that Qatar would not interfere in the domestic affairs of other states, and so a clear challenge of reconciling this with the pillar of self-determination becomes apparent. However, it is possible to detect from this article an early articulation of Qatar's desire to play a role in conflict resolution thereby supporting international peace and cooperation.

Whilst Qatar's broader foreign policy ambitions may be clear, the achievement of security was a key component that needed to come first. The US has played a key role in providing Qatar with a security umbrella by virtue of its forces being stationed at the Al-Udeid air base. Relations with the US were initially slow to develop, as it was not until 1973 that an embassy was opened in Qatar. After the 1991 liberation of Kuwait by a UN coalition led by the US, the US military remained in the region and were primarily located at the Prince Sultan air base in Saudi Arabia. On account of increased domestic pressures within Saudi Arabia, the US military deployment became untenable. Yet it was only after the September 11 2001 terrorist attacks that Al-Udeid took on a greater importance, resulting not only in the first substantial deployment of US forces to Qatar, but also in the positioning of US Central Command in the facility.

The importance of the deployment of US forces to Qatar is highly significant to understanding the manner in which Qatar's foreign relations changed. Following Sheikh Hamad bin Khalifa Al-Thani's 1995 succession through a coup d'état, there was a significant degree of external pressure and threats facing Qatar from neighbouring states. These came because the deposed Emir, Sheikh Khalifa bin Hamad Al-Thani, received support from Abu Dhabi and Saudi Arabia. This culminated in a counter-coup attempt at the behest of the former Emir in 1996, but when that failed the perpetrators were tried in the Qatari courts. It was in the same year that construction of the Al-Udeid air base facility commenced, and thus Hamad's enticing the US to locate its military on the Qatari peninsula was a policy grounded in the period of insecurity that followed the change of leadership. The US relocating to Qatar, the security position of the Qatari state was catered for and allowed for consolidation and implementation of development policies and reforms.

The historical interpretation that Qatar has made use of a foreign entity to afford it security so that it can have autonomy of action is a logical and accurate interpretation, yet recent events indicate that a new dynamic is emerging which challenges this analysis. By virtue of the role Qatar is playing in the supply of natural gas products to a number of countries, the state is increasingly seeking 'diversified security'. In essence the significance of Qatari energy supplies to countries on a global and inter-continental level should not be underestimated: these countries have a vested interest in maintaining a secure and stable flow of energy from the Qatari state and therefore have become stakeholders in its security. That does not mean that this would ever equate to the hard security provided by the US, but it is important as it makes the Qatari state less reliant on the US. Such diversified security gives Qatar a great deal more power on the international stage as it can increasingly rely on political support for its security and initiatives from those countries that are direct consumers of Qatari natural gas products. Qatar's energy capacity and the demand for it by major industrialised countries on a global basis thus demonstrate how a small country can have a geopolitical reach and security considerably beyond what are the norms in international relations. This underlines the interpretation that the grand strategic pillars present in Qatari foreign relations are to maximise independence of action through gaining autonomy and also to have security.

The achievement of autonomy and independence of action has allowed Qatar to engage in a pragmatic foreign policy echoing the principles outlined in the constitution. A clear manifestation can be observed in its efforts to promote conflict resolution and enhance international peace and security. Qatar has focused its conflict resolution efforts amongst members of the Arab League. It has notably engaged in efforts at high profile conflict resolution in Lebanon, Yemen, Sudan, and Libya. Indeed, in 2008, members of the Lebanese parliament were flown to Qatar and engaged in high profile summit style diplomacy. The Emir, Sheikh Hamad bin Khalifa Al-Thani, and also the Prime Minister and Foreign Minister, Sheikh Hamad bin Jassim Al-Thani, were actively involved in the intricacies of the resolution process, and it yielded a successful agreement in Doha that overcame the political deadlock in Beirut. Qatar's engagement in such foreign policy activities underlines the manifestation of autonomy and an independent foreign policy that is a reflection of the national vision. Yet the challenge is one of balancing the strategic relationship it enjoys with the US against its own foreign policy ambitions and priorities.

The reflection of the national vision and the willingness to commit resources towards achieving it took on a new meaning in 2011 in the context of the regional uprisings elsewhere in the Arab world. The Qatar-based television service Al Jazeera played a critical role in informing both regional and international audiences of these revolutions, especially in Egypt and Tunisia. Yet it was with Libya that Qatar demonstrated a willingness to commit actual military resources, in the form of F-16 strike aircraft, in support of UN Security Council resolutions. This action is noteworthy as it broke with Qatar's conformity with GCC foreign policies, and underlined the confidence it now has in taking on a regional leadership role, not just in the GCC but also in the Arab League. Certainly, within the GCC context, Qatar appears more at ease with engaging in such actions than Saudi Arabia, even though the latter has a greater military and economic capacity to do so. Yet Saudi Arabia has shown support for Qatar's newfound role, which indicates that Saudi Arabian and Qatari foreign policies can still be understood as mutually complementary on conflict resolution and other general issues of concern. Indeed, their focus appears well-coordinated so either state can take the lead on a given issue. And in the case of Qatar, the willingness to engage well beyond the Gulf region is clear and underlines Qatar's strong potential to play a key leadership role within the Arab community.

Future challenges

Qatar's future challenges are a product of both its success and the challenge of having to manage carefully future growth and development. Such challenges can be broken down into a few key areas. In the social sphere there is a need to balance traditions, cultural identity and heritage with the rapid pace of modernisation. It is a sensitive yet recognised problem that Qatar has become increasingly integrated into regional and global communities and this has brought with it social and cultural dilemmas. A delicate balancing act is required in order to ensure that future development and expansion are carried out in a sensitive manner. Although issues of this kind are common in any Gulf society, they are particularly acute in Qatar because of the rapid population growth over such a short space of time. According to the Qatar Statistics Authority, the total resident population in 2007 was 907,000, yet by 2009 it had reached over 1,900,000.[26] Such a population explosion not only places a strain on public services and contributes towards inflation, but also makes more visible those cultural practices that are not always compatible with indigenous tradition. The question therefore is how modernisation and development can be achieved in a way that accommodates traditional cultural values and practices, particularly in the context of rapid population growth and increasing density. This is particularly important given that the national population is heavily outnumbered by expatriate foreigners, a problem identified by the Qatar National Vision of 2030. Indeed, with foreigners now able to purchase properties on a freehold basis in Qatar, the question of a permanent rather than a transitory foreign population needs to be considered in terms of how best to accommodate their needs in a culturally sensitive and appropriate manner.

Human development is another key challenge. As noted, the size of Qatar's labour market has grown at a rapid pace. An uncontrolled expansion of the non-national population would be neither desirable nor sustainable. Yet such an issue needs to be figured against the backdrop of the economic growth of the country. Much will depend on the level of economic growth Qatar aims to have, as this will dictate the needs of the expatriate workforce. The problem could perhaps best be managed by controlling the levels of inward public investment, which for Qatar is a main driver of economic growth. Yet the challenge remains one of human development as there is a need for a greater proportion of nationals to become involved in the private sector, since Qatar faces a similar problem to the other Gulf states as the majority of its national population is employed by the public sector. Investment in education and the provision of qualifications that best meet Qatar's national economic and social needs are thus a pressing concern. Indeed, it is a challenge not only to offer such educational opportunities but also to attract nationals to enrol on such courses. Through promoting human capital and development, a greater involvement of Qatari nationals in the private sector can be achieved, thus allowing the rising expatriate population to be better managed.

Linked in with the need for human development is the need for sustainable development. As demonstrated, Qatar's economy has grown rapidly, yet the challenge is for further growth to be managed in a more sustainable manner so that the country becomes less dependent on inward public investment. This is something that will take some time as the private sector will need to develop its ability to attract foreign direct investment, added-value commerce and income from sustainable products. However, Qatar is fortunate to have the cushion of its oil and gas income and also, increasingly, wealth derived from overseas sovereign investments, which can support the economy as the economy diversifies in a sustainable manner.

A further issue linked to Qatar's need for sustainable development is for it to achieve a balanced rate of growth. As discussed, a key problem that has been encountered is very high levels of inflation.[27] The risks associated with this are serious, as if salaries do not keep up with a rising domestic consumer price index further social and economic problems will result. Risks for Qatar can range from the loss of human capital as a result of insufficient wages to low or stagnant productivity and a heightened degree of risk for companies wishing to tender for projects, given their inability to calculate costs of a project over a period of time. Additionally, uncontrolled or unmanaged growth may lead to the wider problem of the economy overheating and going into a cycle of boom and bust, which would also have a clear socio-economic impact.

OMAN

Marc Valeri

State formation

The al-Busa'idi dynasty, of which Qaboos is the fourteenth ruler or sultan, was founded in 1750, when Ahmad al-Busa'idi, governor of Sohar under the Ya'arubi dynasty (1624–1737), expelled the Persian forces from the coast of Oman and proclaimed himself Imam. Ahmad's grandson, Sa'id bin Sultan (r.1806–56), who gave his name to the current royal family, extended Oman's possessions overseas and made Zanzibar his capital in 1832. During the 1840s, Sa'id's fleet made use of the monsoon winds to develop a triangular commercial network between Africa (a source of spices, slaves, precious stones and ivory), India (for manufactured articles and textiles), and Oman (a source of dates and frankincense). On Sa'id's death, the formal sovereignty of the Omani empire covered the whole north-western edge of the Indian Ocean, from Mozambique to Baluchistan. But the inability of Sa'id's sons to regulate the succession led, under British pressure, to the dismemberment of Oman's possessions into the two political entities of Muscat and Zanzibar in 1861.

This regional supremacy explains why the modern history of Oman is punctuated by numerous migration waves from and to Oman. Sa'id bin Sultan encouraged the settlement of Omani people on the eastern African coast, a process which did not dry up until the mid-twentieth century. The return of their descendants started after the 1964 revolution in Zanzibar, which had put an end to the local al-Busa'idi dynasty. A second wave of returnees came following a call made in 1970 by Sultan

135

Qaboos inviting the Omani elite abroad to contribute to the 'awakening' of the country. Today the 'back-from-Africa' Omanis, who are known as 'Swahilis' (referring to their vernacular language) or 'Zanzibaris', are thought to number more than a hundred thousand (out of 2 million Omani nationals). There are also now an estimated 200,000 nationals of Baluchi descent in Oman. Their origin can be explained by the need for the Omani rulers, since the seventeenth century, to raise mercenary armies independent of internal tribal forces. Last but not least, the Omani population of Indian origin was historically involved in maritime trade. Among them the Lawatiyya, a community of Twelver Shia, appear to have settled in Oman from Sind (in present day Pakistan) between 1780 and 1850. They are estimated to number only about 30,000, but they enjoy a large economic influence.

The end of the nineteenth century and the beginning of the twentieth were marked by the complete dereliction of official duties by Sultan Faisal (r.1888–1913) and his son Taimur (r.1913–32)—both were rulers in name only. Their feeling of powerlessness regarding Omani political issues soon deteriorated into a lack of interest in involvement in public affairs. The economic difficulties, linked in people's minds to the British tutelage over Muscat authority, led the sheikhs of Inner Oman to elect an Ibadi Imam in Nizwa in June 1913 (Ibadism is a distinct form of Islam found chiefly in Oman). Jihad was immediately proclaimed against the Sultan and his British allies but the Imam's forces suffered a severe defeat by British Indian regiments when attacking Muscat, in January 1915. The Government of India, not satisfied with a precarious stability that placed an unpopular Sultan at the mercy of a new attack, which obliged the British to provide constant support for him, thought it necessary to secure official mutual recognition. Following the Seeb agreement signed on 25 September 1920 by two powers (Sultan Taimur and the Ibadi sheikhs) each of which were too weak to do without the British tutelage, the tribes were left to enjoy effective control over Inner Oman. Sultan Taimur could consider that he had preserved authority over the whole Omani territory, even if his full sovereignty was restricted to the northern coast and Salalah. Essentially, with this arrangement, the British had kept the upper hand over a divided and weakened Oman.

In 1932, Taimur abdicated in favour of his son Sa'id. Like his father and his grandfather, Sa'id did not have any kind of political legitimacy, but he stood out from his predecessors by his determination to exercise actual political authority. He succeeded first in driving the other al-

Busa'idis either to accept his authority and become his lieutenants, or to renounce for good any political role in Oman. Moreover Sa'id was aware that as long as his government remained insolvent he would be strangled by the British. On the assumption that he could only spend what he had, all the expenditure, like infrastructure projects, was drastically reduced. Sa'id relied on foreign mercenaries or on individuals who owed everything to him and thus remained loyal. Moreover he developed alliances with the merchants' families, who proved indispensable to the ruler's political survival; not only were they the only ones able to provide the Sultan with liquid assets, but he also deducted from their resources huge taxes, which represented the major sources of the Sultanate's revenue. Sa'id also demonstrated his determination to arrange peaceful coexistence with the Imamate. As Major Chauncy, Britain's Consul General in Muscat, noted in 1951, the Sultan of Muscat and the Imam applied the Seeb agreement 'even more in the spirit than in the letter, and the tribes themselves enjoyed a period of peace without comparison in the history'.[1]

But the introduction of the oil issue into the game disrupted the status quo. In 1949, Ibn Sa'ud awarded a concession to the Arabian American Oil Company (Aramco) south of Buraimi oasis. In May 1954 the Imam of Oman, who had agreed to join forces with the Sultan of Muscat to expel the Saudis from Buraimi, died. The new political line of the Imamate changed in favour of a rapprochement with the Saudis. In the face of the Saudi-American threat, the British took the initiative, convinced that there was no alternative to reunifying Oman. In October 1955 the Trucial Oman Scouts, based in Sharjah, launched a head-on attack on the Imamate, leading to its collapse. But no strategy of development and political stabilisation was started by Sa'id, except the building of a road to the interior—to provide access to the Fahud oil wells. Unsurprisingly this led to the proclamation of the Imamate's swift rebirth in June 1957. The major interior towns flew the Imamate's flag once again but the Trucial Oman Scouts, with the decisive support of the British Royal Air Force, regained control during the summer. The Imam's supporters found shelter in the Jabal Akhdar and were forced to flee to Saudi Arabia in January 1959, after intervention from the elite troops of the Special Air Services. From then on, the struggle turned into both intimidation actions (mines, sabotage, etc.) and the establishment of an Imamate in exile, supported by the Arab League, with offices in Cairo and

Baghdad. Even though the 'Oman question' was regularly discussed in United Nations commissions until 1970, the Imamate authorities in exile were slowly marginalised in the 1960s.

From 1958, Sa'id decided to retire to Salalah, in the south of Oman. The features of his mode of government which emerged in the 1940s—deep suspicion towards the Omanis, aversion to social and economic reforms, and entrusting the daily running of the country to foreign experts—were to be exacerbated. This evolution made it possible to keep this 'ultra-Tibet'[2] safe from the upheavals elsewhere in the Middle East and also explains why, at the end of the 1960s, more than 50,000 Omanis had migrated to other Gulf emirates, where they were looking for better living conditions. The remoteness of Oman was especially apparent in the Dhofar province, which was being administered by Sa'id as a special domain. Under the impulse of the revolution in Yemen, a Dhofar Liberation Front (DLF) formed in 1965 became the Popular Front for the Liberation of the Occupied Arabian Gulf (PFLOAG) in 1968, and declared itself Marxist-Leninist. By early 1970, the Sultan's forces in Dhofar only controlled the Salalah plain and their remaining courses of action were limited to air raids on the positions controlled by the PFLOAG.

When the rebellion threatened to spread to northern Oman in 1970, the British had no other solution to counter this situation than a psychological blow, with Sultan Sa'id's forced abdication in favour of his son Qaboos on 23 July. This coup enjoyed the support of the other Gulf rulers as well as the Shah of Iran, all of whom were worried by potential revolutionary contagion. It also led to a radical change of policy in Oman from 1971, as the authorities both increased defence expenditure to 50 per cent of the State budget and decided to use part of the oil rent (exploited since 1967) in pursuing development programmes in education, health and agriculture. The summer of 1972 represented the turning point of the conflict. Not only was the PFLOAG heavily defeated in the coastal town of Mirbat, but the year also witnessed a dramatic increase in foreign help to the Sultan, with the arrival of fresh Iranian troops, in addition to more British personnel. This extra support proved vital in 1975 when joint offensives of the Sultan's Armed Forces and the Iranians were able to overcome the most solid of the rebel positions, although at a very heavy human and material cost. On 11 December 1975 Sultan Qaboos could proclaim the official end of the war.

Political structures and personalities

Born in 1940, Qaboos returned from military education and training in Europe in 1964 and was placed under house arrest until his accession to the throne. As he was an unknown among the Omani population, the new ruler's room to manoeuvre with regard to the British was reduced to a minimum in 1970, and so was his legitimacy vis-à-vis the Omanis. The Dhofar military campaign gave him only limited time to dedicate to the country's development during the first years of his rule.

In 1975 royal decree number 26/75 established that the Sultan is 'the source of all laws' (*masdar al-qawanin*). Since then all Omani legislation has been promulgated through royal decrees, including the Basic Law of the State, which was issued in November 1996. According to its Article 1, the Sultanate is an Arab and Islamic state. Islam and Arabic are the religion and the official language of the state, while the *sharia* constitutes the basis of legislation (Articles 2 and 3). The system of government is described as a 'hereditary Sultanate [...] based on justice, consultation (*shura*) and equality' (Articles 5, 9). The sultan of Oman, who is 'the symbol of national unity as well as its guardian and defender' (Article 41), and holds concurrently the positions of chief of staff of the armed forces, Minister of Defence, Minister of Foreign Affairs and chairman of the Central Bank, has all the prerogatives of executive and legislative power. Besides his large powers of appointment (especially of judges) and dismissal, he promulgates and ratifies laws, and can grant pardons and commute sentences. Article 41 explicitly states that respecting him is a duty and that his orders must be obeyed. Articles 44 to 55 establish that the sovereign will be helped and advised by the Council of Ministers, to which is given the task of implementing general state policies. Article 45 plans for a possible prime minister, who would theoretically preside over the Council's sessions.

The structure that best symbolises the extreme personalisation of authority in Oman is the Diwan of the Royal Court. Qaboos soon showed his determination to keep control of all matters in the country, while giving the image of a ruler close to his subjects' problems. The Diwan has the role of filtering all cases coming before the ruler, while managing those national and private affairs which do not concern any other department but do not require the Sultan's personal intervention. As such, the Diwan has slowly become a super-ministry above all the other Cabinet departments.

A key element of the regime's legitimisation rests on the nation-building process implemented since 1970, which links the country's economic and social development to the modernising state (as the administrator of the oil rent), on the one hand, and to the person of the Sultan who embodies the state and has become the subject of a personality cult, on the other. By recreating a national identity within the framework of an omnipresent state and by unifying cultural and religious references, Qaboos has legitimised his paternalistic authority. The Sultan portrays himself as the embodiment of modern Oman in general and of the renaissance (*nahda*) ideology in particular. As such, the current nation state is built on the negation of the country's pre-1970 history. Referred to as the 'dark period', these earlier times are only ever evoked as an antonym to the awakening of July 23 1970, the date of Qaboos's accession to the throne, later renamed Renaissance Day. All major contemporary urban achievements bear the Sultan's name: Muscat's main highway that connects the city's quarters is a metaphoric hyphen, the Muscat and Salalah hospitals, the most recent mosques, the country's state-run university, and so on. This omnipresence of the ruler is completed by his effigy on banknotes, his portrait in every shop, the national anthem paying explicit homage to him, and the Omani National Day (18 November) actually being Qaboos' birthday.

Unlike the other Gulf Arab monarchies, Oman is not under the rule of a tribe or a family, but under that of a monarch who has relied on various allies. The Al Sa'id royal family members hold few political positions. Qaboos's paternal uncle, Tariq bin Taimur, was Oman's only Prime Minister under Qaboos but lasted a short time (1970–1) and died in 1980, while serving as Governor of the Central Bank.[3] Among the sons of Tariq, Haitham was appointed in 1996 as undersecretary in the Ministry for Foreign Affairs and has been Minister for National Heritage and Culture since 2002, while his brother Brigadier-General As'ad has held the position of Personal Representative of the Sultan since 2002. Shihab bin Tariq was appointed in 1990 as Commander of the Sultan of Oman's Navy, and since 2004 he has served as Adviser to the Sultan. Another brother of Sa'id bin Taimur, Shabib, held the Environment portfolio (1984–91) before he became Special Adviser to the Sultan for Environmental Affairs, a position he still holds. With his son Tariq he runs one of the leading Omani business groups, Tawoos. Another senior member of the Al Sa'id, Fahd bin Mahmud, has been Deputy Prime Minister for the Council of Ministers' Affairs since 1994.

In order to fill sensitive positions, Qaboos has preferred to use some politically inoffensive collateral branches of the al-Busa'idi tribe. Badr bin Sa'ud al-Busa'idi held the position of Minister for the Interior between 1979 and 1996 and has been Minister in charge of Defence Affairs since then. His nephew, Saif bin Hamad, held the position of Minister for the Diwan of the Royal Court until his death in 2002, and was succeeded by 'Ali bin Hamud al-Busa'idi, who had held the post of Minister for the Interior from 1996. In March 2011 another of Badr bin Sa'ud's nephews, Khalid bin Hilal, replaced 'Ali bin Hamud as Minister for the Diwan of the Royal Court. Another instance of 'traditional al-Busa'idi civil servants'[4] is the al-Sammar branch, which produced regional governors for generations through the twentieth century. Hilal bin Hamad al-Busa'idi, a former Minister of Justice in the 1970s and 1980s, chaired the State Security Court, which in 1994 and 2005 tried people accused of attempting to overthrow the regime. One of his sons, Sa'ud, formerly Governor of Musandam, was appointed in March 2011 as minister of state and Governor of Muscat.

The 1970s also saw the entry into top positions of personalities descended from families who were Sultan Sa'id's closest allies: they belong either to historical political supporters of the Sultans of Muscat or to Muscat's merchant elites. The al-Ma'amari is an example of these tribes allied to the twentieth-century sultans, on which the current ruler relied in security and defence matters. General 'Ali bin Majid, who held the posts of Minister for the Royal Office and head of the office of the chief of staff of the Armed Forces from 1989 until March 2011, was one of the key figures of the regime during the 2000s. His brother Fahd was vice-chairman of the Consultative Council between 2000 and 2007 and his brother-in-law, Muhammad bin Marhun, who was Ambassador to the United Arab Emirates until 2007, has since held the position of minister of state and Governor of Dhofar. Lieutenant General Malik al-Ma'amari, whose father was one of the closest advisers to Sultan Sa'id in the 1960s, was Inspector-General of Police and Customs, with ministerial rank, until 2011.

Because Qaboos has never been able—and willing—to rely on his small family, he has allied with the merchant elites, a practice once again in keeping with the pre-1970 period. He has assured them of the protection of the political authorities, the royal family's limited interference in the business sphere, and privileged access to the oil windfall through public contracts. In return, the merchant families have helped the ruler to finance his nation-building endeavours. Never in Oman have the merchant elites been forced to choose between political decision-making positions and economic activities. Thus some of the merchant families' members have been given strategic political positions. A former chairman (1987–91) of the Chamber of Commerce, Maqbool al-Sultan, whose family acted as representatives in Oman for the British India shipping line and Lloyds in the first half of the twentieth century, held the post of Minister for Commerce and Industry from 1991 till February 2011. His brother Jamil is the current vice-president of the Omani Chamber of Commerce and Industry. The leading al-Sultan family company is WJ Towell, which is involved in more than forty sectors (motors, telecommunications, construction, computer engineering, insurance, etc.) and represents in Oman brands like Mars, Unilever, and Nestlé. Another obvious example of direct participation of business families in the decision-making process is the Zawawi family. Yusuf al-Zawawi was a native of Hijaz and came to Muscat at the end of the nineteenth century to establish a trading company. He became one of the unofficial advisers to Sultan Faisal. Qais al-Zawawi, Yusuf's grandson, held the position of Foreign Minister between 1973 and 1982, then became Deputy Prime Minister for Finance and Economy until his death in 1995. His brother 'Umar currently holds the position of Special Adviser to the Sultan for External Affairs. Economically speaking, the Omar Zawawi Establishment has become one of the leading Omani holding companies. The Zubair family also owes a lot of its economic success to its old connections with the Sultans of Muscat. Zubair al-Hutti acted as Governor of Dhofar in the 1930s and Sultan Sa'id entrusted him with running his real-estate projects. Muhammad bin Zubair, who helped set up the Omani Chamber of Commerce in 1972 and was its first chairman, was appointed in November 1974 to the post of Minister for Commerce and Industry; he left it in 1982 to become Personal Adviser to the Sultan for Economic Affairs, his current position. The nephew of Muhammad Zubair, Juma'a bin 'Ali, was Minister for Manpower until 2008.

But the oil rent has at the same time profoundly changed the boundaries between politics and the economy, as many ministers whose families were not active in the economy before have become personally rich. This process has not been questioned by the ruler, as it has increased both the elites' dependency on the state and the stability of his rule. The symbolic debts owed by Qaboos at the beginning of his rule to those actors (merchant elites, tribal notables, co-opted opponents, etc.) who supported him after 1970 has thus gradually turned into a weapon in his hands, forestalling any challenges to his reign by turning the most powerful societal forces into unfailing allies. By the beginning of the twenty-first century, few members of the Council of Ministers had not personally derived material profit from the oil rent. One of the most illustrative cases is the noble branch of the Khalili family, heirs to a prestigious lineage of Ibadi imams. Sa'ud al-Khalili, the nephew of a former Imam of Oman (Muhammad al-Khalili, 1920–54), became one of the four members of the very first Cabinet appointed in August 1970. In addition he owns the powerful Al Taher business group that he founded in 1973, which is active in construction contracting (Caterpillar), food and drink (Sprite and Coke) and the distribution of Shell products. His nephew Salim bin Hilal, Minister for Agriculture until 2011, was formerly chairman of the Chamber of Commerce, while another of his nephews, 'Abd Al-Malik bin 'Abd Allah—previously both the executive chairman of the Royal Court Pension Fund and the chairman of the first Omani banking group, Bank Muscat—was appointed Minister for Tourism in March 2011.

The first institutional top-down initiative to consult with civil society happened in 1979 with the creation of the purely consultative Council of Agriculture, Fisheries and Industry. Dissolved in 1981, the Council handed its duties over to the State Consultative Council, itself replaced in 1990 by the current Consultative Council (*Majlis al-Shura*). Within each *wilaya* (administrative district), 500 people whose opinions and experience were valued were gathered to designate three male candidates for three years. From these three, one was chosen by the ruler himself. In 1993, *wilaya*s whose population exceeded 30,000 inhabitants were to send two delegates to the *Majlis*, and smaller *wilaya*s just one. In 1997 women were also given the right to vote and to stand for election. The electoral college was extended to 175,000 electors (one adult in four; 30 per cent of them women) in 2000. In October 2003, the delegates' term was increased to four years and universal suffrage was introduced in the country's first free elections. Currently composed of eighty-four members, the *Majlis al-Shura* is chaired by a president appointed by royal decree while an executive bureau is charged with planning the plenary sessions' agenda and supervising the activity of the five permanent committees (on the economy, local communities, health, legal affairs, and education and culture).

These committees can ask for a minister or any official to come and explain himself in front of them, although ministers are not yet compelled to obey.

As its name indicates, this assembly has no legislative power. Unless the Council of Ministers explicitly wishes to pass it on directly to the ruler, any proposed law in the economic and social sectors has to be presented to the *Majlis* to be discussed and, if necessary, amended. The bill is then voted upon by the assembly and returned to the ministry. Afterwards, the ruler ratifies the bill, choosing whether or not to take into account the recommendations introduced. In addition, the *Majlis* submits proposals to the Council of Ministers for legislation in the economic, social and environmental fields and to contribute to preparation and implementation of the development plans as well as of the national budget. As freedom of association is very strictly limited by the Basic Law and the establishment of political parties is prohibited, the criteria of choice most commonly used by electors have been related to primordial solidarities, especially in rural areas where choice mainly follows lines of tribal belonging. Revealing is the absence of any members of the royal family, noble lineages of the al-Busaʻidi tribe, or leading merchant families among the candidates. This is due to the regime's unwillingness to face the implications of symbolic over-investment in such candidatures: voters and observers would be tempted to interpret the results as a referendum on the authorities' general policies, which is inconceivable for the regime. These elections do not, in any case, question the legitimacy of the ruler and the leading political figures, but that of the local actors only.

Despite the pre-eminence of conservative and rural forces in the Consultative Council, Qaboos decided to set up an upper chamber in 1996. The fifth part of the Basic Law created the Council of Oman, composed of both the Consultative Council and the State Council (*Majlis al-Dawla*). It is currently composed of seventy-three members (including fourteen women) who are appointed by the Sultan one week after the *Majlis al-Shura* elections for a term of four years. Its members are recruited from among former ministers and undersecretaries, retired officers and judges, businessmen, and 'any person His Majesty the Sultan may deem fit'.[5] While the two assemblies are officially given comparable prerogatives, in practice the job of the State Council is to counterbalance the *Majlis al-Shura*, as the latter's legitimacy, which comes from elections, seems broader and 'independent' of the ruler's will. The way the members are appointed and the social composition of the assembly are expected to prevent the emergence of any radical political proposals and thus ensure the unfailing loyalty of State Council members to the Sultan. In March 2011, popular pressure led the Sultan to announce by royal decree his intention to grant the Council of Oman greater legislative and regulatory powers.

Economic development and diversification

The exploitation of Oman's oil resources was started in July 1967 by Petroleum Development Oman (PDO), which was 85 per cent owned by Shell. In 1969 oil rent already represented forty times the total annual revenue of the Sultanate in the early 1960s. In July 1974 the Omani state took a 60 per cent stake in PDO's capital. Even though Oman's oil production costs are still high by comparison with the other Gulf producers, especially because of the extreme dispersal of resources over many small fields, the Omani state took advantage of the 1970s oil crisis to multiply its revenue fifteenfold over the decade.

The oil rent has been the indisputable cornerstone of Omani socioeconomic development, since it enabled the new regime to implement an extensive redistribution policy. Between 1980 and 2000, state expenditure amounted to 40–45 per cent of GDP. The state penetrated materially and symbolically every aspect of daily life, through new information and communication infrastructure (asphalted roads, government television network, etc.) and extensive social and educational systems covering the whole territory (with schools and health centres being built even in the smallest of villages). This has gone in hand with an explosion of jobs and possibilities of income offered within the public sector (in the army, the police, and the new government services). As a consequence of improved conditions, life expectancy at birth rose from 40 in the 1960s to 66 in 1990 and 72 in 2008, while the rate of illiteracy stood at 17.8 per cent in 2003, having been 41.2 per cent ten years before; 96 per cent of Omani families are now connected to electricity and/or gas, and almost 95 per cent of the population is supplied by piping or tanks with drinkable water. This boom coincided with a massive influx of workers from the Indian subcontinent and Middle Eastern countries (such as Egypt, Sudan, and Jordan). Such foreigners, who represented just 7 per cent of the workforce (in both public and private sectors) in 1970, amounted to 65 per cent of the workforce ten years later. Between 1980 and 1985, the number of foreign workforce doubled again.

Nevertheless debates over the need to rethink the economic model of development based on oil rent are not new in Oman. An economic slowdown in the 1980s, combined with the emergence of endemic unemployment among the younger generations, led to the early implementation of policies favouring nationals in employment (Omanisation [*ta'min*] policies). In October 1994, the Ministry for Labour and Social Affairs announced quotas to be respected in various branches of the private sector. The following year, a tax to finance Omanis' vocational training was deducted from companies in proportion to their numbers of expatriate employees. More broadly, a 1995 long-term programme entitled 'Oman 2020: Vision for Oman's Economy' established two series of objectives. The first was economic diversification: the oil sector's share in GDP had to fall from 41 per cent in 1996 to 9 per cent by 2020, while that of non-oil industries was to increase from 7.5 per cent to 29 per cent. The second had to do with human resources and employment. It was planned to raise the rates of nationals in public and private sectors from 68 to 95 per cent and from 7.5 to 75 per cent respectively, while the share of expatriates in the whole population would be reduced from 25 per cent in 1995 to 15 per cent by 2020.

The all-time peak in the country's oil production (85 per cent by PDO and 10 per cent by the American company Occidental) came in August 2000, with 1,010,000 barrels per day, and it experienced a drop of 26 per cent between 2001 and 2007. Nevertheless, high crude prices on the world market explain why the share of oil in public revenue (between 70 and 75 per cent since 2001) has not decreased. Also, the country's total production (864,600 barrels per day in 2010) has been slowly increasing again since 2007, given that some fields, temporarily unexploited, are becoming profitable again. In this context, Oman's sixth (2001–5), seventh (2006–2010), and eighth (2011–2015) five year development plans have emphasised three main priority areas for economic diversification: the development of the gas sector, tourism, and the non-oil industries.

The production of liquefied natural gas started in February 2000. To promote the use of gas resources, Oman launched several large-scale industrial projects. The most important is the Sohar industrial port, under development since 1998. On the site, various activities, including an oil refinery, an aluminium smelter, petrochemical infrastructure and a steel plant, are scheduled to generate more than 8,000 stable jobs and 30,000 other jobs indirectly in the region. And if all goes according to plan, there will be a total investment of $12 billion. In addition, a fertiliser plant operated in partnership between Oman and India was inaugurated in 2006 in Qalhat. However, while the prospects for gas give grounds for optimism, there remain substantial uncertainties. Natural gas will never replace oil for public revenue, and this has been recognised by the authorities.[6] Moreover, contracts on the gas market are determined before production, and thus do not allow for adjustment of production according to the political and economic context. Besides, activities in relation to natural gas are characterised by high financial and material capital intensity, and require a very small workforce, most of it highly qualified.

'Selective quality tourism'—that is, tourism aimed at predominantly wealthy and easily controllable Western elites—is another priority for diversification. A Ministry for Tourism, the first of its kind in any of the Gulf Cooperation Council (GCC) states, was created in June 2004. Since November 2004, a decree from the Ministry for Housing has authorised non-Omanis to own land or homes in special areas devoted to tourism and established by law. A number of major tourism and real estate projects were thus set up, such as The Wave near Muscat, along 7 km of sea shore. The state, in partnership with the Dubai-based al-Futtaim group, launched in 2005 the first phase of this complex, which is intended to host 4,000 residential properties and is expected to be completed by 2013. Even more ambitious is the Blue City project, between Sohar and Muscat, which is costing $15 billion. Covering 35 square kilometres, this tourism-devoted new city will accommodate 200,000 residents by 2020. The authorities plan for the creation of 7,000 jobs on the site and another 25,000 indirect jobs. In addition, there are several other projects such as the construction of several luxury resorts in Dhofar, Musandam, and Ra's al-Hadd (near Sur).

In addition to gas and tourism, the non-oil industrial sector is another area of focus. Since 1985 the government has built up the Rusail industrial area, west of Muscat, which benefits from exemptions from customs duty. Five other zones (Raysut, Sohar, Nizwa, Buraimi, and al-Mazyuna) have been set up since then. Port activities play a central role in this strategy of diversification. By making Salalah port the leading element in the south's economic development following the opening of a free zone in 2006, the government signalled its intention to compete with Dubai for container shipping. In Muttrah, Sohar and Khasab, lengthy work will increase port capacities further, while a deep water port at Duqm, on the Indian Ocean coast, is also under construction.

The plan to widen the state's financial resources explains also why several taxes—not only customs duties—have been established since the 1990s. Since 1994 all companies, whether Omani or foreign, pay taxes on profits. Moreover various indirect taxes on citizens, like municipal taxes on restaurants, on leasing or on real estate transactions, as well as direct taxes, like a tax on crossing the UAE border (currently three riyals per light vehicle going), are in force. Even total exemption from health care payment for nationals has been abandoned, with the introduction of an annual family medical card (costing one riyal) together with a small fee for each medical consultation. More and more drugs that are no longer provided freely by hospitals must be now bought at pharmacies with no refunds.

This diversification policy has been supported by a strong desire to promote the private sector, aimed both at supporting the role of local companies in economic diversification and at attracting foreign capital. In July 2004 two privatisation laws were promulgated, one dealing especially with water, electricity, and the planning that was formerly the responsibility of the Ministry for Electricity and Water. Another important axis of the Oman privatisation process is the telecommunications sector. In March 2002 an enabling law on telecommunications promulgated by royal decree established the Telecommunications Regulation Authority to be in charge of competition regulation in the sector, the privatisation of the sole operator Omantel, the granting of new licenses and the implementation of tariffs. Since 1996, besides fiscal alignment with the Omani companies law, foreign investors in Oman have also had exemptions from taxes (for the first five years) and from customs duties (for imports for processing in Oman), and finally the possibility of repatriation of profits. Foreign shareholding allowed in an Omani company was extended in 2001 to 70 per cent in all sectors, and even 100 per cent in banking and insurance since 2003 and in telecommunications since 2005.

In parallel to this diversification policy Qaboos convened in 2001 a symposium on the national workforce, in which private sector representatives were invited to comply strictly with regulations on the recruitment of expatriates and the attainment of Omanisation quotas. Two months later a Ministry for Manpower was set up, by amalgamating the Ministry for Labour with the one for Social Affairs and Vocational Training. The sixth Five Year Plan (2001–5) provided for total Omanisation over five years in twenty-four low skilled occupations. Other more technical professions were supposed to follow suit. The new Labour Law, issued by royal decree on 26 April 2003, illustrates these priorities. The employer gets a permit from the Ministry for Manpower to bring in foreign workers only if there are not enough Omanis available for the post on the job market and if the company has complied with the prescribed percentage of Omanisation in its branch. Once the permit is granted, to join the work position a non-Omani can obtain a labour card delivered by the Ministry on condition that the worker has the professional skill or the qualifications needed by the position. Moreover, nationals enjoy a set of benefits expatriates do not, including a minimum wage (raised by 43 per cent to 200 riyals per month in February 2011 for full-time unskilled jobs), a monthly allowance (150 riyals) for job seekers registered at the Ministry for Manpower (introduced in 2011), and strict protection against dismissal. And an employer can terminate the contract of an Omani only during the three-month probation period or if the employee absents himself or herself from work for more than seven consecutive days, or in case of a major mistake.

Thus, the challenge of employing young Omanis, of whom 50,000 every year leave school and university (with or without degrees) and enter the labour market, led to a national mobilisation driven from above. By comparison with neighbouring countries, Oman can be proud of some successes. In December 2008 the civil service sector showed an average Omanisation rate of 85.5 per cent, constantly rising for the last decade. Similarly, 91 per cent of employees in the private banking sector were Omani in late 2008. The number of active expatriates in the private sector stabilised progressively while the rate of nationals in the private sector and the overall rate of Omanisation (security and defence forces excluded) increased to 19 per cent and 32 per cent respectively by the end of 2005. Since 2006, however, the authorities seem to consider that Omanisation does not boil down any more to a post-for-post substitution of expatriate manpower with Omanis, but is rather a question of comparative skills and added-value of local and expatriate workforces. In 2005, while official rates are not available, civil servants of the Ministry for Manpower spoke privately of 300,000 job seekers[7]—an unemployment rate around 25 per cent.

As a symbol of the change of era, the Omani authorities have focused on economic liberalisation in recent years, by giving prominence to a stronger role for private (national and foreign) capital, even if it means the emergence of lasting inflation and the acceptance of a pause in the Omanisation policy in employment. For instance, in order to lure more foreign investment, the new tax system (which came into force in January 2010) cancelled the previous distinction between Gulf-based and foreign companies, by establishing a fixed tax rate on profits of 12 per cent for all companies, both foreign and local, after an initial tax-free exemption of 30,000 riyals of profits. Foreign investment flows doubled between 2005 and 2007, from $540 million in 2003 (2.5 per cent of GDP) to $1.5 billion in 2005 (5.9 per cent of GDP), and more than $3.1 billion in 2007, amounting to 25 per cent of gross fixed capital formation in 2007.[8] In January 2006 Oman signed a bilateral free trade agreement with the US, which came into force in January 2009; many services are excluded from it, in order to preserve the local network of small and medium-sized enterprises, while the Omanisation requirements are still valid, even in the sectors concerned by the agreement. As a consequence, the Omanisation rate in the private sector decreased from 18.8 per cent at the end of 2005 to 15.6 per cent in January 2011, given that the number of active expatriates has more than doubled since the end of 2005 (reaching 969,000 in January 2011), especially because of construction and infrastructure projects.

From this viewpoint, the Omanisation 'national challenge' goes far beyond the employment issue and calls into question the whole economic structure on which Oman has relied for forty years. Most of the decision-making elite are directly involved in business and must avoid questions being asked about the conflict of interest between the nation's general interests they have been supposed to promote (like the Omanisation policy) and the particular interests they have defended as businessmen. Policies of privatisation and economic liberalisation (which mainly benefit already leading actors) and Omanisation of private sector jobs (which directly damages these interests) are reliable indicators of the role that the business elite holds at the moment in the country's balance of power. The priority granted since 2005 to the private sector and to investment in major projects, like Sohar port and tourism infrastructure, to the detriment of openly claimed objectives like Omanisation in employment and control of immigration of workers, clearly indicates on which side the balance has been tilting for several years now.

Foreign policy and security

Omani diplomacy since the end of the Dhofar war is usually labelled as pragmatic and balanced, when it is not being praised for its initiatives in favour of peaceful settlements of disputes in the region. At the same time Oman has never lost its title of 'Britain's oldest friend on the Arabian Peninsula'[9] and, like all major political issues, its foreign policy has directly depended on the ruler and 'his interpretation of the State's national interest'.[10] Indeed Oman's diplomatic guidelines have always been conditioned by the prerequisite of the regime's stability in a troubled regional arena. In this perspective, Oman has displayed under Qaboos a two-sided aim: preserving the country from foreign interference in internal issues, while striving for maintaining stability in the region.

In Omani officials' perception, the two strongest examples of foreign interference in the internal affairs of the country were Communism, until the changes symbolised by the fall of the Berlin Wall, and then political Islamism (especially after the September 2001 attacks). Just as Communism was for a long time used as a label to discredit anyone questioning the current political model, nowadays the 'fight against Islamism'—an enemy all the more 'politically correct' since 2001—is invoked by the regime in order to blame every 'breach of national security'. This double hatred, which Qaboos inherited from his father, for both socialist movements and Islamist ones, explains why, despite the historical connections between Oman and East Africa, Muscat waited until 2005 to establish official diplomatic relations with Tanzania, out of dislike for the latter's 'African socialism' ideology. Similarly, Oman has been reluctant to grant work permits to Nepalese, Palestinians, Syrians or Yemenis because of the obsession with a danger of Oman being infected by socialist ideas.

This fear of foreign interference explains why Oman has often stood up to its powerful Saudi neighbour. The Omani ambition to make the Gulf Cooperation Council something more than a ratification instrument for Saudi policy is often evident. In the religious field, Oman usually starts the month of Ramadan one day later than Riyadh. The *fatwas* fixing the date, which are proclaimed by the highest religious authorities in Oman and are officially justified by longitude, have a clear political meaning. Similarly, Oman has never joined the Organisation of Petroleum Exporting Countries out of a desire to keep its—more symbolic than real—independence over calculation of its energy and budget needs.

But the fluctuating climate since 1970 never led to major disagreements between Muscat and Riyadh, as the latter often granted substantial financial help to Oman and an agreement on delimitation of the common border was signed in 1995.

The other priority of Omani diplomacy under Qaboos has been pragmatism, emphasising geo-strategic realities and the promotion of negotiations instead of showdown and confrontation. Because regional instability has been perceived as a factor feeding internal instability, Oman has regularly taken initiatives in international crises in order to open bilateral negotiations—during the Qatar-Bahrain crisis in 1986, for instance. In this quest for regional stability, Qaboos decided in 1976 to invite the Gulf states' Ministers for Foreign Affairs (including those of Iraq and Iran) to discuss a regional joint security policy. In 1981, at the Abu Dhabi summit which established the GCC, Oman reiterated its proposal for close collaboration between the six countries in security and defence domains, which would be based on a special partnership with the US, but said it was hostile to any transformation of the organisation into an anti-Iran coalition. Less inclined than his GCC counterparts to see in his domestic Shia minority an Iranian Trojan Horse, Qaboos did not break diplomatic relations with Tehran after the Islamic Revolution in 1979, and maintained them during the Iraq-Iran war. He considered that he had no interest in presenting Iran as the sole source of regional tensions, as such an attitude could not lead to any opportunity for long-term stability and mutual cooperation. In the summer of 1987 the Sultan's special representative acted to smooth the way for diplomatic contacts between Iran and Iraq, and later Oman tried to convince Tehran to approve the UN resolution putting an end to the war. Oman also regularly offered itself to the United States as a go-between to help improve US-Iran relations. When Iraq invaded Kuwait in 1990, Oman disapproved of this as a violation of international law, but it proved unwilling to agree to a military solution and did not break its relations with Baghdad. Muscat held the view that the Iraq-Kuwait crisis should be a lesson for the rulers of the region to prevent the emergence of future conflicts by strengthening multilateral links.

This pragmatism was also present throughout Oman's relations with Yemen. In 1982, talks initiated in Kuwait with South Yemen led to diplomatic and economic exchanges from the late 1980s. As soon as a lull occurred in relations with Aden, Oman's first informal contacts took place with the Soviet Union. Not only did the Sultan consider Moscow as a bringer of détente to South Yemen, he also viewed drawing closer to the Soviet Union as an opportunity to strengthen stability in Dhofar and to demonstrate the independence of his diplomacy vis-à-vis the GCC. In 1994, when the civil war broke out in Yemen, the Sultan initiated talks between the two sides in Salalah; then, despite his own convictions, he agreed to host several Southern leaders in exile. For the past ten years, Oman has considered that the proper course for the GCC in the long term is to extend its membership not only to Yemen but also to Iran and Iraq.

As for the Arab-Israeli conflict, just as Oman supported the Israel-Jordan peace treaty, it displayed solidarity with Egypt on the occasion of the 1978 Camp David agreement and refused to participate in the 1979 Arab League summit that expelled Egypt from League membership. In the 1990s Oman, which recognised the existence of a Palestinian leadership only in 1988, began to give financial aid to the Palestinian Authority, but established relations with Israel in 1993. Prime Minister Yitzhak Rabin was a guest in Muscat in December 1994 to discuss regional developments in the aftermath of the Oslo accords. In October 1995 Oman and Israel opened trade offices; however, these closed after the eruption of the September 2000 Intifada. Since then, Omani and Israeli officials have continued to meet, albeit unofficially.

The inescapable corollary of the desire to perpetuate an independent policy towards its regional neighbours has been that Oman has never been able—and has certainly not wanted—to question the strategic and economic privileged partnership with Britain and the US. The British influence in Oman was already responsible for Tariq bin Taimur's resignation from his position of Prime Minister in 1971. Although British forces officially left their Masirah and Salalah bases in 1977 at the end of the Dhofar War, these bases were again used in 2003 for operations by the Anglo-American coalition during the Iraq air offensive. Moreover, the renewal of military co-operation agreements with Britain in 1985 and 1995, and the signature of the US Facilities Access Agreement in 1980 (in exchange for providing Oman with $100 million annually for several years in various forms of security assistance), confirmed Oman's strategic dependency on the US and Britain. Since then, renewals of these agreements and various joint exercises in the desert have continued to underlined the central importance of this relationship. After September

11 2001 the US military presence in Oman dramatically increased from a pre-2001 level of 200 personnel to more than 4,300 personnel in support of Operation Enduring Freedom in Afghanistan. Even if this special relationship grants the ruler very wide freedom of action against recalcitrant social forces in Oman, it causes recurrent criticism from the Sultan's Gulf counterparts and even at home. In 2004 Qaboos called for 'security and stability' in Iraq, but this was all he opted to state in public about the US invasion, even though Omani citizens were regularly demonstrating against it.

Logically, the Omani ruler has maintained an equally long-lasting relationship with two other pro-US Arab countries: Egypt and Jordan. The similar political obstacles King Hussein and Sultan Qaboos had to face certainly brought them close to each other. This personal proximity was unfailing after Hussein's support during the Dhofar War, one illustration being their shared vision of the Israel-Palestine conflict. Likewise, under Hosni Mubarak's presidency, the close relations between Oman and Egypt never faltered, as was demonstrated by Qaboos's frequent visits to Egypt in a private or official capacity and the constant help provided by the Egyptian intelligence services in dismantling opposition cells in Oman since 1994.

One of the major current issues of Omani diplomacy is the Oman-UAE bilateral issue. While mutual relations remained tense after the UAE's independence in 1971, Qaboos and Sheikh Zayed bin Sultan Al-Nahyan, president of the federation, came closer personally during the 1980s. This led to enhanced economic relations and to the first exchange of ambassadors in 1991. Two years later an official of the Omani Ministry for Foreign Affairs declared that 'Oman and the UAE were twin palm trees on the same land',[11] while the Dubai-based *Al-Khaleej* newspaper ran the headline: 'One nation, two states'.[12] An agreement on total delimitation of the border was finally ratified by the rulers in 2002. Since Zayed's death in 2004, however, the political situation became steadily more tense, especially regarding the Al-Ayn and Buraimi shared oasis. While there had never been a physical border between the twin towns, as it was historically the same unit of settlement, the UAE nonetheless erected a fence to mark the border in 2004: UAE officials criticised Muscat's lax policy on migration control, as many illegal immigrants from South Asia were said to be passing illegally through Oman to find jobs in the UAE. This issue led Oman to make Buraimi a special governorate in December 2006, while the area has been given special attention in Oman's seventh Five-Year Plan (2006–10), with ambitious public investment plans as well as tax concessions to the private sector to encourage investment projects. Indeed, the Omani authorities have to face the issue of the strong extraversion of north-western Omani districts towards UAE development poles. This historical obsession of Muscat rulers about the very populated areas of Dhahira and West Batina escaping their allegiance, to the profit of Saudi Arabia half a century ago and the UAE nowadays, is still present under Qaboos. It is not without significance that Qaboos' annual tours across the country in 2005 and 2007 were concentrated on the north-west, where a majority of the active population works in the UAE, and whose local sheikhs are linked to the Sharjah and Dubai families by marriage, family agreements, or business interests. Renewed tensions with Abu Dhabi in January 2011, following Omani official reports linking the UAE to a spy ring allegedly uncovered in Muscat, should not have substantial damaging effects on Oman's relations with its neighbours, as the GCC has set up an aid package worth more than $20 billion to help Oman cope with anti-government protests since March 2011 and Oman has given its full support to the Saudi Arabian and UAE deployment of troops to Bahrain.

In terms of both funding and equipment, the Omani army has, since 1970, been one of the better-trained in the region. Defence and national security forces consume 24 per cent of the state's expenditure, 9 per cent of 2009's GDP—one of the world's highest rates. Foreign personnel have always occupied a leading role in the Omani security forces. Until the Dhofar rebellion ceased to represent a direct threat, in the early 1980s all the high-ranking army officers and the vast majority of holders of sensitive positions in the security, immigration, police and intelligence services were British. The Omanisation of the armed forces, and especially of commanding positions, is now almost total. Qaboos' distrust of individuals not fully dependent on his goodwill is illustrated by the security departments' separation into structures that counterbalance each other, avoiding the concentration of too much power under one authority. Thus, besides the regular army, which itself comes under the Ministry for Defence, several units are directly connected to the Sultan. For example the Royal Guard, which is in charge of protection of the Sultan, the royal family and their property, or the Sultan's Special Forces, conceived on the model of the British SAS, are all elite units attached to the Royal Office.

No command structure, except Qaboos himself, coordinates the action of the regular army and those units.

Future challenges

The post-1970 *état de grâce* experienced by Oman has long since come to an end. For more than ten years now, Oman has faced a series of social and economic challenges which are calling into question the order established in the 1970s. The Omani population is one of the youngest in the world: 35 per cent of nationals are less than fifteen years old and 49 per cent are less than twenty. As these young educated people arrive on the labour market, the economy remains extremely dependent on oil-derived revenue. At the same time, the limited results of the Omanisation policy for private sector jobs cannot hide the slowness of the process of diversifying sources of revenue, which, as described above, remain centred on tourism and the gas industry.

Whereas until the 1970s the only available reference of identity was the tribe or local group, the new state, both as a territory and as a scene of ambitions and encounters, has favoured the promotion of a collective framework of belonging with fellow countrymen whose values may be different. A state of abundance—of material resources, public sector jobs, etc.—combined with the subtle action of the authorities to integrate and co-opt actors into the modern state, has contributed to moderating the tribal politics or *'asabiyya* game.[13] However, the current economic uncertainties have added to the authorities' intransigence about sharing any part of the political decision-making process, and this has led to frustrations and thus an increase in particularistic claims. Oman is crossed by multiple identity and social dividing lines, and these have been made sharper by the economic difficulties, which have restricted room for manoeuvre for the regime and for the oil rent's redistribution. This repolarisation has taken place both in the socio-economic field, through clientelism and favouritism, and on a more symbolic level through competitive bidding in declarations of 'Omaniness' and questioning of loyalty to the nation of other groups. At the heart of this strategy lies the shared purpose of strengthening the political or economic positions of power within the state apparatus and then benefiting from the material and then symbolic dividends (administrative posts, financial advantages, public contracts, etc.) to which these positions give title. These mutual prejudices particularly involve groups that can be described as 'peripheral' in the demographic and historical structure, as they do not belong to the Arab and Ibadi heart of the territory.[14] The paradox—or the explanation—is that these groups have a central position in the socio-political architecture erected by Sultan Qaboos. According to their political and economic role (as in the case of the Shia of Muscat, the 'Swahili' Omanis, etc.) or their military role (as with the Baluchis), they have made themselves allies that the new authority cannot do without.

The 2005 waves of arrests involving personnel of the Education and Islamic Studies colleges of Sultan Qaboos University as well as senior military and civil officials, such as the son-in-law of the Mufti, and leading to sentences on more than seventy people can only be understood in the context of these debates on Oman's national identity. All those arrested belonged to the Ibadi school and most of them held graduate and postgraduate university qualifications. The public prosecution accused them of having been members of a banned secret organisation that was attempting to overthrow the regime by force in order to establish an Ibadi imamate. Presumably a very small minority of the individuals arrested had political objectives. Most of them were certainly not involved in politics, but were motivated rather by religious goals and by the conviction that the promotion of an Omani consensual Islam was a threat to the Ibadi legacy. No connection with networks abroad or with international organisations was demonstrated during the trial. Thus, for the first time since the Imamate fell in the 1950s, Ibadism seemed to have arisen as a rallying reference for political mobilisation, which could openly contradict the legitimacy of the nation state built by and around Sultan Qaboos since 1970. The strong reaction on the part of the regime is therefore not surprising. Within the government itself differences of interpretation were perceptible, between the officials considering that a harsh answer was necessary against these individuals threatening the stability of the country, and those pushing for more tolerance and benevolence. The latter argued that the people arrested were first and foremost 'sons of Oman', and had been animated by laudable intentions, even if the means they employed were condemnable.

Such an event was a sign that growing sectors of society, particularly among the young educated generation, have been reluctant to guarantee the perpetuation of a system in which they feel excluded from political and economic decisions that determine the future of their country. They no longer agree to be politically incapacitated, nor to give up—as their parents did in the name of social welfare—their right to take part in national debates. Mass abstention from the 2007 *Majlis al-Shura* elections, and also the sustained mobilisation of intellectuals and human rights activists since January 2011 (calling for the promulgation of a new constitution leading to a parliamentary monarchy), illustrate the widespread refusal to endorse a consultative body without real power. In order to curb this popular disillusionment with current institutions and appease the demand of political reform, the regime has promised to grant the Council of Oman wider legislative and regulatory powers in the forthcoming October 2011 elections. But the practical implementation of these promises in Oman's Basic Law and in the concrete redistribution of political powers will takes much longer to be realised.

At the same time, a growing proportion of the population has become aware of the symbolic centrality of the person of Qaboos in Omani nation-building; he has been a reassuring paternal figure for forty years. This awareness poses questions for the future, given that Qaboos has no direct descendant has and has not designated an heir. The principles and the procedures of succession to the throne are formalised in the Basic Law. Only Muslim male descendants of Sultan Turki Al Sa'id (r.1871–88) who are legitimate sons of Omani Muslim parents are eligible to become Sultan. When the throne is vacant, the Ruling Family Council is required to meet within three days to designate a successor. If it fails to choose someone, the Defence Council, exclusively composed of security officials who do not belong to the Al Sa'id, will confirm the person designated beforehand by the Sultan in a message addressed to the Ruling Family Council. In 1997, Qaboos announced that he had 'already written down two names, in descending order, and put them in sealed envelopes in two different regions',[15] probably in order to avoid the possibility that a single individual could manipulate the royal will. The central role of the Defence Council, a body external to the royal family, in the procedure of succession raises questions. Up to what point is the royal family ready to be deprived of supreme decision-making by a body composed of members who owe their position to Qaboos only? Moreover, in spite of the precautions taken by the ruler, is not there a risk of seeing contradictory messages emerging, a situation which would involve political confusion? This only makes the succession more delicate because it is more open. Fahd bin Mahmud, whose children's mother is of French origin, does not seem to be able to plan to pass the kingship to one of them after his death. The more probable candidates are thus the three sons of Tariq bin Taimur, who are Qaboos's first cousins: Haitham, As'ad and Shihab.

However, one of Qaboos's major achievements is considered to be the inculcation of the idea of an Omani nation as the horizon of all social and political actors' strategies. Even re-polarisation based on infranational identities (ethno-linguistic groups, regionalism, etc.) observed in the past ten years is not opposed to that of the nation, but complementary to it. While the wealth creation opportunities that the state can offer are dwindling, everyone seeks to consolidate his anchoring into the Omani nation by asserting a greater acknowledgment of its belonging to the 'Oman' entity. Such strategies have been carried out in the name of the Omani nation and within the framework defined by it. They are the proof that both national feeling and the Omani state are fully working as references of thought. If the expression of these particular identities on the public scene represents a threat, it is a threat to the political system itself, to the rules imposed by the regime—a monarchy in the hands of a single man, without counterbalance and without any possibility of alternative expression—and not to the firmly-established framework in which it is held: the nation.

The fundamental question for the regime's future relates to the political-economic 'conflict of interest' at the top levels in the country. Most cabinet members are involved directly or indirectly in business. While this elite has held the levers of power since 1970 and has predominantly benefited from the oil rent, a growing number of voices attack a supposed 'economic resistance to change' and are calling into question the whole economic structure on which Oman has relied since 1970, a structure that few among the elites have a real motivation to reform. As a consequence, the tacit pact that the ruler and these families contracted at the beginning of the former's rule is more difficult to accept for a new generation who are more educated and well aware of the challenges they will have to face.

A strong hint of this shared aspiration for structural change has been evident since January 2011, as most of the big cities (mainly Sohar, Muscat, and Salalah) have been scenes of protests by Omanis, many of whom have organised themselves using websites and online social networks. They have demanded higher salaries, better living conditions, and tougher controls on corruption. Attempts by the ruler to quell protests and to show his supposed benevolence towards the protestors led to an extensive reshuffle of the cabinet, with the removal of long-serving ministers widely perceived as embodying corruption and obstacles to reform (such as 'Ali bin Majid Al-Ma'amari, the Minister for the Royal Office; Ahmed Makki, the Minister for National Economy; and Maqbool Al-Sultan, the Minister for Commerce and Industry). But these reshuffles as well as the promised economic measures have not substantially brought the established authoritarian order into question. They have also done little to remedy the feeling of anxiety among the population concerning the state's perceived lack of long-term vision. Fundamentally the ruler does not seem to be ready to prime a successor by either nominating an heir or transferring some of his powers to a prime minister. Moreover, repression remains an active strategy to choke off dissenting voices, as demonstrated by the recent arrests of journalists and human rights activists, and by the police firing on protestors in Sohar in March 2011.

NOTES

INTRODUCTION

1. This being the original make-up of the GCC, prior to the 2011 suggested inclusion of Morocco and Jordan.

2. For a discussion of rational-legal authority, see Max Weber's tripartite classification of authority in which 'legal authority' is predicated on modern law and bureaucracy. See Max Weber, *The Theory of Social and Economic Organisation* (New York: Free Press, 1997).

3. See for example the discussion of the ruling bargain in the context of Abu Dhabi and Dubai: Christopher M. Davidson, *Abu Dhabi: Oil and Beyond* (London: Hurst & Co., 2009), p. 2; Christopher M. Davidson, *Dubai: The Vulnerability of Success* (London: Hurst & Co., 2008), pp. 4–6.

4. In November 2010 this stance was underscored by the leaking of dozens of US diplomatic cables from Saudi Arabia and the UAE, which reported on their rulers' wishes for military action to be taken against Iran: *The Guardian*, 28 November 2010.

5. For a discussion of the rent-based or 'rentier' state, see Beblawi, Hazem. 'The Rentier State in the Arab World' in Hazem Beblawi and Giacomo Luciani (eds), *The Rentier State* (New York: Croom Helm, 1987).

THE UNITED ARAB EMIRATES

1. For a full discussion see James Onley, *The Arabian Frontier of the British Raj: Merchants, Rulers, and the British in the Nineteenth Century Gulf* (New York: Oxford University Press, 2007).

2. For a full discussion see Christopher M. Davidson, 'Arab Nationalism and British Opposition in Dubai, 1920–1966', *Middle Eastern Studies*, vol. 43, no. 6, 2007.

3. Christopher M. Davidson, *Dubai: The Vulnerability of Success* (London: Hurst & Co., 2008), pp. 39–67.

4. Christopher M. Davidson, *Abu Dhabi: Oil and Beyond* (London: Hurst & Co., 2009), pp. 39–41.
5. Davidson, *Dubai*, pp. 27–8.
6. Ibid., pp. 272–5.
7. Comprising Abu Dhabi, Dubai, Sharjah, Ajman, Umm al-Qawain, and Fujairah.
8. Davidson, *Abu Dhabi*, pp. 56–61.
9. Ibid., pp. 61–9.
10. Gavin Brown, *OPEC and the World Energy Market* (London: Longman, 1998), p. 361.
11. Davidson, *Dubai*, pp. 289–97.
12. For a full discussion see Davidson, *Abu Dhabi*, pp. 61–9.
13. See Najat Abdullah Al-Nabeh, 'United Arab Emirates: Regional and Global Dimensions' (PhD thesis, Claremont Graduate School, 1984).
14. Article 49. See Easa Saleh Al-Gurg, *The Wells of Memory* (London: John Murray, 1998), p. 140; Joseph A. Kéchichian, *Power and Succession in Arab Monarchies: A Reference Guide* (Boulder: Lynne Rienner, 2008), p. 284.
15. Kéchichian, p. 206.
16. Sultan bin Said Al-Mansuri.
17. Muhammad bin Dhaen Al-Hamili.
18. Kéchichian, p. 285.
19. S. Rizvi, 'From Tents to High Rise: Economic Development of the United Arab Emirates', *Middle Eastern Studies*, vol. 29, no. 4, 1993, p. 665.
20. These have normally been over concerns that were already shared by the COM, such as the need for tightening anti-drug legislation and for further modifying the UAE's property laws. Shamma bint Muhammad Al-Nahyan, *Political and Social Security in the United Arab Emirates* (Dubai: 2000), pp. 122–3.
21. Especially in cases where the FNC's views were likely to diverge from the relevant minister's outlook, such as over the price of petrol or the cultural content of terrestrial television. Ibid., p. 121.
22. There have been examples of the FNC's letters to ministers remaining unanswered for several months, and occasions when the FNC has been unable to persuade ministers to attend their sessions and answer basic questions on their policies. Ibid., pp. 178–9, 188.
23. Davidson, *Abu Dhabi*, p. 125.
24. Ibid., pp. 44–9.
25. For a full discussion see Christopher M. Davidson, 'After Shaikh Zayed: The Politics of Succession in Abu Dhabi and the United Arab Emirates', *Middle East Policy*, vol. 13, no. 1, 2006.
26. Davidson. *Abu Dhabi*, pp. 96–105.

27. Ibid.
28. Emirates Towers complex.
29. Davidson, *Dubai*, pp. 137–47.
30. Ibid., pp. 249–55.
31. Ibid., pp. 255–63.
32. *The Guardian*, 27 October 2010.
33. Davidson, *Abu Dhabi*, pp. 69–71.
34. The remainder being oil and liquid fuelled. *Gulf News*, 31 July 2008.
35. Economist Intelligence Unit 2000; Oxford Business Group, 'United Arab Emirates: The Report 2000', pp. 54–5. The second phase of the project will involve an underwater pipeline from Oman to Pakistan.
36. Oxford Business Group, 'Abu Dhabi: The Report 2007'.
37. *Middle East Economic Digest*, 8 January 2010; David A. Stott, 'South Korea's Global Nuclear Ambitions', *The Asia-Pacific Journal*, vol. 12, March 2010.
38. Oxford Business Group, 'Abu Dhabi: The Report 2007', p. 202.
39. Ibid. p. 202; Oxford Business Group, 'United Arab Emirates: The Report 2000', pp. 94–5.
40. Oxford Business Group, 'Abu Dhabi: The Report 2007', p. 212.
41. The latter being built at Ruwais in cooperation with Rio Tinto. *The National*, 24 July 2008.
42. Oxford Business Group, 'Abu Dhabi: The Report 2007', p. 204.
43. *Gulf Today*, 18 July 2007; personal interviews, Abu Dhabi, August 2007.
44. *The National*, 15 March 2010, quoting ADIA's first fund review, published in March 2010.
45. ADIA is based in the new Samsung building on the Corniche, which was completed in 2006.
46. *The Economist*, 17 January 2008; Sovereign Wealth Fund Institute, data for 2008.
47. It was reported in January 2009 that ADIA had lost about $125 billion. *Bloomberg*, 15 January 2009.
48. *Business Week*, 6 June 2008; *Arabian Business*, 8 June 2008.
49. Davidson, *Abu Dhabi*, pp. 73–6.
50. *Middle East Economic Digest*, 6 June 2008.
51. *The National*, 22 July 2008.
52. *The National*, 12 July 2008; personal interviews, Abu Dhabi, April 2008.
53. *The National*, 31 July 2008.
54. *The National*, 9 December 2008.
55. Davidson, *Abu Dhabi*. pp. 82–3.
56. Ibid., pp. 84–5.
57. Dubai Department of Ports and Customs, 'Dubai: Non-oil Foreign Trade' in Dubai Department of Economic Development, *Development Statistics* (Dubai, 2002), p. 109.

58. Davidson, *Dubai*, pp. 114–19.
59. Ibid., pp. 119–28.
60. Ibid., pp. 128–35.
61. Ibid., pp. 135–7.
62. Tamweel and Amlak were merged in November 2008. *Gulf News*, 22 November 2008.
63. *Al-Arabiya*, 24 November 2008.
64. *New York Times*, 20 February 2009.
65. *The National*, 12 October 2008.
66. *Wall Street Journal*, 23 February 2009.
67. *The Guardian*, 25 November 2009.
68. *The Times*, 5 January 2010.
69. *Jane's Defence Weekly*, 7 February 2007; personal interviews, London, May 2008. At least $2.5 billion per annum, but likely to be much more.
70. Personal interviews, Abu Dhabi, April 2008; Abdulkhaleq Abdulla, 'Political Dependency: The Case of the United Arab Emirates' (PhD thesis. Georgetown University, 1985), p. 208.
71. *Jane's Defence Weekly*, 7 February 2007.
72. Oxford Business Group, 'United Arab Emirates: The Report 2000', pp. 58–9.
73. *Jane's Defence Weekly*, 7 February 2007
74. Personal interviews, Dubai, January 2007; *Counterpunch*, 4 December 2004.
75. Many Yemenis and Egyptians serve in the UAE Armed Forces, perhaps over 20,000.
76. Al-Hakeem precision guided missiles.
77. MBDA Corporation.
78. *The National*, 12 August 2008; *Gulf News*, 30 July 2008; *AFP*, 9 September 2008.
79. Manufactured by Northrop Grumman.
80. The submarine system is being set up by Germany's Konigsberg Corporation. Personal interviews, London, May 2008.
81. Oxford Business Group, 'United Arab Emirates: The Report 2000', pp. 58–9. The agreement may involve 75,000 troops being promised to the UAE in the event of an invasion.
82. (*In Arabic*) Nayef Obaid, *The Foreign Policy of the United Arab Emirates* (Abu Dhabi: 2004), pp. 155–6.
83. *Jane's Defence Weekly*, 7 February 2007; personal interviews, London, July 2006. Perhaps over 100 US personnel are stationed at Dhafrah air base.
84. *International Herald Tribune*, 22 June 2005. RQ-4 Global Hawk unmanned reconnaissance aircraft have been stationed there. KC-10 tanker aircraft also use the base to support operations in Afghanistan.
85. Davidson, *Dubai*, pp. 270–1.

86. *Workers World*, 17 May 2007.

87. John Duke Anthony, *Arab States of the Lower Gulf: People, Politics, Petroleum* (Washington, DC: Middle East Institute, 1975), p. 152.

88. Obaid, p. 155.

89. Personal interviews, Kuwait, November 2005; Frauke Heard-Bey, *From Trucial States to United Arab Emirates* (London: Longman, 1996), pp. 388–91.

90. Heard-Bey, pp. 511–13.

91. Donald Hawley, *The Emirates: Witness to a Metamorphosis* (Norwich: Michael Russell, 2007), p. 30.

92. *Jane's Defence Weekly*, 7 February 2007.

93. Amr Moussa.

94. *The National* 28 July 2008; *(in Arabic)* Khalid Mutawwa, *The Arabic Falcon* (Sharjah, 2005), p. 99.

95. Oxford Business Group, 'Abu Dhabi: The Report 2007', p. 25.

96. *Reuters*, 11 May 2007; *BBC News*, 13 May 2007.

97. In contrast, Jordan's soldiers are restricted to base camp security duties. *BBC News Online*, 28 March 2008.

98. *Gulf News*, 18 July 2008.

99. Abdullah Ibrahim Al-Shehhi (the UAE's former Ambassador to India), *AFP*, 6 July 2008.

100. *The National*, 8 August 2008.

101. Hendrik Van der Meulen, 'The Role of Tribal and Kinship Ties in the Politics of the United Arab Emirates' (PhD thesis, Fletcher School of Law and Diplomacy, 1997), p. 238.

102. Oxford Business Group, 'United Arab Emirates: The Report 2000', pp. 98–9.

103. *Telegraph*, 5 August 2008.

104. Oxford Business Group, 'Abu Dhabi: The Report 2007', p. 51.

105. *The National*, 27 July 2008.

106. *Gulf News*, 8 December 2006.

107. *Gulf News*, 28 July 2008.

108. *Oxford Analytica*, February 2007.

109. *The National*, 3 June 2008.

110. *Masdar Research Journal* (vol. 5, no. 2, 2007).

111. Nasser bin Ghaith was a professor at the UAE Armed Forces College and a lecturer in economics at the Abu Dhabi branch of Paris-I (Sorbonne) University.

112. Ahmed bin Mansour Al-Shehhi.

113. Growth rates for the UAE national population are estimated to be between 4.5 and 6 per cent. A 2005 report by the National Human Resource Devel-

opment and Employment Authority (Tanmia) estimated it to be 5.6 per cent.

114. In 2002 it was estimated that 85 per cent of the UAE's population was urbanised, and it was predicted that by 2030 over 96 per cent would be urbanised. *Emirates News Agency* (WAM), 9 April 2002.

115. In 2005 the National Human Resource Development and Employment Authority (Tanmia) estimated that female participation in the labour force had risen to over 16 per cent. This compares with just 5 per cent in 1995.

116. Personal interviews with employees of the Dubai Chamber of Commerce and Industry, Dubai, February 2006.

117. For a discussion of anthropological reality in the region see Olivier Roy, *The Politics of Chaos in the Middle East* (London: Hurst & Co., 2008), p. 43.

118. Abu Dhabi Law 14 of 2008 was confirmed by *Emirates News Agency* (WAM), 20 December 2008.

119. Article 13.

120. Andrew Wheatcroft, *With United Strength: Sheikh Zayed bin Sultan Al-Nahyan, the Leader and the Nation* (Abu Dhabi: Emirates Centre for Strategic Studies and Research, 2005), p. 202.

121. Ibid.

122. Oxford Business Group, 'Abu Dhabi: The Report 2007', p. 35.

123. *The National*, 28 July 2008.

124. It is estimated that over the past decade the four poorest emirates have only accounted for between 6 and 15 per cent of the UAE's GDP. Crown Prince Court Department of Research and Studies, 'Statistical Book' (Abu Dhabi: 1996), p. 54; personal interviews, Dubai, January 2007.

125. The Shihuh tribe.

BAHRAIN

1. The word 'Bahrain' was used in the past to refer to the eastern coastline of Saudi Arabia as well as the modern-day country of Bahrain.

2. These are held in Exeter University.

3. Reprinted in *Ruling Families of Arabia: the Al-Khalifa* (London: Archive Editions, 2008), p. 136.

4. Charles Belgrave, *Personal Column* (a heavily edited version of his diary).

5. In a 1952 feature on Charles Belgrave, *Life Magazine* in the US described Major Daly's views thus: 'Under treaties between Britain and the Persian Gulf sheikhdoms, [Daly] was one of several men designated to help the sheikhs with foreign affairs. He had no authority to meddle in internal troubles, a limitation Daly found intolerable because Bahrain had almost no foreign relations and almost nothing but trouble internally.' James Bell, 'He Said Forward! To The Backward', *Life Magazine*, 17 November 1952.

6. A detailed account can be found in Mahdi Abdalla Al-Tajir, *Bahrain, 1920–1945: Britain, the Sheikh, and the Administration* (London: Croom Helm, 1987).

7. Analysed in detail in James Onley, *The Arabian Frontier of the British Raj: Merchants, Rulers, and the British in the Nineteenth Century Gulf* (New York: Oxford University Press, 2007).

8. Nelida Fuccaro, *Histories of City and State in the Persian Gulf: Manama since 1800* (Cambridge University Press, 2009)

9. Al-Tajir, p. 173.

10. Falah Al-Mdaires, 'Shi'ism and Political Protest in Bahrain', *Digest of Middle East Studies*, vol. 11, no. 1, 2002.

11. Fuccaro, pp. 178–80.

12. F. Khuri, *Tribe and State in Bahrain: The Transition of Social and Political Authority in an Arab State* (University of Chicago Press, 1981).

13. Miriam Joyce, 'The Bahraini Three on St Helena: 1956–1961', *Middle East Journal*, vol. 54, no. 4, 2000.

14. Fuccaro, p. 174.

15. Al-Tajir, p. 178.

16. David Winkler, *Amirs, Admirals, and Desert Sailors* (Annapolis: Naval Institute Press, 2007), p. 54.

17. The agreement was officially terminated in 1973 as a result of the Arab-Israeli war that year, but the government quietly allowed the termination notice to lapse, and the declared eviction did not take place.

18. Three decades later Al-Alawi is the Bahraini government's Housing Minister, while Al-Jamri became the editor of a newspaper in Bahrain and Al-Shehabi remains in exile in London.

19. Winkler, p. 122.

20. See Munira Fakhro, 'The Uprising in Bahrain: An Assessment' in G. Sick and L. Potter (eds), *The Persian Gulf at the Turn of the Millennium* (New York: St. Martins Press, 1997); Louay Bahry, 'The Opposition in Bahrain: A Bellwether for the Gulf?', *Middle East Policy*, vol. 5, no. 2, 1997; Fred Lawson, 'Repertoires of Contention in Contemporary Bahrain' in Quintan Wiktorowicz (ed.), *Islamic Activism; a Social Movement Theory Approach* (Bloomington: Indiana University Press, 2004).

21. Lawson, p. 98.

22. This came three weeks before the Khobar Towers bombing in Saudi Arabia, which was also blamed on a Gulf offshoot of Hezbollah.

23. See *Gulf News*, 21 October 2010.

24. The National Action Charter on Democratic Life states that 'It is in the interest of the state of Bahrain to adopt a bicameral system whereby the legislature will consist of two chambers, namely one that is constituted through free, direct elections whose mandate will be to enact laws, and a second one that would have people with experience and expertise who would give advice

as necessary'. The full text can be obtained from the UNDP's Programme on Governance in the Arab Region, via http://www.pogar.org/publications/other/constitutions/bahrain-charter-01e.pdf

25. Mansoor Jamri, 'Shia and the State in Bahrain: Integration and Tension', *Alternative Politics*, vol. 2, no. 1, 2010.

26. Steve Monroe, 'Salafis in Parliament: Party Politics and Democratic Attitudes in the Gulf', unpublished paper delivered at the Gulf Research Meeting, University of Cambridge, July 2010.

27. Author interview, Manama, September 2010.

28. The role of these clubs is analysed in detail in Emile Nakhleh, *Bahrain: Political Development in a Modernising Society* (Lexington: Lexington Books, 1976) and Khuri.

29. The Bahrain Centre for Human Rights has questioned why such international finance would be necessary for a fairly low-tech forum of a type that typically costs around $200 per year to register and is moderated by volunteers. Meanwhile, Abdulemam was freed for less than a month in early 2011, then rearrested in the March crackdown.

30. Central Bank of Bahrain, 'Financial Sector Fact Sheet, July 2010'. Available from Central Bank of Bahrain website: http://www.cbb.gov.bh

31. Bahrain Economic Development Board, September 2010. http://www.bahrainedb.com/bahrain-why.aspx

32. It has also had an impact on the standard of living of the middle classes, many of whom are accustomed to having domestic servants.

33. Detailed first-hand accounts can be found in Andrew Gardner, *City of Strangers: Gulf Migration and the Indian Community in Bahrain* (Ithaca, NY: Cornell University Press, 2010).

34. Central Bank of Bahrain, 'Economic Indicators', March 2010.

35. S. Rizvi, 'Shi'ism in Bahrain: Marja'iyya and Politics', *Orient* IV, 2009.

36. US State Department, 'Human Rights Report: Bahrain', 2008. See http://www.state.gov/g/drl/rls/hrrpt/2008/nea/119113.htm

SAUDI ARABIA

1. Madawi Al-Rasheed, *Contesting the Saudi State: Islamic Voices From a New Generation* (Cambridge University Press, 2007), p. 2.

2. Guido Steinberg, 'The Wahhabi Ulama and the Saudi State: 1745 to the Present' in Paul Aarts and Gerd Nonneman (eds), *Saudi Arabia in the Balance: Political Economy, Society, Foreign Affairs* (London: Hurst & Co., 2005), pp. 17–19, 24.

3. Adherents of the more conservative trend within Sunni Islam which hearkens for a return to the purity of Islam's early years, particularly strong in the Najdi region of the Arabian Peninsula.

4. Mai Yamani, 'The Two Faces of Saudi Arabia', *Survival*, vol. 50, no. 1, 2008, p. 144.

5. Gwenn Okruhlik, 'Rentier Wealth, Unruly Law, and the Rise of Opposition: the Political Economy of Oil States', *Comparative Politics*, vol. 31, no. 3, 1999, pp. 297–8.

6. Tim Niblock, with Monica Malik, *Political Economy of Saudi Arabia* (London: Routledge, 2007), p. 35.

7. Abd Al-Aziz ibn 'Abd Allah Al-Khwaiter, 'King Abdul Aziz: His Style of Administration' in Fahd Al-Semmari (ed.), *History of the Arabian Peninsula* (London: I.B. Tauris, 2009), p. 202.

8. Simon Bromley, *Rethinking Middle East Politics: State Formation and Development* (Cambridge: Polity Press, 1994), pp. 144–5.

9. Hazem Beblawi, 'The Rentier State in the Arab World' in Giacomo Luciani (ed.), *The Arab State* (London: Routledge, 1990), pp. 87–9.

10. Giacomo Luciani, 'Allocation vs Production States: A Theoretical Framework' in Luciani (ed.), *The Arab State*, pp. 71–2.

11. Ibid., p. 76.

12. Niblock with Malik, *Political Economy of Saudi Arabia*, p. 56, 75, 91.

13. Steffen Hertog, *Princes, Brokers, and Bureaucrats: Oil and the State in Saudi Arabia* (Ithaca, NY: Cornell University Press, 2010), pp. 28–9.

14. Madawi Al-Rasheed, 'Circles of Power: Royals and Society in Saudi Arabia' in Aarts and Nonneman (eds.), *Saudi Arabia in the Balance*, pp. 199–208.

15. Okruhlik, 'Rentier Wealth, Unruly Law, and the Rise of Opposition', pp. 297–8.

16. Robert Vitalis, *America's Kingdom: Mythmaking on the Saudi Oil Frontier* (Stanford University Press, 2007), pp. 218–24.

17. Onn Winckler, 'Labor and Liberalization: The Decline of the GCC Rentier System' in Joshua Teitelbaum (ed.), *Political Liberalization in the Persian Gulf* (London: Hurst & Co., 2009), pp. 65–6.

18. Ibid., p. 68.

19. Roger Hardy, 'Ambivalent Ally: Saudi Arabia and the War on Terror' in Madawi Al-Rasheed (ed.), *Kingdom Without Borders: Saudi Arabia's Political, Religious and Media Frontiers* (London: Hurst & Co., 2008), p. 101.

20. Okruhlik, 'Rentier Wealth, Unruly Law, and the Rise of Opposition', p. 299.

21. For the seminal work on inter-Arab divisions, see Malcolm Kerr, *The Arab Cold War, 1956–1964: A Study of Ideology in Politics* (Oxford University Press, 1965).

22. Yaroslav Trofimov, *The Siege of Mecca: The Forgotten Uprising in Islam's Holiest Shrine and the Birth of al-Qaeda* (London: Penguin, 2008), p. 252.

23. Toby Craig Jones, 'Rebellion on the Saudi Periphery: Modernity, Marginalization, and the Shi'a Uprising of 1979', *International Journal of Middle East Studies*, vol. 38, no. 2, 2006, p. 219.

24. Mahan Abedin, 'Saudi Shia Wait and See as New Light Falls on Islam's Old Divide' in Joshua Craze, and Mark Huband (eds), *The Kingdom: Saudi Arabia and the Challenge of the 21ˢᵗ Century* (London: Hurst & Co., 2010), p. 68.

25. Benjamin Schwarz, 'America's Struggle Against the Wahhabi/Neo-Salafi Movement', *Orbis*, vol. 51, no. 1, 2007, p. 116.

26. Fred Halliday, *The Middle East in International Relations: Power, Politics and Ideology* (Cambridge University Press, 2005), p. 150.

27. *The Economist*, 15 July 2010.

28. Marina Ottaway, 'Evaluating Middle East Reform: How Do We Know When It Is Significant?' *Carnegie Paper*, no. 56 (Washington, DC: Carnegie Endowment for International Peace, 2005), p. 6.

29. Okruhlik, 'Rentier Wealth, Unruly Law, and the Rise of Opposition', pp. 302–5.

30. Gregory Gause, *Oil Monarchies: Domestic and Security Challenges in the Arab Gulf States* (New York: Council on Foreign Relations Press, 1994), pp. 106–7.

31. Giacomo Luciani, 'Democracy vs Shura in the age of the Internet' in Abdulhadi Khalaf and Giacomo Luciani (eds), *Constitutional Reform and Political Participation in the Gulf* (Dubai: Gulf Research Centre, 2006), p. 278.

32. Ibid.

33. Gerd Nonneman, 'Security and Inclusion: Regimes Responses to Domestic Challenges in the Gulf' in Sean McKnight, Neil Partrick and Francis Toase (eds), *Gulf Security: Opportunities and Challenges for the New Generation* (London: RUSI Whitehall Paper Series 51, 2000), pp. 108–9.

34. Anoushivaran Ehteshami and Steven Wright, 'Political Change in the Arab Oil Monarchies: From Liberalisation to Enfranchisement', *International Affairs*, vol. 83, no. 5, 2007, pp. 914–16.

35. Yamani, *Two Faces of Saudi Arabia*, p. 145.

36. Ana Echague and Edward Burke, 'Strong Foundations? The Imperatives for Reform in Saudi Arabia' (Madrid: FRIDE Working Paper 84, 2009), p. 5.

37. Abdullah Ansary, 'Judicial Reform and the Principle of Independence', *Arab Reform Bulletin*, May 2009.

38. Kristian Ulrichsen, *Insecure Gulf: The Challenge of Transition and the End of Certainty* (London: Hurst & Co., 2011).

39. Vincent Romani, 'The Politics of Higher Education in the Middle East: Problems and Prospects', *Middle East Brief*, no. 36, May 2009, p. 1.

40. Zvika Krieger, 'Reforms in Higher Education Raise Questions', *Arab Reform Bulletin*, December 2007.

41. Echague and Burke, 'Strong Foundations', p. 5.

42. Ibid., p. 4.

43. *The Economist*, 15 July 2010.

44. Eleanor Gillespie (ed.), 'Politics, Succession and Risk in Saudi Arabia', *Gulf States Newsletter Special Report*, January 2010, p. 27.

45. Simon Henderson, 'Bandar is Back', *Foreign Policy*, 21 October 2010.

46. Gillespie, *Politics, Succession and Risk*, p. 26.

47. Ulrichsen, *Insecure Gulf*.

48. Echague and Burke, 'Strong Foundations', p. 4.

49. Gillespie, *Politics, Succession and Risk*, pp. 27–8.

50. CIA World Factbook, 'Saudi Arabia: Economy Overview', updated 24 June 2010.

51. Halliday, *Middle East in International Relations*, p. 271.

52. BP *Statistical Review of World Energy*, June 2010, p. 6.

53. Anoushivaran Ehteshami, *Globalization and Geopolitics in the Middle East: Old Games, New Rules* (London: Routledge, 2007), p. 110.

54. Gary Donn and Yahya Al-Manthri, *Globalisation and Higher Education in the Arab Gulf States* (Oxford: Symposium Books, 2010), p. 37.

55. CIA World Factbook, 'Saudi Arabia: People Overview', updated 24 June 2010.

56. Paul Dresch, 'Societies, Identities and Global Issues' in Paul Dresch and James Piscatori (eds), *Monarchies and Nations: Globalisation and Identity in the Arab States of the Gulf* (London: I.B. Tauris, 2005), p. 16.

57. Donn and Al-Manthri, *Globalisation and Higher Education*, p. 37.

58. Niblock with Malik, *Political Economy of Saudi Arabia*, pp. 57–8.

59. Ibid., pp. 181–5.

60. Ibid., pp. 91, 140, 199.

61. Ibid., p. 198.

62. http://www.kingabdullahcity.com/en/Home/index.html

63. Rodney Wilson, 'Economic Governance and Reform in Saudi Arabia' in Anoushivaran Ehteshami, and Steven Wright (eds), *Reform in the Middle East Oil Monarchies* (Reading: Ithaca Press, 2008), pp. 137, 144.

64. Ibrahim Saif, 'The Oil Boom in the GCC Countries, 2002–2008: Old Challenges, Changing Dynamics' (Washington, DC: Carnegie Endowment for International Peace, 2009), p. 14.

65. *Saudi Gazette*, 25 August 2009.

66. Giacomo Luciani, 'From Private Sector to National Bourgeoisie: Saudi Arabian Business' in Aarts and Nonneman (eds), *Saudi Arabia in the Balance*, p. 144.

67. Gerd Nonneman, 'Political Reform in the Gulf Monarchies: From Liberalization to Democratization? A Comparative Perspective' in Ehteshami and Wright (eds), *Oil Monarchies*, pp. 19, 41.

68. Luciani, 'Private Sector to National Bourgeoisie', pp. 180–81.

69. Chatham House. 'The Gulf as a Global Financial Centre: Growing Oppor-

tunities and International Influence' (London: Chatham House Report, 2008), p. 48.

70. *The Peninsula*, 23 June 2009.

71. *The Gulf: Business News and Analysis*, 19 September 2009, pp. 16–19.

72. Wilson, 'Economic Governance and Reform', p. 137.

73. Jean-François Seznec, 'The Gulf Sovereign Wealth Funds: Myths and Reality', *Middle East Policy*, vol. 15, no. 2, 2008, p. 103.

74. Steffen Hertog, 'Gulf Countries: The Current Crisis and Lessons of the 1980s', *Arab Reform Bulletin*, July 2009.

75. Kristian Ulrichsen, 'Gulf States' Perspectives on Global Governance', *Global Policy*, vol. 2, no. 1, 2011.

76. *Saudi Gazette*, 5 November 2010.

77. *New York Times*, 19 March 2010.

78. Ben Simpfendorfer, *The New Silk Road: How a Rising Arab World is Turning Away From the West and Rediscovering China* (Basingstoke: Palgrave Macmillan, 2009), pp. 30–32.

79. Steve Yetiv and Chunlong Lu, 'China, Global Energy and the Middle East', *Middle East Journal*, vol. 61, no. 2, 2007, pp. 207–8.

80. Mahmoud Ghafouri, 'China's Policy in the Persian Gulf', *Middle East Policy*, vol. 16, no. 2, 2009, p. 88.

81. Shahram Chubin, 'Iran's Power in Context', *Survival*, vol. 51, no. 1, 2009, p. 165.

82. Gerd Nonneman, 'Determinants and Patterns of Saudi Foreign Policy: "Omnibalancing" and "Relative Autonomy" in Multiple Environments' in Aarts and Nonneman (eds), *Saudi Arabia in the Balance*, pp. 350–51.

83. Gregory Gause, *The International Relations of the Persian Gulf* (Cambridge University Press, 2010), p. 9.

84. J.E. Peterson, *Saudi Arabia and the Illusion of Security* (Oxford University Press, 2002), pp. 32–3.

85. Quoted in Thomas Hegghammer, 'Saudi Militants in Iraq: Backgrounds and Recruitment Patterns', Norwegian Defence Research Establishment (FFI) report, February 2007, p. 9.

86. Henner Furtig, 'Conflict and Cooperation in the Persian Gulf: The Interregional Order and US Policy', *Middle East Journal*, vol. 61, no. 4, 2007, p. 628.

87. Anthony Cordesman, *Saudi Arabia: Guarding the Desert Kingdom* (Boulder: Westview Press, 1997), pp. 113–14.

88. Gause, *Oil Monarchies*, p. 90.

89. Laurence Louer, *Transnational Shia Politics: Religious and Political Networks in the Gulf* (London: Hurst & Co., 2008), pp. 297–8.

90. Jones, *Rebellion on the Saudi Periphery*, p. 213.

91. Abdulaziz Sager, 'The GCC States and the Situation in Iraq' (Dubai: Gulf Research Centre, July 2008).

92. Halliday, *The Middle East in International Relations*, p. 150.
93. Bruce Riedel and Bilal Y. Saab, 'Al Qaeda's Third Front: Saudi Arabia', *The Washington Quarterly*, vol. 31, no. 2, 2008, p. 44.
94. Thomas Hegghammer, 'Islamist Violence and Regime Stability in Saudi Arabia', *International Affairs*, vol. 84, no. 4, 2008, p. 708.
95. Schwarz, *America's Struggle*, p. 124; Furtig, *Conflict and Cooperation*, p. 638.
96. Christian Koch, 'Gulf States Plan for Day that Oil Runs Dry', *Jane's Intelligence Review*, December 2006, p. 22.
97. Christopher Blanchard and Alfred Prados, 'Saudi Arabia: Terrorist Financing Issues' in *Congressional Research Service Reports for Congress*, Washington, DC, 14 September 2007, p. 2.
98. Kristian Coates Ulrichsen, 'Bahrain: Evolution or Revolution?' in *OpenDemocracy*, 1 March 2011, www.opendemocracy.net.
99. 'Affordable Homes Become as Important as Democracy in Saudi Arabia', *Gulf States Newsletter*, vol. 35, no. 898, 8 April 2011, p. 11.
100. *The National*, 11 March 2011.
101. 'Eastern Province Shia Take to the Streets in Support of Bahrain and Domestic Reform', *Gulf States Newsletter*, Special Bulletin, 18 March 2011.
102. Salman Al-Rashid, 'What Next After King Abdullah?', *Foreign Policy*, 14 April 2011.
103. Kristian Coates Ulrichsen, 'Gulf States: Studious Silence Falls on Arab Spring' in *OpenDemocracy*, 25 April 2011, www.opendemocracy.net.
104. Gregory Gause, *Saudi-Yemeni Relations: Domestic Structures and Foreign Influence* (London: Hurst & Co., 1990).
105. Nonneman, *Security and Inclusion*, pp. 108–9.
106. Saif, *Oil Boom*, pp. 6–7.

KUWAIT

1. For the most comprehensive account of Kuwait's earliest days see Ahmed Mustafa Abu-Hakima, *The Modern History of Kuwait, 1750–1965* (London: Luzac, 1983).
2. Jacqueline S. Ismael, *Kuwait: Dependency and Class in a Rentier State*, 2nd. edn. (Miami: University Press of Florida, 1993), p. 20.
3. Ahmed Abu-Hakima, arguably the outstanding expert on the history of Eastern Arabia, believes that 1752 is the correct date. Alan Rush, the author of an exhaustive study of the Al-Sabah, agrees. However, Jacqueline Ismail quotes Khazal stating that by 1716 politics, trade, and maritime security had been divided among the key tribes. See Abu-Hakima, *The Modern History of Kuwait*, p. 23.
4. Jill Crystal, *Kuwait: The Transformation of an Oil State* (Boulder, CO and Oxford: Westview Press, 1992), p. 9.

5. For an overview of Kuwait during the First World War see Michael S. Casey, Frank W. Thackeray and John E. Findling, *The History of Kuwait* (Westport, CT: Greenwood; Oxford: Harcourt Education [distributor], 2007), pp. 52–5.

6. Jill Crystal, *Oil and Politics in the Gulf: Rulers and Merchants in Kuwait and Qatar* (Cambridge University Press, 1995), p. 23.

7. For the best explanation and analysis of these attacks see Lori Plotkin Boghardt, *Kuwait Amid War, Peace and Revolution: 1979–1991 and New Challenges* (Basingstoke: Palgrave Macmillan, 2006), pp. 70–102.

8. Ibid., p. 53.

9. Coincidentally, Iraq charged that Kuwait had cost Iraq $14 billion in lost earnings by over-producing; very close to the amount of funding that Kuwait gave Iraq during the war.

10. Ismael, *Kuwait: Dependency and Class in a Rentier State*, p. 174.

11. For a thorough assessment of the coalition actions see Majid Khadduri and Edmund Ghareeb, *War in the Gulf, 1990–91: The Iraq-Kuwait Conflict and Its Implications* (New York and Oxford: Oxford University Press, 1997), pp. 169–79.

12. Ismael, *Kuwait: Dependency and Class in a Rentier State*, p. 175.; Crystal, *Kuwait: The Transformation of an Oil State*, p. 162.

13. David Pollock, 'Actions, Not Just Attitudes: A New Way to Assess U.S.-Arab Relations', *Washington Institute for Near East Policy Papers*, 11 March 2010; base 'fact' from 'Background Note: Kuwait', US State Department http://www.state.gov/r/pa/ei/bgn/35876.htm.

14. Mary Ann Tetreault, 'Autonomy, Necessity, and the Small State: Ruling Kuwait in the Twentieth Century', *International Organization* 45, no. 4, 1991, p. 574.

15. Alan de Lacy Rush, *Al-Sabah: History & Genealogy of Kuwait's Ruling Family, 1752–1987* (London: Ithaca, 1987), p. 52. Quoted in Tetreault, 'Autonomy, Necessity, and the Small State: Ruling Kuwait in the Twentieth Century', p. 574.

16. On the 1921 Council see Ismael, *Kuwait: Dependency and Class in a Rentier State*, pp. 71–3.

17. Crystal, *Oil and Politics in the Gulf: Rulers and Merchants in Kuwait and Qatar*, p. 81.

18. See Peter Mansfield, *Kuwait: Vanguard of the Gulf* (London: Hutchinson, 1990), pp. 37–53.

19. See Jill Crystal, 'Coalitions in Oil Monarchies: Kuwait and Qatar', *Comparative Politics* 21, no. 4, 1989.

20. Crystal, *Kuwait: The Transformation of an Oil State*, p. 95.

21. Ismael, *Kuwait: Dependency and Class in a Rentier State*, p. 82.

22. See Abdo I. Baaklini, 'Legislatures in the Gulf Area: The Experience of Kuwait, 1961–1976', *International Journal of Middle East Studies* vol. 14, no. 3, 1982.

23. Shafeeq Ghabra, 'Voluntary Associations in Kuwait: The Foundation of a New System?', *Middle East Journal* 45, no. 2 (1991), p. 206.

24. Crystal, *Oil and Politics in the Gulf: Rulers and Merchants in Kuwait and Qatar*, p. 88.

25. He did not call for elections within the set time frame, thus its dissolution was unconstitutional.

26. Crystal, *Oil and Politics in the Gulf: Rulers and Merchants in Kuwait and Qatar*, p. 97.

27. Mary Ann Tetreault, *Stories of Democracy: Politics and Society in Contemporary Kuwait* (New York and Chichester: Columbia University Press, 2000), p. 110. Crystal, *Oil and Politics in the Gulf: Rulers and Merchants in Kuwait and Qatar*, p. 103.

28. Ismael, *Kuwait: Dependency and Class in a Rentier State*, p. 178.

29. References to secularists, conservatives, and Islamists are necessarily broad terms designed to simplify complex group structures.

30. Ismael, *Kuwait: Dependency and Class in a Rentier State*, p. 183.

31. Here three elite managers were prosecuted; their sentences ranged from fifteen to forty-five years in jail and they had to collectively pay back $130 million. Sheikh Ali Al-Khalifah Al-Athbi Al-Sabah, the minister involved, resorted to legal technicalities to save himself from a public trial.

32. Mary Ann Tetreault, Katherine Meyer and Helen Rizzo, 'Women's Rights in the Middle East: A Longitudinal Study of Kuwait', *International Political Sociology* vol. 3, Issue 2 (2009), p. 229.

33. Oxford Business Group, 'The Report: Kuwait 2007', *County Intelligence Report* (Oxford Business Group, 2010).

34. Nathan J. Brown, 'Moving out of Kuwait's Political Impasse', *Web Commentary* (Washington, DC: Carnegie Endowment for International Peace, June 2009).

35. Oxford Business Group, 'The Report: Kuwait 2007', p. 15.

36. Michael Herb, 'Emirs and Parliaments in the Gulf', *Journal of Democracy* vol. 13, no. 4 (October 2002), p. 44.

37. Asil merchants are the 'grand families' of the merchant world and include the Al-Sagr, Al-Nisf, Al-Ghanim, Al-Hamad, Al-Mudhaf, Al-Khalid, Al-Khourafi, and Al-Marzouq: Pete W. Moore, *Doing Business in the Middle East: Politics and Economic Crisis in Jordan and Kuwait* (Cambridge University Press, 2004), p. 32.

38. AGOC became British Petroleum (BP) in 1954.

39. Crystal, *Kuwait: The Transformation of an Oil State*, p. 38.

40. Ibid., p. 39.

41. See M.W. Khouja and P.G. Sadler, *The Economy of Kuwait:Development and Role in International Finance* (London: Macmillan, 1979), p. 25.

42. Crystal, *Oil and Politics in the Gulf:Rulers and Merchants in Kuwait and Qatar*, p. 74.

43. Merchants (or, indeed, other Kuwaitis) could now sit back and wait for foreign companies to come in, and take their percentage whilst potentially doing nothing. Moore, *Doing Business in the Middle East: Politics and Economic Crisis in Jordan and Kuwait*, p. 45.

44. Farouk El Kharouf, Sulayman Al Qudsi and Shifa Obeid, 'The Gulf Cooperation Council Sovereign Wealth Funds: Are They Instruments for Economic Diversification or Political Tools?' *Asian Economic Papers*, vol. 9, no. 1 (2010), p. 125.

45. Khouja and Sadler, *The Economy of Kuwait: Development and Role in International Finance*, p. 36.

46. Muhammad Sani Salisu and Semen Y. Yagudin, 'Investments and Vertical Integration—Catalyst for Developments in the Oil Industry of an Emerging Market. The Case of Refining in Kuwait', *Oil and Gas Business* (2007), p. 3.

47. Crystal, *Kuwait: The Transformation of an Oil State*, p. 52.

48. Ibid.

49. Ibid., p. 45.

50. Mary Ann Tetreault, *The Kuwait Petroleum Corporation and the Economics of the New World Order* (Westport, CT: Quorum Books, 1995), pp. 50–75.

51. For a thorough examination of Kuwait's vertical integration initiatives see Ibid.

52. Moore, *Doing Business in the Middle East: Politics and Economic Crisis in Jordan and Kuwait*, p. 85.

53. Beblawi quoted in ibid., p. 87.

54. Ibid., p. 89.

55. Ibid., p. 125.

56. Ibid.

57. Ismael, *Kuwait: Dependency and Class in a Rentier State*, p. 174.

58. 'Kuwait Country Report', in *EIU Country Report* (London: Economist Intelligence Unit, 1st Quarter 1997), p. 18.

59. Ibid., p. 12.

60. Figures from UNCTAD.

61. Khadduri and Ghareeb, *War in the Gulf, 1990–91: The Iraq-Kuwait Conflict and Its Implications*, pp. 9–10.

62. A combination of Byzantine Ottoman bureaucracy and the local governor's strenuous objections prevented his assumption of the title. Frederick F. Ans-

combe, *The Ottoman Gulf: The Creation of Kuwait, Saudi Arabia, and Qatar* (New York and Chichester: Columbia University Press, 1997), pp. 94–9.

63. Crystal, *Kuwait: The Transformation of an Oil State*, p. 135.
64. Ibid.
65. Ibid., p. 133.
66. Tetreault, *The Kuwait Petroleum Corporation and the Economics of the New World Order*, p. 123.
67. Crystal, *Oil and Politics in the Gulf: Rulers and Merchants in Kuwait and Qatar*, p. 164.
68. Ibid., p. 173.
69. 'Public Sector Wages Rise by 22% Annually', *Kuwait Times*, 12 July 2010.
70. 'Kuwait Country Report', in *EIU Country Report* (London: Economist Intelligence Unit, 4th Quarter 1996), p. 11.
71. Herb, 'Emirs and Parliaments in the Gulf', p. 44.

QATAR

1. H. Rahman, *The Emergence of Qatar: the Turbulent Years, 1627–1916* (London: Kegan Paul, 2005), p. 17.
2. Ibid., p. 18.
3. James Onley 'The Politics of Protection in the Gulf: The Arab Rulers and the British Resident in the Nineteenth Century', *New Arabian Studies*, vol. 6, 2004, p. 60.
4. Ibid., p. 44.
5. Ibid., p. 46.
6. H. Rahman, *The Emergence of Qatar*, pp. 42–8.
7. Ibid.
8. W. Palgrave. *Narrative of a Year's Journey through Central and Eastern Arabia (1862–63)* (London: Macmillan, 1865), pp. 231–2.
9. Y. Abdulla, *A Study of Qatari-British Relations, 1914–1945* (Doha: Orient Publishing, 1981), p. 19.
10. John G. Lorimer, *Gazetteer of the Persian Gulf, Oman and Central Arabia.* (London: Gregg International, 1970), pp. 892–4.
11. 'Agreement of the Chief of El-Kutr engaging not to commit any breech of the maritime peace—1868' in C. Aitchison, *Treaties and Engagements Relating to Arabia and the Persian Gulf* (Gerrards Cross, UK: Archive Editions, 1987), p. 255.
12. H. Rahman, *The Emergence of Qatar*, pp. 99–100.
13. Christopher M. Davidson. *Dubai: the Vulnerability of Success* (London: Hurst & Co., 2008), pp. 60–65.
14. Ibid., p. 62.

15. Anoushivaran Ehteshami and Steven Wright, 'Political Change in the Arab Oil Monarchies: from Liberalization to Enfranchisement', *International Affairs*, vol. 83, no. 5, 2007. pp. 918–22.

16. Louay Bahry. 'Elections in Qatar: A Window of Democracy Opens in the Gulf', *Middle East Policy*, vol. 6, no. 4, 1999. pp. 118–27.

17. Ibid., pp. 118–27.

18. J. Dargin, *The Dolphin Project: The Development of a Gulf Gas Initiative* (Oxford: Oxford Institute for Energy Studies, 2008), pp. 29–42.

19. Ibid.

20. See Qatar Statistics Authority, *Gross Domestic Product by Economic Activity*, 14 August 2010. http://www.qix.gov.qa

21. See Dohaland, Musheireb Project, 14 August 2010. http://www.dohaland. com.qa

22. See Qatar Statistics Authority, *Economy—CPI*, 14 August 2010. http://www. qix.gov.qa

23. Ibid.

24. Ibid.

25. Gerd Nonneman, 'Analysing the Foreign Policies of the Middle East and North Africa: A Conceptual Framework' in Gerd Nonneman (ed.), *Analyzing Middle East Foreign Policies and the Relationship with Europe* (London: Routledge, 2005), pp. 6–18.

26. See Qatar Statistics Authority, *Population Structure*, 28 August 2010. http:// www.qix.gov.qa

27. See Qatar Statistics Authority, *Economy—CPI*, 14 August 2010. http://www. qix.gov.qa

OMAN

1. See R.W. Bailey (ed.), *Records of Oman.1867–1947*, 7 volumes (Farnham Common, Archives Editions, 1988) vol. 1, p. 130.

2. Fred Halliday, *Arabia without Sultans* (Harmondsworth: Penguin Books, 1974), p. 266.

3. Qaboos married Tariq's daughter Nawwal in 1976 but the marriage produced no child.

4. John E. Peterson, *Oman in the Twentieth Century. Political Foundations of an Emerging Arab State* (London: Croom Helm, 1978), p. 208.

5. *State Council. Royal Decrees of the State Council* (Muscat: State Council, 2001), p. 22.

6. Public revenue linked to natural gas for 2009 amounted to 731 million Omani riyals, which was only 14 per cent of total hydrocarbon revenue.

7. Personal interviews, Muscat, 30 August 2005.

8. United Nations Conference on Trade and Development, 'World Investment Report 2009'; Economic and Social Commission for Western Asia, 'Foreign Direct Investment Report', September 2008.

9. *The Times*, 18 November 1974.

10. Calvin H. Allen and W. Lynn Rigsbee, *Oman under Qaboos: From Coup to Constitution, 1970–1996* (London: Frank Cass, 2000), pp. 180–1.

11. Personal interviews, Muscat, 31 May 2003.

12. Quoted by Fatma Al-Sayegh, 'The UAE and Oman: Opportunities and Challenges in the Twentieth-First Century', *Middle East Policy*, vol. 19, no. 3, 2002, p. 134.

13. Introduced by Ibn Khaldun, the notion of *'asabiyya*, usually translated as 'group feeling', is understood as populations tied by blood links or behaviour, acting as a group or defining themselves as such, and most of the time—but not necessarily—organised to achieve common goals (like taking positions of power). See Ibn Khaldun, *The Muqaddimah: An Introduction to History* (Princeton University Press, 1980).

14. Estimates of religious allegiance among the Omani population are not based on official data, because the authorities never mention figures for religion and tribal or ethnic groups. According to calculations based on the results of the 2003 census, Ibadi Omanis appear to constitute 50 to 55 per cent of the population, Sunnis 45 to 50 per cent, and Shia 3 per cent. Ibadis are in a strong majority in Inner Oman, where are located the historical centres of the Imamate (Nizwa, Rustaq, Bahla) and where the most prominent Imamate dynasties originated from.

15. Judith Miller, 'Creating Modern Oman: An Interview with Sultan Qabus', *Foreign Affairs*, vol. 76, no. 3, 1997, p. 17.

BIBLIOGRAPHY

Aarts, Paul and Gerd Nonneman (eds). *Saudi Arabia in the Balance: Political Economy, Society, Foreign Affairs* (London: Hurst, 2005).

Abdulla, Abdulkhaleq. 'Political Dependency: The Case of the United Arab Emirates' (PhD thesis. Georgetown University, 1985).

Abdulla, Y. *A Study of Qatari-British Relations, 1914–1945* (Doha: Orient Publishing, 1981).

Abu-Hakima, Ahmed Mustafa. *The Modern History of Kuwait, 1750–1965* (London: Luzac, 1983).

Aitchison, C. *Treaties and Engagements Relating to Arabia and the Persian Gulf* (Gerrards Cross, UK: Archive Editions, 1987).

Allen, Calvin H. and W. Lynn Rigsbee. *Oman under Qaboos: From Coup to Constitution, 1970–1996* (London: Frank Cass, 2000).

Ansary, Abdullah. 'Judicial Reform and the Principle of Independence', *Arab Reform Bulletin*, 5 May 2009.

Anscombe, Frederick. *The Ottoman Gulf: The Creation of Kuwait, Saudi Arabia, and Qatar* (New York: Columbia University Press, 1997).

Anthony, John Duke. *Arab States of the Lower Gulf: People, Politics, Petroleum* (Washington, DC: Middle East Institute, 1975).

Baaklini, Abdo. 'Legislatures in the Gulf Area: The Experience of Kuwait, 1961–1976', *International Journal of Middle East Studies*, Vol. 14, No. 3, 1982.

Bahry, Louay. 'Elections in Qatar: A Window of Democracy Opens in the Gulf', *Middle East Policy*, Vol. 6, No. 4, 1999.

———— 'The Opposition in Bahrain: A Bellwether for the Gulf?' *Middle East Policy*, Vol. 5, No. 2, 1997.

Bailey, R. (ed.). *Records of Oman.1867–1947*, 7 volumes (Farnham Common: Archives Editions, 1988), Vol. 1.

Beblawi, Hazem and Luciani, Giacomo (eds). *The Rentier State* (New York: Croom Helm, 1987).

Blanchard, Christopher, and Alfred Prados. 'Saudi Arabia: Terrorist Financing Issues' in *Congressional Research Service Reports for Congress*, Washington, DC, 14 September 2007.

Boghardt, Lori Plotkin. *Kuwait Amid War, Peace, and Revolution: 1979–1991 and New Challenges* (Basingstoke: Palgrave Macmillan, 2006).

Bromley, Simon. *Rethinking Middle East Politics: State Formation and Development* (Cambridge: Polity Press, 1994).

Brown, Gavin, *OPEC and the World Energy Market* (London: Longman, 1998).

Casey, M., F. Thackeray and J. Findling. *The History of Kuwait* (Oxford: Harcourt Education, 2007).

Chubin, Shahram. 'Iran's Power in Context', *Survival*, Vol. 51, No. 1, 2009.

Cordesman, Anthony. *Saudi Arabia: Guarding the Desert Kingdom* (Boulder: Westview Press, 1997).

Craig Jones, Toby. 'Rebellion on the Saudi Periphery: Modernity, Marginalization, and the Shi'a Uprising of 1979', *International Journal of Middle East Studies*, Vol. 38, No. 2, 2006.

Craze, Joshua and Mark Huband (eds). *The Kingdom: Saudi Arabia and the Challenge of the 21ˢᵗ Century* (London: Hurst, 2010).

Crystal, Jill. *Oil and Politics in the Gulf: Rulers and Merchants in Kuwait and Qatar* (Cambridge University Press, 1995).

——— *Kuwait: The Transformation of an Oil State* (Boulder: Westview Press, 1992).

——— 'Coalitions in Oil Monarchies: Kuwait and Qatar', *Comparative Politics*, Vol. 21, No. 4, 1989.

Dargin, J. *The Dolphin Project: The Development of a Gulf Gas Initiative* (Oxford: Oxford Institute for Energy Studies, 2008).

Davidson, Christopher M. *Abu Dhabi: Oil and Beyond* (New York: Columbia University Press, 2009).

——— *Dubai: The Vulnerability of Success* (New York: Columbia University Press, 2008).

——— 'Arab Nationalism and British Opposition in Dubai, 1920–1966', *Middle Eastern Studies*, Vol. 43, No. 6, 2007.

——— 'After Shaikh Zayed: The Politics of Succession in Abu Dhabi and the United Arab Emirates', *Middle East Policy*, Vol. 13, No. 1, 2006.

Donn, Gary and Yahya Al-Manthri. *Globalisation and Higher Education in the Arab Gulf States* (Oxford: Symposium Books, 2010).

Dresch, Paul and James Piscatori (eds). *Monarchies and Nations: Globalisation and Identity in the Arab States of the Gulf* (London: I.B. Tauris, 2005).

Echague, Ana and Edward Burke. 'Strong Foundations? The Imperatives for Reform in Saudi Arabia' (Madrid: FRIDE Working Paper 84, 2009).

Ehteshami, Anoushivaran. *Globalization and Geopolitics in the Middle East: Old Games, New Rules* (London: Routledge, 2007).

Ehteshami, Anoushivaran and Steven Wright. 'Political Change in the Arab Oil Monarchies: From Liberalisation to Enfranchisement', *International Affairs*, Vol. 83, No. 5, 2007.

Ehteshami, Anoushivaran and Steven Wright (eds). *Reform in the Middle East Oil Monarchies* (Reading: Ithaca Press, 2008).

Furtig, Henner. 'Conflict and Cooperation in the Persian Gulf: The Interregional Order and US Policy', *Middle East Journal*, Vol. 61, No. 4, 2007.

Gardner, Andrew. *City of Strangers: Gulf Migration and the Indian Community in Bahrain* (Ithaca, NY: Cornell University Press, 2010).

Gause, Gregory. *The International Relations of the Persian Gulf* (Cambridge University Press, 2010).

———— *Oil Monarchies: Domestic and Security Challenges in the Arab Gulf States* (New York: Council on Foreign Relations Press, 1994).

Ghabra, Shafeeq. 'Voluntary Associations in Kuwait: The Foundation of a New System?', *Middle East Journal*, Vol. 45, No. 2, 1991.

Ghafouri, Mahmoud. 'China's Policy in the Persian Gulf', *Middle East Policy*, Vol. 16, No. 2, 2009.

Gillespie, Eleanor (ed.). 'Politics, Succession and Risk in Saudi Arabia', *Gulf States Newsletter Special Report*, January 2010.

Al-Gurg, Easa Saleh. *The Wells of Memory* (London: John Murray, 1998).

Halliday, Fred. *The Middle East in International Relations: Power, Politics and Ideology* (Cambridge University Press, 2005).

———— *Arabia without Sultans* (Harmondsworth: Penguin Books, 1974).

Hawley, Donald. *The Emirates: Witness to a Metamorphosis* (Norwich: Michael Russell, 2007).

Heard-Bey, Frauke. *From Trucial States to United Arab Emirates* (London: Longman, 1996).

Hegghammer, Thomas. 'Islamist Violence and Regime Stability in Saudi Arabia', *International Affairs*, Vol. 84, No. 4, 2008.

———— 'Saudi Militants in Iraq: Backgrounds and Recruitment Patterns', Norwegian Defence Research Establishment (FFI) report, February 2007.

Herb, Michael. 'Emirs and Parliaments in the Gulf', *Journal of Democracy*, Vol. 13, No. 4, 2002.

Hertog, Steffen. *Princes, Brokers, and Bureaucrats: Oil and the State in Saudi Arabia* (Ithaca, NY: Cornell University Press, 2010).

———— 'Gulf Countries: The Current Crisis and Lessons of the 1980s', *Arab Reform Bulletin*, July 2009.

Ismael, J.S. *Kuwait: Dependency and Class in a Rentier State* (Miami: University Press of Florida, 1993).

Jamri, Mansoor. 'Shia and the State in Bahrain: Integration and Tension', *Alternative Politics*, Vol. 2, No. 1, 2010.

Joyce, Miriam. 'The Bahraini Three on St Helena: 1956–1961', *Middle East Journal*, Vol. 54, No. 4, 2000.

Kaldor, Mary, Terry Lynn Karl and Yahia Said (eds). *Oil Wars* (London: Pluto Press, 2007).

Kéchichian, Joseph A. *Power and Succession in Arab Monarchies: A Reference Guide* (Boulder: Lynne Rienner, 2008).

Kerr, Malcolm. *The Arab Cold War, 1956–1964: A Study of Ideology in Politics* (Oxford University Press, 1965).

Khadduri, Majid and Edmund Ghareeb. *War in the Gulf, 1990–91: The Iraq-Kuwait Conflict and Its Implications* (New York: Oxford University Press, 1997).

Khalaf, Abdulhadi and Giacomo Luciani (eds). *Constitutional Reform and Political Participation in the Gulf* (Dubai: Gulf Research Centre, 2006).

Ibn Khaldun. *The Muqaddimah: An Introduction to History* (Princeton University Press, 1980).

El-Kharouf, Farouk, Sulayman Al-Qudsi and Shifa Obeid. 'The Gulf Cooperation Council Sovereign Wealth Funds: Are They Instruments for Economic Diversification or Political Tools?' *Asian Economic Papers*, Vol. 9, No. 1, 2010.

Khouja, M. and P. Sadler. *The Economy of Kuwait: Development and Role in International Finance* (London: Macmillan, 1979).

Khuri, F. *Tribe and State in Bahrain: The Transition of Social and Political Authority in an Arab State* (University of Chicago Press, 1981).

Al-Khwaiter, Abd Al-Aziz ibn 'Abd Allah, 'King Abdul Aziz: His Style of Administration' in Fahd Al-Semmari (ed.), *History of the Arabian Peninsula* (London: I.B. Tauris, 2009).

Krieger, Zvika. 'Reforms in Higher Education Raise Questions', *Arab Reform Bulletin*, December 2007.

Kwarten, Leo. 'Why the Saudi Shias Won't Rise Up Easily' (Beirut: A Conflicts Forum Monograph, 2009).

Lorimer, John G. *Gazetteer of the Persian Gulf, Oman and Central Arabia* (London: Gregg International, 1970).

Louer, Laurence. *Transnational Shia Politics: Religious and Political Networks in the Gulf* (London: Hurst, 2008).

Love, Roy. 'Economic Drivers of Conflict and Cooperation in the Horn of Africa: A Regional Perspective and Overview' (London: Chatham House Africa Programme Briefing Paper, December 2009).

Luciani, Giacomo (ed.). *The Arab State* (London: Routledge, 1990).

Mansfield, Peter. *Kuwait: Vanguard of the Gulf* (London: Hutchinson, 1990).

McKnight, Sean, Neil Partrick and Francis Toase (eds). *Gulf Security: Opportunities and Challenges for the New Generation* (London: RUSI Whitehall Paper Series 51, 2000).

Al-Mdaires, Falah. 'Shi'ism and Political Protest in Bahrain', *Digest of Middle East Studies*, Vol. 11, No. 1, 2002.

Miller, Judith. 'Creating Modern Oman: An Interview with Sultan Qabus', *Foreign Affairs*, Vol. 76, No. 3, 1997.

Moore, Pete. *Doing Business in the Middle East: Politics and Economic Crisis in Jordan and Kuwait* (Cambridge University Press, 2004).

BIBLIOGRAPHY

(*in Arabic*) Mutawwa, Khalid. *The Arabic Falcon* (Sharjah, 2005).

Al-Nabeh, Najat Abdullah. 'United Arab Emirates: Regional and Global Dimensions' (PhD thesis, Claremont Graduate School, 1984).

Al-Nahyan, Shamma bint Muhammad. *Political and Social Security in the United Arab Emirates* (Dubai: 2000).

Nakhleh, Emile. *Bahrain: Political Development in a Modernising Society* (Lexington: Lexington Books, 1976).

(*in Arabic*) Obaid, Nayef. *The Foreign Policy of the United Arab Emirates* (Abu Dhabi: 2004).

Niblock, Tim, with Monica Malik. *The Political Economy of Saudi Arabia* (London: Routledge, 2007).

Nonneman, Gerd (ed.). *Analyzing Middle East Foreign Policies and the Relationship with Europe* (London: Routledge, 2005).

Okruhlik, Gwenn. 'Rentier Wealth, Unruly Law, and the Rise of Opposition: the Political Economy of Oil States', *Comparative Politics*, Vol. 31, No. 3, 1999.

Onley, James. *The Arabian Frontier of the British Raj: Merchants, Rulers, and the British in the Nineteenth Century Gulf* (New York: Oxford University Press, 2007).

———— 'The Politics of Protection in the Gulf: The Arab Rulers and the British Resident in the Nineteenth Century', *New Arabian Studies*, Vol. 6, 2004.

Ottaway, Marina. 'Evaluating Middle East Reform: How Do We Know When It Is Significant?' *Carnegie Paper*, No. 56 (Washington, DC: Carnegie Endowment for International Peace, 2005).

Palgrave, W. *Narrative of a Year's Journey through Central and Eastern Arabia (1862–63)* (London: Macmillan, 1865).

Peterson, J.E. *Saudi Arabia and the Illusion of Security* (Oxford University Press, 2002).

Pollock, David. 'Actions, Not Just Attitudes: A New Way to Assess US-Arab Relations', *Washington Institute for Near East Policy Papers*, 11 March 2010.

Rahman, H. *The Emergence of Qatar: the Turbulent Years, 1627–1916* (London: Kegan Paul, 2005).

Al-Rasheed, Madawi. *Contesting the Saudi State: Islamic Voices From a New Generation* (Cambridge University Press, 2007).

Al-Rasheed, Madawi (ed.). *Kingdom Without Borders: Saudi Arabia's Political, Religious and Media Frontiers* (London: Hurst, 2008).

Riedel, Bruce and Bilal Y. Saab. 'Al Qaeda's Third Front: Saudi Arabia', *The Washington Quarterly*, Vol. 31, No. 2, 2008.

Rizvi, S. 'Shi'ism in Bahrain: Marja'iyya and Politics', *Orient IV*, 2009.

———— 'From Tents to High Rise: Economic Development of the United Arab Emirates', *Middle Eastern Studies*, Vol. 29, No. 4, 1993.

Romani, Vincent. 'The Politics of Higher Education in the Middle East: Problems and Prospects', *Middle East Brief*, No. 36, May 2009.

Roy, Olivier. *The Politics of Chaos in the Middle East* (London: Hurst, 2008).

Rush, Alan. *Al-Sabah: History and Genealogy of Kuwait's Ruling Family, 1752–1987* (London: Ithaca, 1987).

Sager, Abdulaziz. 'The GCC States and the Situation in Iraq' (Dubai: Gulf Research Centre, July 2008).

Saif, Ibrahim. 'The Oil Boom in the GCC Countries, 2002–2008: Old Challenges, Changing Dynamics' (Washington, DC: Carnegie Endowment for International Peace, 2009).

Salisu, Muhammad and S. Yagudin. 'Investments and Vertical Integration—Catalyst for Developments in the Oil Industry of an Emerging Market: The Case of Refining in Kuwait', *Oil and Gas Business*, issue 1, 2007.

Al-Sayegh, Fatma. 'The UAE and Oman: Opportunities and Challenges in the Twentieth-First Century', *Middle East Policy*, Vol. 19, No. 3, 2002.

Schwarz, Benjamin. 'America's Struggle Against the Wahhabi/Neo-Salafi Movement', *Orbis*, Vol. 51, No. 1, 2007.

Seznec, Jean-François'. The Gulf Sovereign Wealth Funds: Myths and Reality', *Middle East Policy*, Vol. 15, No. 2, 2008.

Sick, G. and L. Potter (eds). *The Persian Gulf at the Turn of the Millennium* (New York: St. Martins Press, 1997).

Simpfendorfer, Ben. *The New Silk Road: How a Rising Arab World is Turning Away From the West and Rediscovering China* (Basingstoke: Palgrave Macmillan, 2009).

Stott, David A. 'South Korea's Global Nuclear Ambitions', *The Asia-Pacific Journal*, Vol. 12, March 2010.

Al-Tajir, Mahdi Abdalla. *Bahrain, 1920–1945: Britain, the Shaikh, and the Administration* (London: Croom Helm, 1987).

Teitelbaum, Joshua (ed.). *Political Liberalization in the Persian Gulf* (London: Hurst, 2009).

Tetreault, Mary Ann, Katherine., Meyer and Helen Rizzo. 'Women's Rights in the Middle East: A Longitudinal Study of Kuwait', *International Political Sociology*, Vol. 3, No. 2, 2009.

——— *Stories of Democracy: Politics and Society in Contemporary Kuwait* (New York: Columbia University Press, 2000).

——— *The Kuwait Petroleum Corporation and the Economics of the New World Order* (Westport: Quorum Books, 1995).

——— 'Autonomy, Necessity, and the Small State: Ruling Kuwait in the Twentieth Century', *International Organization*, Vol. 45, No. 4, 1991.

Trofimov, Yaroslav. *The Siege of Mecca: The Forgotten Uprising in Islam's Holiest Shrine and the Birth of al-Qaeda* (London: Penguin, 2008).

Ulrichsen, Kristian. *Insecure Gulf: The Challenge of Transition and the End of Certainty* (London: Hurst, 2011).

BIBLIOGRAPHY

———'Gulf States' Perspectives on Global Governance', *Global Policy*, Vol. 2, No. 1, 2011.

Van der Meulen, Hendrik. 'The Role of Tribal and Kinship Ties in the Politics of the United Arab Emirates' (PhD thesis, The Fletcher School of Law and Diplomacy, 1997).

Vitalis, Robert. *America's Kingdom: Mythmaking on the Saudi Oil Frontier* (Stanford University Press, 2007).

Weber, Max. *The Theory of Social and Economic Organisation* (New York: Free Press, 1997).

Wheatcroft, Andrew. *With United Strength: Sheikh Zayed bin Sultan Al-Nahyan, the Leader and the Nation* (Abu Dhabi: Emirates Centre for Strategic Studies and Research, 2005).

Wiktorowicz, Quintan (ed.). *Islamic Activism; a Social Movement Theory Approach* (Bloomington: Indiana University Press, 2004).

Winkler, David. *Amirs, Admirals, and Desert Sailors* (Annapolis: Naval Institute Press, 2007).

Yamani, Mai. 'The Two Faces of Saudi Arabia', *Survival*, Vol. 50, No. 1, 2008.

Yetiv, Steve and Chunlong Lu. 'China, Global Energy and the Middle East', *Middle East Journal*, Vol. 61, No. 2, 2007

INDEX

NOTES ON CONTRIBUTORS

Christopher M. Davidson Dr. Christopher M. Davidson is a reader in Government and International Affairs at Durham University. He was formerly an assistant professor at Zayed University in the United Arab Emirates and a visiting associate professor at Kyoto University in Japan. He is a listed expert with the United Nation's Alliance of Civilisations, has been consulted by the UN's Special Rapporteur on Human Rights, and his work has been cited by the UNHCR—the UN Refugee Agency. He is the author of four single authored books: *The United Arab Emirates: A Study in Survival*; *Dubai: The Vulnerability of Success*; *Abu Dhabi: Oil and Beyond*; and *The Persian Gulf and Pacific Asia: From Indifference to Interdependence*. He has delivered public lectures at a number of leading universities, including Stanford, Yale, and Oxford. He has written articles for the *Guardian*, the *Daily Telegraph*, the *New Statesman*, *Foreign Policy*, *Al-Akhbar*, and *OpenDemocracy*. He has appeared on most mainstream current affairs television and radio shows, including BBC 2's *Newsnight*, BBC Radio 4's *PM* and *Today* shows, Sky's *Jeff Randall Show*, CNN's *Connect the World*, and NPR's *All Things Considered*. He can be followed at *twitter.com/dr_davidson*.

Jane Kinninmont Jane Kinninmont is a senior research fellow on the Middle East and North Africa Programme at London's Chatham House. She was formerly an associate director at the Economist Group and a managing director at Business Monitor International. She specialises in the study of reform and opposition movements in the Arab world, with focuses on Egypt and Bahrain. She has contributed a large number of articles to the *Economist*, and has also written for both *Foreign Policy* and *Foreign Affairs*. Her book, *Bahrain in Focus*, is shortly forthcoming. She has appeared on a number of TV and radio shows, including BBC 2's *Newsnight*. She can be followed at *twitter.com/janekinninmont*.

Kristian Coates Ulrichsen Dr. Kristian Coates Ulrichsen is a research fellow at the London School of Economics and serves as deputy director of the LSE's Kuwait Research Programme on Development, Governance and Globalisation in the Gulf States. His research focuses on political and security trends in the Arabian Peninsula, the changing position of the Gulf States in the global order, and their transition toward post-oil structures of governance. His recent books include *Insecure Gulf: The End of Certainty and the Transition to the Post-Oil Era* and, co-edited with David Held, *The Transformation of the Gulf: Politics, Economics and the Global Order*. He has also published numerous articles and policy studies, most recently 'The Geopolitics of Insecurity in the Horn of Africa and the Arabian Peninsula' in *Middle East Policy*, 'Rebalancing Global Governance: Gulf States' Perspectives on the Governance of Globalisation' in *Global Policy*, and 'The GCC States and the Shifting Balance of Global Power' in *Georgetown University School of Foreign Service in Qatar Occasional Papers*. He can be followed at *twitter.com/dr_ulrichsen*.

David Roberts David Roberts has lived, studied and researched throughout the Middle East, including several years spent in Kuwait and Qatar. He is currently the Deputy Director of the Royal United Services Institute's (RUSI) Qatar office. He is also completing his PhD at Durham University where he was awarded a full scholarship by the Centre for the Advanced Study of the Arab World (CASAW). He obtained another scholarship to spend the 2009–10 academic year on an Arabic programme at Qatar University while also conducting research into Qatar's foreign policy. In addition to writing various book chapters, numerous opinion editorials and analysis articles typically focusing on the Gulf (appearing in *Kuwait Times, Foreign Policy, Daily News Egypt*, etc), he is frequently sought for commentary by the international print, TV and radio media (including Al-Jazeera, the *Financial Times*, Reuters, and the BBC). He is also the author of thegulfblog.com and presently serves as the president of the British Society for Middle Eastern Studies' (BRISMES) graduate section. He can be followed at *twitter.com/thegulfblog*.

Steven Wright Dr. Steven Wright is an assistant professor and head of the Department of International Affairs at Qatar University. He is also an honorary research fellow at Exeter University's Institute for Arab and Islamic studies. He has previously held visiting research fellowships at the London School of Economics and at Durham University, where he was the Sir William Luce Fellow in 2006. He currently serves as the assistant editor of the Journal of Arabian Studies (published by Routledge). His research focuses on the politics and international relations of the Gulf Cooperation Council states, in addition to US foreign policy in the Middle East. He is the author of the recent book *The United States and Persian Gulf Security* and was co-editor of *Reform in the Middle East Oil Monarchies*.

Marc Valeri Dr. Marc Valeri is a lecturer in the Political Economy of the Middle East and director of the MA Programme in Gulf Studies at Exeter University's Institute for Arab and Islamic Studies. His main areas of interest are the social, political and economic transformations and reform in the Arabian Peninsula. Moreover he is developing research interests in the stability and legitimacy of authoritarian regimes in the Middle East. He is the author of the recent book *Oman: Politics and Society in the Qaboos-State*.